PENGUIN BOOKS

Baking
bible

Baking
bible

Introduction

Baking is an old-fashioned skill that never goes out of style. Anyone who's tried it knows just how rewarding it is to bake delicious treats at home, and to watch with satisfaction as they are enjoyed by loved ones.

Baking Bible brings together an outstanding collection of sweet and savoury recipes for cakes, puddings, biscuits, tarts, pies, slices and muffins. There are traditional favourites, as well of plenty of new ideas, so you'll never run short of inspiration. With gluten-free, dairy-free and no-bake options, there's something to suit everybody.

All the recipes in this book are easy to follow and are designed to be baked in a standard home oven, with no need for fancy equipment or hard-to-find ingredients. And most of the recipes are quick and easy to prepare, so even if you've never baked before, you'll find yourself turning out perfectly baked goodies every time.

General baking tips

- Whatever you are baking, preparation is important. Use good quality ingredients and pay attention to measurements.

- Make sure you have a suitable baking tin or tray and grease, line or dust it with flour before you begin cooking. (See also Greasing and Lining Tins and Trays, page 4.)

- Preheat the oven to the required temperature.

- Measure out all ingredients first, before starting. All cup and spoon measurements should be level, unless stated otherwise in the recipe.

- Eggs, butter and oil are best used at room temperature.

- Butter is generally considered better for baking than margarine, but you can substitute one for the other if you wish.

- The egg size used in all these recipes is large (65 g eggs).

- When creaming butter and sugar use a wooden spoon or electric mixer and beat until light and fluffy.

- Unless specified otherwise, eggs should be added one at a time and, to prevent curdling, each should be beaten in well before the next is added.

- Always sift dry ingredients before using, as this helps incorporate air and gives a lighter result.

- For better tasting cakes, muffins, biscuits and slices, use vanilla extract rather than its synthetic imitation, vanilla essence.

- When folding whipped egg whites into a mixture, use a metal spoon.

How to . . .

BEAT: mix vigorously with a spoon or electric mixer.

BLEND: combine one ingredient with another until completely mixed together, either using a fork, wooden spoon or electric mixer.

CREAM: beat butter or fat, alone or mixed with sugar, until light, pale yellow and fluffy.

FOLD: carefully incorporate one mixture into another – usually a light one such as whipped egg whites into a heavier mixture. Folding involves gently 'drawing' a figure of eight with a metal spoon and being careful not to knock the air out of the lighter mixture.

STIR: mix carefully in a circular motion to combine.

WHIP: beat rapidly with a whisk or electric mixer to incorporate as much air as possible. Cream or egg whites are examples of ingredients that are whipped.

BAKE BLIND: precook pastry by lining it with non-stick baking paper, weighing it down with uncooked rice or dried pulses and baking it in the oven.

COOK IN A 'BAIN-MARIE' (WATER BATH): Place the baking tin or mould into a baking dish, and pour boiling water into the dish until it reaches halfway up the sides of the tin or mould. Then bake for the stated time. This method is suitable for delicate mixtures that require a gentle, indirect heat – e.g. custards, puddings and soufflés.

MELT CHOCOLATE: microwave or use a double boiler. To microwave, place chopped chocolate into a microwave-safe bowl and heat on MEDIUM until partially melted. Remove and stir until melted and smooth. To use a double boiler, place chopped chocolate into a double boiler and stir over simmering water until melted and smooth. Alternatively, place chocolate into a metal bowl and stir over a saucepan of simmering water until melted (the water should not touch the base of the bowl). Be careful not to let any water get into the chocolate.

Greasing & lining tins and trays

- Clarified butter was traditionally used to grease tins and trays, as it gives the best tasting results, but vegetable oil brushed (or sprayed) evenly will do almost as well and is easier for the busy home cook.

- To use clarified butter, melt some butter slowly until it separates, then use a brush to spread the clear oil lightly over the tin or tray. Take care not to use the milky white solids, which can cause sticking (these should be discarded).

- Whether using oil or clarified butter, it's important not to grease tins and trays too thickly, as this may actually cause sticking.

- If required to line a baking tin or tray, cut a strip of non-stick baking paper that covers the base and sides of the tin. Lightly grease the tin, place the paper inside, then brush or spray with oil, or brush with clarified butter. (For slices, use a piece of baking paper that slightly overhangs the sides of the tin — this way you can grasp the baking paper to easily remove the slice after baking.)

- To dust a tin, grease it lightly, then add a small amount of flour and rotate the tin until the sides and base are lightly coated.

Gluten-free flour

The gluten-free recipes included in this book require gluten-free flour. Gluten-free flour mixes are now available in many supermarkets, or from health food shops and specialist suppliers. However, you can also mix up your own — just make sure to store it in a sealed container in the freezer if only using occasionally.

The flours below are perfect for general baking of cakes, slices, muffins, puddings and biscuits.

GENERAL PURPOSE GLUTEN-FREE FLOUR MIX

175 g rice flour
100 g maize flour or dry polenta
175 g sorghum flour

SWEET GLUTEN-FREE FLOUR MIX 1

175 g rice flour
175 g cornflour
100 g fine potato flour

SWEET GLUTEN-FREE FLOUR MIX 2

250 g rice flour
250 g ground almonds

Hints for baking the best cakes

· It is important that the oven temperature is correct. If the oven is not hot enough, cakes will not rise well and will be heavy. If the oven is too hot the outside of the cake will burn before the inside is cooked.

· Cake mixtures should be baked immediately to give good results.

· To check if a cake is cooked, press the top lightly with a fingertip; most cakes should spring back immediately when cooked, though very rich cakes and chocolate cakes may dent slightly and still be done. Alternatively, insert a thin wooden skewer gently into the centre of the cake; if it comes out clean, then the cake is ready.

· Always remove cakes from the oven once cooked and allow to cool.

Hints for baking the best biscuits & slices

· Be aware that if using a larger baking tin than that specified, your slice will be thinner and take less time to cook. The opposite generally applies if using a smaller tin, and you'll end up with a cakey result rather than a chewy one. For no-bake slices, tin size generally doesn't matter and it is more a matter of personal preference.

· Most biscuits work best if the dough is as soft as possible, so don't use too much flour on the board when rolling out. Or instead of using flour, roll out dough between two sheets of baking paper or cling wrap.

· Most doughs should be chilled for at least 20 minutes before rolling out, to make them easier to handle.

- Place cut-out dough on chilled baking trays to prevent them spreading too much during cooking.

- Bright shiny trays cook more evenly than dark-coloured trays, which may cause biscuits to brown too quickly on the bottom. Line dark trays with heavy-duty aluminium foil to prevent this.

- Avoid using high-sided baking trays to bake biscuits as heat distribution is more uneven.

- Space trays of biscuits evenly throughout the oven, but be aware that most ovens cook unevenly to some degree. You may have to turn or swap the trays around during the cooking process so that all the biscuits are ready at the same time.

- Always cool biscuits on a wire rack after cooking, unless directed otherwise.

- Never overlap the biscuits when cooling, as they may end up misshapen.

- When oats are called for, make sure you use traditional rolled oats, not instant oats (unless specified).

- Always store biscuits and slices in an airtight container once cool. Store different types of biscuits in separate containers, so they keep their individual flavours.

- To crisp up biscuits that have softened, place them on an ungreased tray and heat at 180°C for several minutes.

- If you plan on serving a slice soon after baking, store it in the tin in which you baked it – covered in foil, after cooling and cutting.

- Most biscuits and slices freeze well. Individual pieces of slice can be wrapped in cling wrap and frozen ready for the lunchbox.

- Many biscuit doughs can also be successfully frozen and simply removed and cooked when required – perfect for unexpected visitors.

- Avoid icing slices and biscuits before freezing, as the icing may discolour or separate when defrosted. Instead, freeze un-iced and decorate once thawed.

Hints for baking the best muffins

- The secret to perfect muffins is not to over mix the batter – you should mix just enough to combine the wet and dry ingredients.

- It's important to grease muffin tins well, so that they are easy to turn out once cooked. Alternatively, line muffin tins with paper cases.

- Too much liquid in the muffin mixture will result in soggy and flat muffins. Too little liquid and they'll end up hard and dry.

- Note that using white flour instead of wholemeal flour will give you a lighter muffin.

- Bake muffins in the middle of the oven, and be adaptable with the temperature and timing of cooking – every oven behaves differently. The oven is too hot if the muffin tops are uneven and cracked, and it is too cool if the tops are pale and have not risen.

- To reheat muffins, wrap them loosely in foil and put in the oven for 5–10 minutes at 125°C, or 15–20 minutes at 180°C if they are frozen.

Abernethy biscuits

75 g cold butter, cut into
  small pieces

1½ cups plain flour

⅓ cup castor sugar

½ teaspoon baking powder

1 teaspoon caraway seeds

1 egg, beaten

1½ tablespoons milk

Preheat oven to 180°C. Lightly grease baking trays.

Combine butter and sifted flour in a food processor.
Add sugar, baking powder and caraway seeds and blend.
Mix the egg and milk together, then add them to the dry
ingredients and process to combine.

Turn the dough onto a lightly floured surface. Roll it out
thinly and cut into small rounds. Gather any leftover
dough, roll out again and use to make more biscuits.

Transfer to prepared trays and bake for 10 minutes.

MAKES 40

Afghans

190 g softened butter

⅓ cup soft brown sugar

1¼ cups self-raising flour

2 tablespoons cocoa

1¾ cups Corn Flakes

chocolate glacé icing
(page 680)

white chocolate buttons or
walnut halves, for
decorating (optional)

Preheat oven to 180°C. Lightly grease baking trays.

Cream butter and sugar, then add sifted flour and cocoa. Carefully stir in the Corn Flakes a little at a time.

Drop spoonfuls of mixture onto prepared trays and bake for 12–15 minutes.

When completely cooled, ice with chocolate icing.
Top each biscuit with a white chocolate button or walnut half, if desired.

MAKES 24

Almond biscotti

2 cups plain flour

1½ teaspoons baking powder

½ teaspoon ground
   cinnamon

¾ cup white sugar

1½ cups whole raw almonds

3 eggs

2 teaspoons vanilla extract

Preheat oven to 180°C. Lightly grease baking trays.

In a large bowl, combine sifted flour, baking powder and cinnamon, and sugar. Add almonds and mix to combine.

In a small bowl, whisk together the eggs and vanilla. Fold egg mixture into flour mixture until a stiff dough forms.

Turn dough onto a lightly floured surface and divide into two pieces. Roll each piece into a log about the same length as your baking tray. Place the logs on the baking tray, leaving plenty of room between them, and flatten slightly. Bake for 25 minutes.

Remove from the oven (leave the oven on) and set aside until cool enough to handle.

Using a serrated knife, slice each log diagonally into 1-cm thick slices.

Place biscuits onto the trays and bake for a further 12–15 minutes, until crisp.

VARIATIONS

For anise biscotti, replace the vanilla extract with anise extract and omit the almonds. For chocolate almond biscotti, replace the vanilla extract with almond essence and add ¼ cup cocoa to the flour mix.

MAKES 40

Almond biscuits

100 g softened butter

⅓ cup white sugar

1 cup ground almonds

⅔ cup gluten-free flour mix
  (page 6)

1 egg, separated

½ cup almonds, chopped

Preheat oven to 180°C. Lightly grease baking trays.

Cream butter and sugar until light and fluffy. Add ground almonds and sifted flour and mix well.

Reserve a little of the egg white, then beat the rest of the egg and add to the mixture to form a firm dough.

Roll dough out to a thickness of 3 mm and cut into rounds or shapes using a biscuit cutter. Gather any leftover dough, roll out again and use to make more biscuits.

Brush biscuits with reserved egg white and sprinkle with chopped almonds.

Bake for 10–12 minutes or until golden.

MAKES 24 | GLUTEN FREE

Almond cake

150 g softened butter

1 cup castor sugar

3 eggs

¾ teaspoon almond essence

1½ cups plain flour

3 teaspoons baking powder

70 g ground almonds

¾ cup milk

icing sugar, for dusting

Preheat oven to 160°C. Lightly grease and flour a 20-cm cake tin.

Cream butter and sugar, then beat in eggs and almond essence. Add sifted flour and baking powder and ground almonds alternately with milk. Mix well.

Pour into cake tin and bake for 50–60 minutes. Leave in the tin for 10 minutes before turning out.

Dust with icing sugar to serve.

Almond lace doilies

80 g butter, melted

½ cup finely ground
   almonds

3 tablespoons plain flour

½ cup white sugar

2 tablespoons sour cream

½ teaspoon vanilla extract

Preheat oven to 180°C. Lightly grease baking trays.

Place the melted butter in a large bowl and add the ground almonds, sifted flour, sugar, sour cream and vanilla. Mix well.

Drop teaspoonfuls of the mixture onto prepared trays and bake for 10 minutes, or until golden.

Cool on the trays for a few moments, then gently transfer to a wire rack to cool completely.

MAKES 16

Almond lemon muffins

1¾ cups self-raising flour

2–3 tablespoons castor sugar

1 teaspoon baking powder

½ teaspoon salt

1 egg

¾ cup milk

80 g butter, melted

2 teaspoons grated lemon
zest

½ teaspoon vanilla extract

¾ cup chopped unblanched
almonds

Preheat oven to 200°C. Lightly grease muffin tins.

In a large bowl, sift together flour, sugar, baking powder and salt.

In a small bowl, combine egg, milk, melted butter, grated lemon zest, vanilla and almonds.

Add to flour mixture. With a fork, stir briskly until all dry ingredients are moistened. Batter should look lumpy.

Three-quarters fill greased muffin tins and bake for 20–25 minutes or until golden brown.

MAKES 12–14

Almond lemon shortbread

300 g softened butter

½ cup castor sugar

1½ cups plain flour

1½ cups rice flour

½ cup ground almonds

finely grated zest of 1 lemon

a few drops almond essence

blanched almonds, for
    decorating

Cream butter and sugar until light and fluffy. Sift the flours together and gradually stir into butter mixture.

Add ground almonds, lemon zest and almond essence and mix until smooth.

Refrigerate dough for 30 minutes.

Preheat oven to 150°C. Lightly grease baking trays.

Divide dough into four pieces and roll out on a lightly floured surface to make four rounds, each about 1.5 cm thick. Pinch edges and cut each round into eight triangular pieces. Sprinkle with blanched almonds.

Bake for 20–30 minutes or until shortbread just begins to colour (be careful it doesn't burn). Let cool on the tray for 5 minutes before transferring to a wire rack.

MAKES 32

Almond poppy seed muffins

1 egg

¾ teaspoon salt

⅓ cup white sugar

¼ cup vegetable oil

1 cup milk

2 cups plain flour

1 tablespoon baking powder

¾ cup chopped almonds

⅓ cup poppy seeds

Preheat oven to 200°C. Lightly grease muffin tins.

Beat egg, salt and sugar until light and fluffy. Add oil in a stream and continue beating. Beat in milk.

Sift flour and baking powder together several times and add to batter, stirring until just mixed. Add nuts and poppy seeds.

Bake for 20–25 minutes.

MAKES 16

Almond sponge

6 eggs, separated

⅔ cup castor sugar

¼ cup orange juice

¼ teaspoon vanilla extract

⅔ cup plain flour

1½ cups ground almonds

1 tablespoon finely grated
orange zest

pinch of salt

1 teaspoon cream of tartar

fresh berries, for decorating

icing sugar, for dusting

Preheat oven to 150°C. Lightly grease and flour a 25-cm bundt pan.

Using an electric mixer, whisk together the egg yolks and half the castor sugar until thick and creamy. Add the orange juice and vanilla extract.

In a separate bowl combine the sifted flour, almonds, orange zest and pinch of salt. Fold into the egg-yolk mixture.

Whisk the egg whites and cream of tartar until soft peaks form. Slowly whisk in the remaining sugar until glossy. Fold into the cake batter until combined.

Pour the batter into the prepared pan. Bake for 45–50 minutes.

Cool in the pan, then invert onto a serving platter and spoon the berries into the middle. Dust with icing sugar.

Serve with cream.

American tollhouse cookies

2¼ cups plain flour

1 teaspoon bicarbonate
of soda

1 teaspoon salt

160 g softened butter

¾ cup white sugar

¾ cup soft brown sugar,
firmly packed

1 teaspoon vanilla extract

2 eggs

2 cups chocolate chips

1 cup chopped pecans or
walnuts

Preheat oven to 180°C.

Sift together flour, bicarbonate of soda and salt.

In a separate bowl, cream butter, sugars and vanilla
until light and creamy. Beat in eggs.

Gradually add flour mixture to butter mixture, mixing
until well combined. Stir in chocolate chips and nuts.

Drop teaspoonfuls of dough onto ungreased baking
trays, leaving plenty of room for spreading. Bake for
8–10 minutes.

MAKES 60

Animal biscuits

½ cup wholemeal plain flour

1 cup plain flour

¼ teaspoon ground ginger

¼ teaspoon ground cinnamon

pinch of salt

⅔ cup semolina

75 g cold butter, cut into small pieces

1 ripe banana

1½ tablespoons maple syrup

cream cheese or icing of choice (pages 677–82), for frosting

sultanas or chocolate chips, for decorating

Preheat oven to 200°C. Lightly grease baking trays.

Sift together flours, spices and salt. Stir in semolina. Rub in butter with your fingertips until crumbly. Mash the banana with the maple syrup and stir into the flour mixture to make a smooth, pliable dough.

Roll out dough on a floured surface and cut into animal shapes with biscuit cutters. Gather any leftover dough, roll out again and use to make more biscuits.

Bake for 20 minutes, or until golden and firm. Cool on a wire rack.

Frost with cream cheese that has been beaten with a little icing sugar, or top with coloured icing. Score the frosting with a fork to make it look like fur. Use sultanas or choc chips for eyes.

MAKES 15–20

Anzac biscuits

100 g butter, melted

2 tablespoons boiling water

1 teaspoon bicarbonate
    of soda

2 tablespoons golden syrup

1 cup plain flour

1 cup white sugar

2 cups rolled oats

¾ cup desiccated coconut

Preheat oven to 190°C. Lightly grease baking trays.

Mix together butter, boiling water, bicarbonate of soda and golden syrup.

In a separate bowl, mix the sifted flour, sugar, oats and coconut. Add the liquid and blend until well combined.

Drop spoonfuls of mixture onto trays and cook for 10–12 minutes, or until golden.

MAKES 30

Anzac muffins

1 teaspoon bicarbonate
  of soda

¾ cup warm milk

50 g butter, melted

2 tablespoons golden syrup

⅔ cup soft brown sugar

½ cup desiccated coconut

1 teaspoon baking powder

½ cup rolled oats

1 egg

2 cups plain flour

Preheat oven to 190°C. Grease muffins tins.

Dissolve bicarbonate of soda in milk, then add butter, golden syrup and brown sugar and mix well.

Add coconut, baking powder, oats, egg and sifted flour and stir until just combined.

Three-quarters fill muffin tins and bake for 15–20 minutes.

MAKES 16

Anzac slice

1 cup rolled oats

1½ cups plain flour

1 cup soft brown sugar,
    firmly packed

1 cup desiccated coconut

finely grated zest of 1 orange

125 g butter

2 tablespoons golden syrup

2 tablespoons orange juice

½ teaspoon bicarbonate
    of soda

½ cup marmalade

Preheat oven to 180°C. Lightly grease and line
a 19-cm × 29-cm slice tin.

Combine oats, sifted flour, sugar, coconut and
orange zest in a large bowl. Mix well.

Place butter, golden syrup and orange juice in a
saucepan and stir over low heat, without boiling,
until the butter has melted. Bring to the boil, then
remove from heat and stir in the bicarbonate of soda.

Add liquid to dry ingredients and stir well to combine.

Press two-thirds of the mixture into the tin, then spread
evenly with marmalade. Crumble remaining mixture over
the top.

Cook for about 35 minutes, or until golden brown.
Cool for 5 minutes in the tin, then transfer to a wire
rack to cool. Cut into squares.

MAKES 36

Apple, blackberry & rhubarb blanket pie

1⅓ cups plain flour

125 g cold butter, cut into small pieces

4–5 tablespoons sour cream or chilled water

400 g rhubarb, trimmed and cut into small chunks

250 g apples, peeled, cored and cut into small chunks

250 g fresh blackberries or mulberries (or defrosted frozen berries)

½ cup castor sugar, for sprinkling

2 tablespoons milk or egg wash, for brushing

1 tablespoon castor sugar, for sprinkling

pouring custard (page 683)

For the pastry, place sifted flour into a food processor and add the butter. Process for 1 minute or until the mixture resembles coarse breadcrumbs. Add sour cream or water and pulse until the pastry dough comes together. Remove and shape into a ball. Chill for 20 minutes while you prepare the filling.

Preheat oven to 200°C. Lightly flour a shallow baking tin or pizza tray.

For the filling, mix the rhubarb and fruit together in a bowl and stir in the sugar.

Working on a floured board, roll out the pastry to about 30 cm in diameter.

Using a rolling pin, lift the pastry onto the prepared tin or tray. Spoon the fruit into the middle and carefully bring the pastry up, folding it to make a round free-form shape. Leave a small gap in the centre, exposing some of the fruit.

Brush the pastry with milk or egg and sprinkle over the castor sugar.

Bake for 30–40 minutes or until the pastry is crisp and golden and the fruit is tender. Cool a little before lifting onto a serving plate.

Serve warm with pouring custard.

SERVES 6

Apple, bran & date muffins

2 eggs

½ cup soft brown sugar

¼ cup vegetable oil

2 cups skim milk

1 cup chopped dates

1 cup raisins

2 cups plain flour

½ teaspoon ground
  cinnamon

2 teaspoons bicarbonate
  of soda

2 teaspoons baking powder

1 cup grated green apple

1 cup bran

½ cup wheatgerm

Beat eggs lightly. Add sugar, oil, milk, dates and raisins, and stir to mix.

In a separate bowl, sift together flour, cinnamon, bicarbonate of soda and baking powder. Stir in remaining ingredients, then mix in egg mixture.

Cover and chill for at least 1 hour.

Preheat oven to 190°C. Grease muffin tins.

Three-quarters fill muffin tins and bake for 20 minutes or until firm.

MAKES 16–20

Apple & cinnamon cake

1 cup self-raising flour

2 tablespoons castor sugar

60 g softened butter

1 egg, lightly beaten

⅓ cup milk

TOPPING

200 g green apples, peeled, cored and thinly sliced

½ teaspoon ground cinnamon

1 teaspoon cornflour

30 g butter, melted

Preheat oven to 180°C. Lightly grease a 23-cm round springform cake tin and line the base with non-stick baking paper.

Sift the flour and sugar into a mixing bowl. Add the butter and cut into the flour with a knife until mixture resembles coarse breadcrumbs. Stir in the egg and milk and beat to a smooth batter. Spread over the base of the prepared tin.

Combine the apple, cinnamon and cornflour in a bowl. Arrange on top of the cake batter. Drizzle melted butter over the top.

Bake for 45 minutes or until a skewer inserted into the centre of the cake comes out clean. Cool in the tin on a wire rack. Remove from the tin when cold.

Apple & date chews

450 g apples, peeled, cored
   and chopped

½ cup mixed nuts, chopped

1 cup pitted dates, chopped

1 cup gram flour (besan)

½ cup castor sugar

40 g butter, melted

1 tablespoon honey

1 egg, beaten

pinch of salt

Preheat oven to 180°C. Lightly grease and line
a 19-cm × 29-cm slice tin.

Mix all the ingredients together until well combined.
Spread into the tin.

Bake for 20–30 minutes until golden brown. Cool in
the tin, then cut into fingers before turning out.

MAKES 30 | GLUTEN FREE

Apple & date ring

1 cup chopped pitted dates

½ cup hot water

1 cup plain flour

1 cup castor sugar

1 teaspoon baking powder

1 teaspoon bicarbonate
   of soda

2 eggs

½ cup vegetable oil

2 teaspoons vanilla extract

1½ cups grated apple

TOPPING

1 cup desiccated coconut

¼ cup castor sugar

1 egg

Preheat oven to 180°C. Lightly grease and flour a 20-cm ring tin.

Place chopped dates in a saucepan with the water and bring to the boil. Remove from heat and leave to stand for 15 minutes.

Sift together flour, sugar, baking powder and bicarbonate of soda. Beat eggs lightly with oil and vanilla extract. Add to dry ingredients, together with dates and apple. Mix until just combined.

Pour into ring tin and bake for 30–35 minutes, or until cake springs back when lightly touched. Remove from oven and increase temperature to 190°C.

To make coconut topping, beat together coconut, sugar and egg. Spread over cake and bake for a further 10 minutes or until golden. Allow to cool in tin before turning out onto a wire rack.

Apple muffins

⅓ cup vegetable oil

¾ cup soft brown sugar,
  firmly packed

1 tablespoon honey

2 eggs, lightly beaten

1 cup grated apple

½ cup apple juice

1½ cups All-Bran

1 cup wholemeal plain
  flour

½ cup plain flour

1½ teaspoons baking powder

½ cup buttermilk

Preheat oven to 220°C. Grease muffin tins.

Mix together oil, brown sugar and honey. Add lightly
beaten eggs and beat until thoroughly combined.

Add grated apple and apple juice. Stir in All-Bran.

Sift remaining dry ingredients. Stir into egg mixture
with buttermilk until just combined.

Three-quarters fill muffin tins and bake for 15 minutes
or until firm.

MAKES 12–16

Apple muffins with maple glaze

1⅓ cups plain flour

1 cup oats (quick or
   old-fashioned)

½ cup castor sugar

1 tablespoon baking powder

2 teaspoons ground
   cinnamon

½ cup milk

80 g butter, melted

¼ cup maple syrup

2 egg whites, lightly beaten

1 cup chopped apple

toasted pecan halves,
   for decorating

GLAZE

¼ cup icing sugar

1½ tablespoons maple syrup

Preheat oven to 200°C. Grease muffin tins.

Mix together sifted flour, oats, sugar, baking powder
and cinnamon.

In a separate bowl combine milk, butter, maple syrup
and egg whites.

Mix wet and dry ingredients until just blended. Gently stir
in apple.

Three-quarters fill muffin tins and top each with a pecan
half. Bake 20–25 minutes.

Let stand a few minutes before removing from tins.
Cool on wire racks for about 10 minutes.

For glaze, mix together sifted icing sugar and maple
syrup. Leave muffins sitting on a wire rack under which
you have placed sheets of baking paper. Drizzle over
the glaze.

MAKES 14–16

Apple & nut muffins

1 egg

⅔ cup apple juice or milk

½ cup vegetable oil

1 teaspoon vanilla extract

2 cups plain flour

¼ cup castor sugar

¼ cup soft brown sugar,
   firmly packed

1 tablespoon baking powder

½ teaspoon salt

½ cup chopped nuts

1 apple, peeled, cored and
   chopped

2 tablespoons castor sugar
   mixed with 1 teaspoon
   cinnamon, for sprinkling

Preheat oven to 200°C. Grease muffin tins.

In a large bowl, beat egg with juice, oil and vanilla.

Stir in sifted flour, sugars, baking powder and salt until just moistened.

Stir in nuts and apple.

Three-quarters fill prepared muffin tins. Sprinkle with cinnamon sugar.

Bake for 20 minutes or until golden brown.

MAKES 16

Apple & orange pudding

1 kg Granny Smith apples,
  peeled, cored and cut
  into chunks

grated zest and juice of
  1 orange

¼ cup soft brown sugar

TOPPING

100 g softened butter

100 g soft brown sugar

2 large eggs

1 teaspoon baking powder

1 cup self-raising flour

50 g flaked almonds,
  for decorating

Preheat oven to 180°C. Lightly grease a 2-litre ovenproof dish.

Combine the apple, orange zest and juice, and brown sugar in the ovenproof dish.

Place all the topping ingredients in an electric mixer and blend slowly until combined. Blend on high speed until soft and fluffy (about 1 minute).

Spoon the topping over the apple to cover it, spreading the mixture to the edges. Sprinkle the flaked almonds over the top.

Bake for 35–40 minutes or until lightly browned on top.

Serve immediately with ice-cream or cream.

SERVES 4

Apple, rum & date cake

½ cup chopped pitted dates, soaked in ¼ cup rum

140 g softened butter

1½ cups castor sugar

3 eggs

2 cups self-raising flour

½ teaspoon ground nutmeg

½ teaspoon ground cinnamon

½ teaspoon ground ginger

½ teaspoon ground cloves

pinch of salt

1 teaspoon baking powder

2 cups chopped walnuts

2 cups chopped apple

Preheat oven to 180°C. Lightly grease a 23-cm springform cake tin and line the base with non-stick baking paper.

Place the chopped dates and rum in a small saucepan. Cook for 5 minutes over a gentle heat. Remove and cool.

Cream the butter and sugar in a mixing bowl until light and fluffy. Add the eggs one at a time, beating until well combined.

Sift all the dry ingredients into a mixing bowl. Coat the chopped walnuts and apple with a little flour. Fold the sifted dry ingredients into the butter mixture, then fold in walnuts and apples. Stir through the date mixture.

Pour into the prepared tin and bake for 60–75 minutes or until a skewer inserted into the centre of the cake comes out clean. Cool in the tin and then turn out onto a wire rack. Serve with whipped cream.

Apricot almond cake

1½ cups chopped dried
    apricots

2 cups orange juice

125 g softened butter

½ cup soft brown sugar

½ cup honey

1 egg

1½ cups plain flour

1½ cups wholemeal plain
    flour

½ teaspoon bicarbonate
    of soda

2 teaspoons baking powder

1 cup chopped almonds

¼ cup blanched whole
    almonds

Soak chopped apricots in orange juice overnight.

Preheat oven to 180°C. Lightly grease a 20-cm round tin and line the base with non-stick baking paper.

Cream butter, brown sugar and honey until light and fluffy. Add egg, beating well.

Sift flours, bicarbonate of soda and baking powder into a large bowl, then add chopped almonds. Fold flour mixture into creamed mixture, then fold in apricot mixture.

Pour into prepared tin and arrange whole almonds over the top. Bake for 60–80 minutes.

Apricot & almond muffins

1 cup dried apricots

2 cups plain flour

1 egg

¾ cup milk

75 g butter, melted

1 tablespoon baking powder

½ cup castor sugar

70 g almond slivers

Cover apricots with water in a small saucepan and bring to the boil.

Leave to cool for at least 1 hour then drain, chop and transfer to a large bowl.

Preheat oven to 180°C. Grease muffins tins.

Add sifted flour and remaining ingredients to apricots and mix until just combined.

Spoon into muffin tins and bake for 15 minutes.

MAKES 16

Apricot almond slice

1 cup self-raising flour

125 g cold butter, cut into small pieces

½ cup white sugar

1 egg, beaten

apricot jam, for spreading

milk, to brush

½ cup chopped almonds

Preheat oven to 180°C. Lightly grease a 19-cm square cake tin.

Rub butter into sifted flour until crumbly, then add sugar. Add egg and mix to form a stiff dough.

Turn onto a lightly floured surface and knead gently. Divide dough into two pieces. Roll out one piece to just fit cake tin, and press into tin. Spread with apricot jam.

Roll out remaining dough and place on top. Brush with milk and sprinkle with chopped almonds.

Bake for 20–30 minutes. Cover with foil if the almonds start to burn.

MAKES 16

Apricot, ginger & lemon slice

¾ cup dried apricots

1½ cups self-raising flour

pinch of salt

½ teaspoon ground
　cinnamon

125 g cold butter, cut into
　small pieces

1½ cups white sugar

¼ cup preserved ginger,
　chopped

¼ cup walnuts, chopped

1 egg

½ cup milk

lemon glacé icing
　(page 679)

Soak apricots in warm water for 30 minutes, then drain and chop.

Preheat oven to 180°C. Lightly grease and line a 19-cm × 29-cm slice tin.

Sift together flour, salt and cinnamon. Rub in butter with your fingertips until crumbly. Add sugar, apricots, ginger and nuts and mix until combined.

Beat together egg and milk, then add to mixture and stir until well combined.

Spread mixture into tin and bake for 25–30 minutes.

When cool, top with lemon icing and once set, cut into fingers.

MAKES 36

Apricot & lemon muffins

1 cup plain flour

½ teaspoon salt

1 teaspoon baking powder

1½ cups bran

¼ cup castor sugar

½ cup chopped apricots,
  dried or fresh

2 teaspoons grated lemon
  zest

½ teaspoon bicarbonate
  of soda

1 cup milk

1 egg

1 tablespoon butter, melted

1 tablespoon golden syrup

Preheat oven to 200°C. Grease muffin tins.

Sift together flour, salt and baking powder.

Stir in bran, sugar, apricots and lemon zest.
Make a well in the centre of the dry ingredients.

Dissolve bicarbonate of soda in milk. Beat egg lightly.

Combine milk, melted butter, egg and golden syrup, and
pour into well in dry ingredients. Stir to just combine.

Three-quarters fill muffin tins and bake in the oven for
10–15 minutes or until firm.

MAKES 12

Apricot meringue slice

BASE

175 g softened butter

½ cup white sugar

2 egg yolks

1 cup self-raising flour

1 cup plain flour

⅓ cup milk

1 teaspoon vanilla extract

apricot jam, for spreading

TOPPING

2 egg whites

1 cup castor sugar

1 cup desiccated coconut

Preheat oven to 180°C. Lightly grease a 23-cm square slab tin.

For the base, cream butter and sugar until light and fluffy, then beat in egg yolks. Add sifted flours, milk and vanilla and mix well.

Press into prepared tin and spread with jam.

For the topping, beat egg whites and sugar until stiff peaks form. Carefully fold in coconut. Spread over the base and bake for 30 minutes, making sure the meringue doesn't burn.

When cold, cut into squares.

MAKES 16

Apricot oat biscuits

1½ cups plain flour

1 teaspoon baking powder

1 teaspoon ground
   cinnamon

1 cup rolled oats

½ cup soft brown sugar

¾ cup dried apricots,
   chopped

1 tablespoon flaked almonds

⅔ cup natural yoghurt

¼ cup canola oil

soft brown sugar,
   for sprinkling

Preheat oven to 190°C. Lightly grease a baking tray.

Sift together the flour, baking powder and cinnamon.
Stir in the other dry ingredients.

In a separate bowl, beat together the yoghurt and oil.
Add to the dry ingredients and mix to make a firm dough.

Roll the mixture into about 16 balls, place on prepared
baking tray and flatten slightly with a fork. Sprinkle with
brown sugar.

Bake for 15–20 minutes, until golden brown and firm to
the touch.

MAKES 16

Apricot rough three-layer slice

BASE

¾ cup self-raising flour

¾ cup desiccated coconut

¾ cup soft brown sugar

90 g butter, melted

FILLING

125 g dried apricots,
   chopped

2 cups desiccated coconut

¾ cup condensed milk

TOPPING

125 g dark cooking
   chocolate, chopped

30 g white vegetable
   shortening

Preheat oven to 180°C. Lightly grease a 23-cm square slab tin.

For the base, mix sifted flour with other ingredients until well combined. Press into the tin. Bake for 15 minutes.

For the filling, place apricots into a small saucepan and cover with water. Simmer for a few minutes, until tender. Drain.

Mix apricots with coconut and condensed milk, then spread over the warm biscuit base.

For the topping, melt the chocolate and shortening in a double boiler over simmering water, or on MEDIUM in the microwave. Stir until smooth, then spread over the apricot filling. Chill before cutting into small squares.

MAKES 36

Apricot & sesame slice

40 g butter

2 tablespoons golden syrup

2 tablespoons soft brown
sugar

⅓ cup desiccated coconut

100 g rice flakes
(precooked variety)

⅓ cup chopped dried
apricots

2 tablespoons sesame seeds

½ teaspoon ground
cinnamon

pinch of salt

¼ cup milk chocolate chips

Preheat oven to 150°C. Lightly grease and line a
19-cm × 29-cm slice tin.

Melt the butter and golden syrup over a low heat.
Mix all the other ingredients (except choc chips)
together in a bowl, then stir in the melted butter
and syrup. Mix in the chocolate chips.

Press mixture firmly into the tin.

Bake for 30–35 minutes.

Cool in the tin before cutting into squares or fingers
and turning out.

MAKES 24 | GLUTEN FREE

Apricot & walnut muffins

12 dried apricots

2 tablespoons brandy

2 cups plain flour

1 tablespoon baking powder

½ cup castor sugar

½ cup chopped walnuts

1 egg

½ cup milk

50 g butter, melted

Preheat oven to 200°C. Grease muffin tins.

Cook apricots in brandy over medium heat for 5 minutes and then chop roughly.

Sift together flour and baking powder and stir in sugar, apricots and walnuts.

Combine egg and milk and add melted butter.

Make a well in the centre of the dry ingredients and pour in egg mixture. Stir quickly until just combined.

Three-quarters fill muffin tins and bake in the oven for 15–20 minutes.

MAKES 16

Arabian date & nut cake

¾ cup hot strong coffee

1 cup chopped pitted dates

½ cup chopped walnuts

125 g softened butter

1 cup castor sugar

2 eggs

1¾ cups plain flour

½ teaspoon bicarbonate
   of soda

½ teaspoon salt

1½ teaspoons baking powder

pinch of salt

1 teaspoon vanilla extract

icing sugar, for dusting

Preheat oven to 180°C. Grease a 25-cm × 15-cm loaf tin and line the base with non-stick baking paper.

Pour hot coffee over chopped dates and walnuts and allow to cool.

Cream butter and sugar until light and fluffy, then add eggs and beat well. Sift in dry ingredients. Lastly mix in date and nut mixture and vanilla extract.

Pour into cake tin and bake for 50–60 minutes. Dust with icing sugar to serve.

Artichoke heart with bacon & garlic muffins

¾ cup fresh breadcrumbs

1 clove garlic, crushed

40 g butter

1 egg, beaten

½ cup plain flour

¼ teaspoon salt

1 tablespoon baking powder

½ cup grated tasty cheese

1 cup marinated artichoke hearts, quartered

2 rashers bacon, cooked and chopped

Preheat oven to 200°C. Grease muffin tins.

Fry breadcrumbs and garlic in butter until crisp.

Make egg up to 1 cup with water and mix with sifted flour, salt, baking powder, cheese, artichoke hearts and bacon until just combined.

Three-quarters fill muffin tins and sprinkle with fried breadcrumbs.

Bake for 12–15 minutes.

MAKES 12

Auntie Ruth's lemon slice

BASE

1½ cups Corn Flakes, crushed

120 g butter, melted

¼ cup white sugar

TOPPING

1 × 395-g tin condensed milk

½ cup lemon juice

finely grated zest of 1 lemon

1 egg yolk

Lightly grease a 23-cm square slice tin.

For the base, mix all ingredients together. Press into the tin. Refrigerate for about 10 minutes.

For the topping, beat ingredients together until thick and fluffy. Pour evenly over base. Return to refrigerator until set, then cut into squares.

MAKES 36 | NO BAKE

Bacon & tomato muffins

2 cups plain flour

1 tablespoon baking powder

4 rashers bacon

2 tomatoes

2 tablespoons tomato paste

1 egg

¾ cup milk

50 g butter, melted

Preheat oven to 200°C. Grease muffin tins.

Sift together flour and baking powder.

Cut rind off bacon and chop flesh.

Skin and de-seed tomatoes, and chop roughly.

Mix together bacon, tomatoes, tomato paste, egg and milk.

Add tomato mixture and melted butter to dry ingredients. Stir until just combined.

Three-quarters fill muffin tins and bake in the oven for 15–20 minutes.

MAKES 16

Baileys, cream cheese & chocolate muffins

90 g cream cheese

1½ tablespoons Baileys
  Irish Cream

1 egg

¾ cup milk

⅓ cup water

50 g butter, melted

100 g dark cooking
  chocolate, grated

1½ cups plain flour

2 teaspoons baking powder

½ teaspoon salt

⅓ cup cocoa

½ cup castor sugar

Preheat oven to 190°C. Grease muffin tins.

Beat cream cheese until smooth, add Baileys and beat again.

In a separate bowl whisk together egg, milk, water and butter, then add chocolate.

Sift remaining dry ingredients into egg mixture and stir until just combined.

One-third fill muffin tins with muffin mixture, make a hollow in the centre of each, and fill with 1 teaspoon cream cheese mixture.

Top up to three-quarters full with remaining muffin mixture.

Bake for 20 minutes.

MAKES 14–16

Baked date pudding

TOPPING

40 g butter, melted

⅓ cup soft brown sugar,
    firmly packed

PUDDING

2 eggs

¾ cup soft brown sugar

1½ cups plain flour

1½ teaspoons baking powder

pinch of salt

¾ cup chopped pitted dates

2 tablespoons chopped
    walnuts

⅓ cup milk

cream, ice-cream or
    pouring custard
    (page 683), to serve

Preheat oven to 180°C. Grease a 20-cm cake tin.

Combine topping ingredients and spread evenly over
the bottom of prepared cake tin.

In a bowl standing in a sink of hot water, beat eggs and
brown sugar until doubled in volume and light, white
and fluffy. Stir in sifted dry ingredients, dates, walnuts
and milk. Pour over topping.

Bake in a bain-marie (see page 3) for 60 minutes or until
pudding comes away from sides. Turn pudding out onto
a serving plate so that topping shows uppermost.

Serve sliced in wedges with whipped cream, ice-cream
or pouring custard.

SERVES 6

Baked rice pudding with lemon

⅓ cup short-grain rice

½ cup castor sugar

1 litre milk

1 tablespoon butter

finely grated zest of 1 lemon

Preheat oven to 175°C. Grease a 2-litre ovenproof dish.

Sprinkle the rice over the bottom of the prepared dish. Combine the sugar and milk and pour over the rice. Dot the top with butter.

Bake for 60 minutes. Stir in the lemon zest and bake for a further 15–20 minutes. Allow to stand for 10 minutes.

Serve warm with cream.

SERVES 6

Baked stuffed peaches

¾ cup ground almonds

6 amaretti biscuits (almond macaroons), crushed

2 tablespoons castor sugar

1 egg, lightly beaten

½ cup ricotta

6 large, ripe, firm peaches, halved and pitted

½ cup white wine

¼ cup orange juice

1 tablespoon butter

ice-cream or pouring custard (page 683), to serve

Preheat oven to 180°C. Lightly grease a shallow ovenproof dish.

Combine the ground almonds, crushed biscuits and sugar. Stir in the egg and ricotta. Mix to form a sticky ball. Spoon mixture into the cavities of the halved peaches.

Place peach halves into the prepared dish and pour the wine and orange juice over the top. Dot the top of each peach with butter.

Bake for 25–30 minutes or until lightly browned on top.

Serve warm or cold with ice-cream or pouring custard.

SERVES 6

Banana bread pudding

½ cup orange marmalade

5 thick slices white bread

3 large bananas, peeled and
 cut into thick slices

4 eggs, lightly beaten

1 litre milk

2 cups castor sugar

2 teaspoons vanilla extract

1 teaspoon ground nutmeg

1 tablespoon ground
 cinnamon

80 g butter, melted

icing sugar, for dusting

Preheat oven to 180°C. Lightly grease a 2-litre ovenproof dish.

Spread the marmalade on the bread slices and then cut the bread into small chunks. Lay half of the bread chunks over the base of the prepared dish. Arrange the banana slices over the bread and then place the remainder of the bread chunks on top.

Combine the eggs, milk, sugar, vanilla extract and spices. Whisk in the melted butter. Pour the mixture over the bread and banana.

Cover the dish with foil and place into a bain-marie (see page 3). Bake for 30 minutes. Remove the foil and bake for a further 30 minutes or until the pudding is firm and lightly browned on top.

Remove from the bain-marie and cool a little. Dust with icing sugar before serving.

SERVES 8

Banana & buttermilk cake

200 g softened unsalted
  butter

1 cup castor sugar

3 large eggs

1 cup mashed banana

2 teaspoons vanilla extract

1 cup buttermilk

1¾ cups self-raising flour

1 teaspoon bicarbonate
  of soda

pinch of salt

butterscotch sauce
  (page 682)

Preheat oven to 180°C. Lightly grease a 23-cm springform cake tin and line the base with non-stick baking paper.

Cream the butter and sugar until light and fluffy. Add the eggs, mashed banana, vanilla extract and buttermilk. Sift the flour, bicarbonate of soda and salt into another bowl. Stir the flour mixture into the batter and mix until smooth.

Pour into the prepared tin and bake for 45 minutes or until a skewer inserted comes out clean.

Cool in the tin for 10 minutes. Turn out onto a wire rack and cool for 10 minutes more.

Serve warm with butterscotch sauce.

Banana choc-chip muffins

1½ cups self-raising flour

⅓ cup castor sugar

60 g cold butter, cut into
    small pieces

⅔ cup mashed banana

½ cup chocolate chips

1 egg

½ cup milk

FILLING

sliced banana

whipped cream

Preheat oven to 190°C. Grease muffin tins.

In a large bowl rub butter into sifted flour and sugar until mixture resembles fine breadcrumbs.

Stir in mashed banana, chocolate chips, egg and milk to combine.

Spoon mixture into prepared tins and bake for 20 minutes.

For the filling, fold sliced banana into whipped cream. Once muffins have cooled a bit, slice each in half and fill with banana cream filling.

MAKES 12

Banana & date muffins

2½ cups oat bran

1½ cups wholemeal plain flour

1½ tablespoons baking powder

2 teaspoons mixed spice

1 teaspoon ground cinnamon

500 g finely chopped banana

100 g finely chopped pitted dates

½ cup apple juice concentrate

½ cup cold-pressed grapeseed oil

1 cup evaporated milk

3 egg whites

Preheat oven to 180°C. Grease muffin tins.

Place oat bran in a bowl. Add sifted flour, baking powder, mixed spice and cinnamon. Mix flour and spices through oat bran with hands.

Add banana and dates and toss well to break up and coat with flour.

Combine apple juice concentrate, oil and milk, and combine with flour and oat mixture.

Beat egg whites until soft peaks form, then gently fold through the mixture.

Three-quarters fill muffin tins and bake in the oven for 25–30 minutes.

MAKES 16

Banana & fresh fig gratin

4 fresh figs, quartered

4 ripe, firm bananas,
   thickly sliced

3 eggs

1½ tablespoons ground
   almonds

1 teaspoon vanilla extract

300 ml cream

¼ cup soft brown sugar

icing sugar, for dusting

Preheat oven to 180°C. Lightly grease a square 1-litre ovenproof dish.

Place the fruit in the bottom of the prepared dish.

Beat together the eggs, ground almonds, vanilla extract, cream and brown sugar. Pour over the fruit.

Place dish on a preheated baking tray and bake for 10–15 minutes or until nearly set.

Then place under a hot grill until lightly browned.

Dust liberally with icing sugar before serving warm.

SERVES 4

Banana & ginger muffins

60 g softened butter

2 tablespoons castor sugar

1 egg

1 ripe banana, mashed

1 cup plain flour

1 teaspoon ground ginger

2 tablespoons golden syrup

1 teaspoon bicarbonate
  of soda

⅓ cup milk

FILLING

whipped cream

icing sugar

ground ginger

Preheat oven to 200°C. Grease muffin tins.

Cream butter and sugar, then beat in egg and mashed banana.

Sift in flour and ginger.

Dissolve golden syrup and bicarbonate of soda in milk and add to mixture. Mix lightly.

Spoon batter into prepared muffin tins and bake for 15 minutes.

Serve filled with fresh whipped cream flavoured with a little sugar and ground ginger.

MAKES 12

Banana layer cake

65 g softened butter

½ cup castor sugar

2 eggs, beaten

2 tablespoons milk

1 cup mashed banana

1⅓ cups wholemeal
   self-raising flour

FILLING

125 g softened butter

1 egg white

¾ cup demerara sugar

1 teaspoon liqueur

2 bananas, sliced

Preheat oven to 200°C. Grease and flour two sandwich tins.

Cream butter and sugar, then add eggs gradually. Combine milk and mashed banana and add to mixture alternately with sifted flour.

Pour into prepared tins and bake for 25 minutes.

To make butter cream filling, cream butter thoroughly. In a separate bowl whisk egg whites until soft peaks form. Add whisked egg white to the creamed mixture by the spoonful. Beat in sugar gradually and flavour with liqueur.

Spread one cake half with butter cream and top with half the sliced banana. Place remaining cake half on top then decorate top of cake in the same way.

Banana mousse pie

PASTRY

100 g cold butter, cut into
    small pieces

1½ cups plain flour

1 teaspoon finely grated
    lemon zest

⅓ cup icing sugar

1 egg, lightly beaten

2–3 tablespoons cold water

FILLING

4 ripe bananas, chopped

½ cup soft brown sugar

2 tablespoons rum

3 eggs, separated

TOPPING

2 ripe bananas, sliced

½ cup flaked almonds

2 tablespoons castor sugar

icing sugar, for dusting

For the pastry, pulse the butter and sifted flour in a food processor until the mixture resembles fine breadcrumbs. Add the lemon zest and icing sugar and pulse for about 1 minute.

Combine the egg and water and, with the motor running, slowly pour enough liquid into the food processor to draw the mixture together. Remove and roll into a ball. Chill for 30 minutes.

Preheat oven to 200°C. Lightly grease a 20-cm pie dish.

On a floured board, roll out the pastry and fit it into the prepared dish, cutting away any excess. Blind-bake the pastry shell (see page 3) on a preheated baking tray for 10–15 minutes or until lightly browned at the sides.

Remove pastry and reduce the oven temperature to 175°C.

For the filling, blend bananas with sugar, rum and egg yolks in the food processor until smooth. Whip the egg whites until stiff. Carefully fold through the banana mixture. Pour into the pastry case.

For the topping, arrange banana slices over the top of the pie. Bake for 20 minutes or until firm.

Sprinkle with flaked almonds and castor sugar.

Preheat grill until hot and grill the pie for 2–3 minutes to caramelise the nutty topping.

Serve warm or cold dusted with icing sugar.

SERVES 6

Banana nut biscuits

125 g softened butter

½ cup soft brown sugar

½ cup peanut butter

½ cup mashed banana

1 cup self-raising flour

pinch of salt

Cream butter and sugar until light and fluffy. Add peanut butter and banana and mix well.

In a separate bowl, sift together dry ingredients. Add to banana mixture, and stir well to combine.

With floured hands, roll mixture into long logs, about 3 cm in diameter. Wrap in foil and chill until cold.

Preheat oven to 180°C. Lightly grease baking trays.

Cut the logs into 8-mm slices, then transfer to baking trays and bake for 12–15 minutes.

MAKES 40

Banana walnut cake

125 g softened butter

1 cup castor sugar

2 eggs

1 cup mashed banana

1 teaspoon vanilla extract

2¼ cups self-raising flour

¼ teaspoon bicarbonate
of soda

½ cup water

TOPPING

50 g softened butter

2 tablespoons self-raising
flour

2 tablespoons castor sugar

1 teaspoon ground
cinnamon

2 tablespoons chopped
walnuts

Preheat oven to 180°C. Lightly grease a 23-cm square tin and line the base with non-stick baking paper.

Cream butter and sugar until light and fluffy. Add eggs one at a time, beating well after each addition. Add banana and vanilla extract, and beat well.

Sift flour and bicarbonate of soda and add to creamed mixture with the water.

Pour mixture into prepared tin.

To make topping, rub butter into flour, add remaining ingredients and mix well.

Spread topping evenly over cake mixture and bake for 40–45 minutes.

Berry cake

1 cup plain flour

100 g butter, melted

1 egg

½ cup castor sugar

1½ teaspoons baking powder

1 teaspoon vanilla extract

3 cups fresh or frozen
   berries (blackberries,
   blueberries, raspberries)

TOPPING

2 cups sour cream

½ cup castor sugar

1½ tablespoons custard
   powder

2 egg yolks

1 teaspoon vanilla extract

Preheat oven to 180°C. Lightly grease and flour a 23-cm springform tin.

For cake, mix together sifted flour and all other cake ingredients except berries. Pour into prepared tin. Cover with berries.

Beat topping ingredients together and pour on top of berries. Bake for 50–60 minutes.

Serve with whipped cream and more berries if desired.

Billionaire shortbread bars

BASE

100 g softened butter

¼ cup castor sugar

1½ cups self-raising flour

FILLING

125 g butter

½ cup castor sugar

2 tablespoons golden syrup

1 × 395-g tin condensed
milk

TOPPING

75 g white cooking
chocolate, chopped

75 g dark cooking chocolate,
chopped

Preheat oven to 180°C. Lightly grease and line a 19-cm × 29-cm slice tin.

For the base, cream butter and sugar until light and fluffy. Fold in sifted flour. Press mixture evenly into base of tin. Bake for 15 minutes or until golden. Set aside to cool.

For filling, combine butter, sugar, golden syrup and condensed milk in a saucepan. Stir over low heat until dissolved, then boil for several minutes, stirring vigorously, until caramel in colour. Spread over cooked base and leave to cool.

For the topping, melt white and dark chocolate separately, in a double boiler or on MEDIUM in the microwave. Pour over the slice one at a time, spreading evenly. Use a fork to create a swirly pattern through the chocolate.

Once the chocolate has set, cut into bars.

MAKES 16

Blackberry lattice fingers

1½ cups plain flour

½ teaspoon baking powder

125 g cold butter, cut into
   small pieces

½ cup castor sugar

½ teaspoon vanilla extract

1 egg, beaten

¼ cup blackberry jam
   (or other fruit jam)

Preheat oven to 180°C. Lightly grease and line a 19-cm × 29-cm baking tray.

Sift together flour and baking powder. Add butter and rub in with your fingertips until crumbly. Stir in sugar and vanilla and add enough egg to work into a dough.

Knead dough lightly on a floured surface. Roll out two-thirds of the dough to make a rectangle that's about 18 cm × 28 cm in size. Place on the prepared tray and spread evenly with the jam.

Roll out remaining dough into an 18-cm square. Cut into strips 1.5-cm wide with a sharp knife and place in a lattice pattern over the jam.

Bake for about 25 minutes or until golden brown. Cool and then cut into fingers.

MAKES 20

Blackberry muffins

¾ cup natural yoghurt

½ cup water

2 eggs

2 cups blackberries
(fresh, frozen or tinned)

3 cups plain flour

1 tablespoon baking powder

½ teaspoon bicarbonate
of soda

1½ cups castor sugar

icing sugar, for dusting

Preheat oven to 180°C. Grease muffin tins.

Mix together yoghurt, water and eggs. (If using tinned blackberries, reserve juice from berries and use ½ cup of this in place of water.)

Add sifted flour and remaining ingredients and mix until just combined.

Spoon into muffin tins and bake for 15–20 minutes.

Dust with icing sugar just before serving.

MAKES 24

Black bottom cake

225 g cream cheese

1 egg

⅓ cup castor sugar

pinch of salt

175 g dark chocolate chips

BASE

1½ cups plain flour

1 teaspoon bicarbonate
  of soda

½ cup cocoa

½ teaspoon salt

1 cup castor sugar

100 g butter, melted

1 cup water

1 teaspoon vanilla extract

1 tablespoon vinegar

ICING

65 g dark cooking chocolate

⅔ cup cream

Preheat oven to 190°C. Lightly grease and flour a 20-cm cake tin.

For the topping, beat together cream cheese, egg, sugar and a pinch of salt. Stir in chocolate chips.

For base, sift together flour, bicarbonate of soda, cocoa and salt, then add sugar, melted butter, water, vanilla extract and vinegar.

Pour base mixture into prepared cake tin. Spread cream cheese topping mixture on top. Bake for 45 minutes. Allow to cool before removing from tin.

To make chocolate icing, melt together chocolate and cream in a double boiler or on MEDIUM in the microwave. Pour over cake.

Black bottom muffins

1¼ cups plain flour

¾ cup castor sugar

⅓ cup cocoa

½ teaspoon bicarbonate
of soda

¼ teaspoon salt

⅔ cup buttermilk

¼ cup vegetable oil

60 g butter, melted and
cooled slightly

1 egg

1 teaspoon vanilla extract

⅓ cup chocolate chips

TOPPING

200 g cream cheese

¼ cup castor sugar

1 egg

few drops almond essence

¼ cup toasted slivered
almonds

Preheat oven to 190°C. Grease muffin tins.

In a large bowl mix together sifted flour, sugar, cocoa, bicarbonate of soda and salt.

In a separate bowl mix together buttermilk, oil, butter, egg and vanilla until well combined.

Make a well in the centre of the dry ingredients and add buttermilk mixture. Stir to combine, then mix in chocolate chips.

To make topping, beat together cream cheese, sugar, egg and almond essence, then fold in almonds.

Spoon muffin batter into prepared tins, then cover with topping. Bake for 20 minutes.

MAKES 12

Black forest muffins

2 cups plain flour

2 teaspoons baking powder

1 tablespoon cocoa

1 egg

150 g dark cooking chocolate melted in 1 cup boiling water

75 g softened butter

½ cup castor sugar

1 cup glacé cherries

FILLING

100 g dark cooking chocolate, chopped

100 ml sour cream

1½ cups icing sugar

raspberry jam, for spreading

Preheat oven to 180°C. Grease muffin tins.

Sift together flour, baking powder and cocoa. Add remaining muffin ingredients and mix until just combined.

Three-quarters fill prepared muffin tins and bake for 15–20 minutes. Leave to cool.

To make filling, melt chocolate in a double boiler over simmering water, or on MEDIUM in the microwave. Mix chocolate, sour cream and sifted icing sugar.

Remove muffins from tins, make a diagonal cut into each, spread cuts thinly with raspberry jam and fill with icing.

MAKES 16

Black & white muffins

50 g softened butter

½ cup castor sugar

1 egg

1 cup milk

2 cups plain flour

2 teaspoons baking powder

80 g white chocolate,
  chopped

1 tablespoon cocoa

80 g dark cooking chocolate,
  chopped

Preheat oven to 190°C. Line muffin tins with paper cases.

Cream butter and sugar until fluffy.

Add egg and milk, then mix in sifted flour and baking powder until just combined.

Divide mixture between two bowls. Add white chocolate to one, and to the other add cocoa and dark chocolate.

Half fill each paper case with white mixture, then top with dark mixture.

Bake for 20 minutes.

MAKES 16

Blueberry cake

60 g butter, melted

½ cup castor sugar

1 egg

¾ cup sour cream

½ teaspoon vanilla extract

1 cup self-raising flour

TOPPING

1 cup icing sugar

225 g ricotta

1 egg

2 tablespoons freshly
squeezed lemon juice

2 cups fresh blueberries

Preheat oven to 180°C. Lightly grease and flour a 22-cm springform cake tin.

Using an electric mixer, beat the butter, sugar and egg together for about 1 minute until pale and thick. Mix in the sour cream, vanilla extract and sifted flour.

Spoon the batter into the prepared tin and bake for 20 minutes or until lightly browned and risen. Remove cake but leave oven on.

To make topping, beat the sifted icing sugar, ricotta, egg and lemon juice together until smooth. Pour onto the hot cake and sprinkle the blueberries over the top. Return to the oven and bake for a further 30 minutes or until the cake topping is set and lightly browned. Cool in the tin on a wire rack.

Serve warm or at room temperature.

Blueberry fat-free muffins

1¾ cups rolled oats

½ cup oat bran

¾ teaspoon bicarbonate of soda

½ teaspoon ground cinnamon

¾ cup unsweetened apple sauce

½ cup honey

1 teaspoon vanilla extract

½ cup skim milk

3 egg whites, lightly beaten

1 cup blueberries

Preheat oven to 180°C. Grease muffin tins.

Pulse rolled oats and oat bran in food processor for 10 seconds. Reserve 2 tablespoons of the oat mixture.

In a medium bowl, combine remaining oat mixture, bicarbonate of soda and cinnamon. Mix well and set aside.

In a small bowl, combine apple sauce, honey, vanilla and milk. Pour into oat mixture. Stir until just blended.

Gently mix in egg whites.

Dust well-drained blueberries with 2 tablespoons reserved oat mixture. Gently fold the blueberries into the batter.

Spoon mixture into muffin tins and bake for 20–25 minutes.

MAKES 12–16

Blueberry maple muffins

1 cup bran flakes, lightly
  crushed

1 cup sour cream

1 cup maple syrup

2 eggs

2 cups plain flour

2 teaspoons bicarbonate
  of soda

1 cup blueberries

1 cup walnuts, chopped

The night before baking, combine bran flakes with
sour cream and maple syrup and refrigerate overnight.

Preheat oven to 200°C. Grease muffin tins or line with
paper cases.

Beat eggs until frothy and blend into bran flake mixture.

Combine sifted flour with bicarbonate of soda and stir
into batter until blended. Fold in blueberries.

Spoon batter into prepared tins, then sprinkle walnuts
evenly over muffins. Bake for 15–20 minutes.

MAKES 16–18

Bran biscuits

1 cup wholemeal plain flour

1 teaspoon baking powder

2 cups unprocessed
(natural) bran

⅓ cup castor sugar

125 g cold butter, cut into
small pieces

2 eggs, lightly beaten

Preheat oven to 180°C. Lightly grease baking trays.

Sift together flour and baking powder. Mix in bran and sugar, then rub butter through dry ingredients with your finger tips. Add eggs and mix in thoroughly with a fork.

Turn mixture onto a lightly floured surface and knead gently into a smooth dough.

Roll dough out thinly and cut into strips or squares. Prick all over with a fork.

Bake for 10–15 minutes or until golden brown.

MAKES 36

Brandy apple spice cake

1 cup raisins

¾ cup brandy

4 cups chopped Granny
    Smith apples

2 cups raw sugar

½ cup vegetable oil

2 eggs

2 cups plain flour

2 teaspoons bicarbonate
    of soda

1 teaspoon salt

2 teaspoons ground
    cinnamon

1 teaspoon freshly grated
    nutmeg

¼ teaspoon ground cloves

1 cup chopped walnuts

Soak raisins in brandy for 2 hours to plump them.

Preheat oven to 160°C. Lightly grease and flour a 23-cm square fluted flan tin or 23-cm springform tin.

Add apple to raisin mixture and mix well.

Beat sugar, oil and eggs until pale and creamy.

Sift flour, bicarbonate of soda, salt and spices into oil mixture. Add apple mixture and chopped walnuts, combining well.

Pour into prepared tin. Bake for 90 minutes.

Allow to cool in the tin before turning out onto a wire rack. Serve with whipped cream.

Brandy snaps

1 cup plain flour

1 teaspoon ground ginger

½ teaspoon ground
  cinnamon

100 g butter

⅓ cup golden syrup

½ cup castor sugar

1 tablespoon brandy

whipped cream, to serve

Preheat oven to 160°C. Line baking trays with baking paper.

Sift together the flour, ginger and cinnamon.

Place the butter, golden syrup and sugar into a saucepan over medium heat and stir until the butter has melted. Simmer for 1 minute, then add to the dry ingredients. Stir well, then mix in the brandy.

Drop tablespoons of the mixture onto trays, leaving 4 cm between each to allow for spreading.

Bake for 15–18 minutes or until golden. Cool for 5 minutes on the trays before transferring to a wire rack.

Allow to cool flat, or, while still warm, roll around the handle of a large wooden spoon to form a tube. Remove from handle while still warm, then allow to cool.

Fill tubes with sweetened whipped cream or your choice of filling.

MAKES 18

Brazil nut & fruit muffins

2 cups plain flour

⅔ cup soft brown sugar,
  firmly packed

2 teaspoons baking powder

½ teaspoon salt

1 cup chopped dried apricots

¾ cup boiling water

½ cup vegetable oil

½ cup mashed banana

1 egg

1 teaspoon vanilla extract

1 cup chopped brazil nuts

Preheat oven to 200°C. Grease muffin tins.

In a large bowl mix together sifted flour, brown sugar, baking powder and salt.

In a separate bowl combine apricots and boiling water and allow to soak for 5 minutes.

Stir oil, banana, egg and vanilla into apricot mixture.

Make a well in the centre of the dry ingredients and add apricot mixture. Stir to combine, then fold in nuts.

Spoon batter into prepared muffin tins and bake for 16–20 minutes.

Serve with butter while still warm.

MAKES 16

Brown walnut cake

75 g softened butter

125 g castor sugar

2 eggs, beaten

1½ cups plain flour

1 teaspoon ground ginger

1 teaspoon ground
   cinnamon

1 teaspoon bicarbonate
   of soda

¾ cup milk

⅓ cup golden syrup

1 cup chopped walnuts

icing sugar, for dusting

Preheat the oven to 180°C. Lightly grease and flour a 20-cm cake tin.

Cream butter and sugar, and add beaten eggs. Stir in sifted flour and spices. Fold in chopped walnuts. Dissolve bicarbonate of soda in milk and add to mixture. Warm golden syrup and mix in.

Pour mixture into prepared cake tin and bake for 40–45 minutes, or until a skewer inserted into the centre of the cake comes out clean.

Dust with icing sugar or ice as required.

Butterscotch brownies

125 g softened butter

125 g soft brown sugar

2 eggs, beaten

1 teaspoon vanilla extract

¾ cup self-raising flour

50 g walnuts, chopped

Preheat oven to 170°C. Lightly grease an 18-cm square baking tin.

Cream butter and sugar until light and fluffy. Beat in eggs and vanilla, then gently fold in sifted flour. Add the walnuts and mix well.

Pour mixture into tin and bake for 35–40 minutes. Cut into squares when cool.

MAKES 16

Butterscotch date biscuits

125 g softened butter

2 cups soft brown sugar,
  firmly packed

2 eggs, beaten

1 teaspoon vanilla extract

3½ cups plain flour

½ teaspoon salt

1 teaspoon bicarbonate
  of soda

1 teaspoon baking powder

FILLING

500 g pitted dates, chopped

½ cup soft brown sugar

½ cup water

½ cup blanched almonds,
  chopped

Cream butter and sugar until light and fluffy. Add eggs and vanilla and beat well.

Sift together all dry ingredients, then add to creamed mixture and stir until thoroughly combined.

Roll the dough into a log about 4 cm in diameter, wrap in foil and refrigerate for several hours, until cold.

Preheat oven to 180°C. Lightly grease baking trays.

For the filling, heat dates, sugar and water in a saucepan until thickened. Stir in nuts.

Cut the log into slices. Place half the slices on prepared baking trays. Top each with a dollop of the date filling and place a second slice of dough on top. Press edges together with a fork to seal.

Bake for about 10 minutes, or until lightly browned.

MAKES 60

Cappuccino choc-chip muffins

2 cups plain flour

¾ cup castor sugar

2½ teaspoons baking
powder

2 teaspoons instant coffee
granules

½ teaspoon salt

½ teaspoon ground
cinnamon

1 cup milk

125 g butter, melted and
cooled slightly

1 egg

1 teaspoon vanilla extract

¾ cup chocolate chips

grated chocolate, for
sprinkling

FILLING

100 g cream cheese

1 tablespoon castor sugar

½ teaspoon vanilla extract

½ teaspoon instant coffee
granules

Preheat oven to 190°C. Grease muffin tins.

In a large bowl mix together sifted flour, sugar, baking
powder, coffee, salt and cinnamon.

In a separate bowl mix together milk, butter, egg and
vanilla.

Make a well in the centre of the dry ingredients and
add milk mixture. Stir to combine, then fold in the
chocolate chips.

Spoon batter into prepared muffin tins and bake for
15–20 minutes.

To make filling, cream all ingredients together.

Cut muffins in half, spread with filling and sprinkle
with grated chocolate.

MAKES 16

Caramel cake

125 g softened butter

1 cup castor sugar

1 egg

1½ cups plain flour

½ teaspoon salt

1 teaspoon baking powder

1 tablespoon golden syrup

1 cup milk

1 teaspoon bicarbonate
of soda

½ cup raisins

1 tablespoon cocoa

chocolate butter icing
(page 678)

Preheat oven to 200°C. Lightly grease and flour a 23-cm cake tin.

Cream butter and sugar, and beat in egg.

Sift flour, salt and baking powder into a separate bowl.

Melt golden syrup and milk, then add bicarbonate of soda.

Add milk mixture and sifted dry ingredients alternately to the creamed mixture.

Pour half the mixture into prepared cake tin, then sprinkle over raisins. Stir cocoa into remaining mixture and pour this on top of raisins.

Bake for 35–40 minutes. Ice with chocolate icing when cake is cool.

Caramel crackle squares

250 g jersey caramels,
    chopped

1 tablespoon golden syrup

60 g butter

250 g dark cooking
    chocolate, chopped

3 cups Rice Bubbles

100 g white marshmallows,
    chopped

Grease and line a 23-cm square slab tin.

Put jersey caramels, golden syrup, butter and half
the chocolate in a bowl. Microwave on MEDIUM for
2 minutes, then stir until smooth. Mix in Rice Bubbles.

Press into prepared dish.

Put remaining chocolate and marshmallows in a bowl.
Microwave on MEDIUM for 45 seconds, then stir until
smooth. Spread over the caramel mixture. Leave to
set then cut into small squares.

MAKES 36 | NO BAKE

Caramel-crusted fruit slice

125 g butter

1 cup soft brown sugar

1 egg, lightly beaten

225 g mixed dried fruit

1 cup self-raising flour

Preheat oven to 180°C. Lightly grease and line a 19-cm × 29-cm slice tin.

Melt butter in a large saucepan. Add sugar, and stir over low heat until dissolved. Remove from heat and cool for a few minutes so egg doesn't scramble when added. Stir in egg, then add fruit and sifted flour. Mix well.

Press into baking tin and bake for 20 minutes, or until a crust has formed but the centre is still not completely set. Be careful not to overcook or the slice will be crisp and biscuit-like, rather than chewy.

Cool slightly and score 4-cm squares in the top with a sharp knife. Allow to cool completely in the tray, then cut into squares.

MAKES 24

Caramel slice

BASE

1 cup self-raising flour

½ cup white sugar

½ cup desiccated coconut

½ cup Corn Flakes

125 g butter, melted

FILLING

1 × 395-g tin condensed
  milk

2 tablespoons golden syrup

40 g butter

1 tablespoon white sugar

TOPPING

3 tablespoons white
  vegetable shortening

½ cup drinking chocolate
  powder

Preheat oven to 180°C. Lightly grease and line a
19-cm × 29-cm slice tin.

For the base, sift flour into a bowl, then mix in sugar,
coconut and Corn Flakes. Pour melted butter over
dry ingredients and mix well.

Press into tin and bake for 10 minutes.

For the filling, put all ingredients in a saucepan and boil
for 10 minutes, stirring constantly. Pour over the base.

For the topping, melt vegetable shortening and mix in
sifted drinking chocolate. Pour over the caramel layer,
and leave to set. Cut into squares or fingers when cold.

MAKES 36

Caraway & cheese muffins

2 cups plain flour

1 tablespoon baking powder

¼ teaspoon salt

1 teaspoon mustard powder

1 cup grated tasty cheese

1 tablespoon caraway seeds

1 egg

¾ cup milk

50 g butter, melted

Preheat oven to 200°C. Grease muffin tins.

Sift together flour, baking powder and salt.

Stir in mustard, grated cheese and caraway seeds.

Combine egg and milk. Stir melted butter, egg and milk into dry ingredients until just combined.

Three-quarters fill prepared muffin tins and bake for 15–20 minutes.

MAKES 16

Caraway crisps

120 g softened butter

1 cup cream cheese

¼ cup white sugar

1 cup self-raising flour

¼ teaspoon salt

2 tablespoons caraway seeds

1 tablespoon sea salt

Cream butter and cream cheese until smooth, then add the sugar. Gradually stir in sifted flour and salt.

Roll dough into logs 5 cm in diameter, wrap in foil and chill for at least 30 minutes.

Preheat oven to 220°C. Lightly grease baking trays.

Cut logs into thin slices, place on baking trays and sprinkle with caraway seeds and sea salt.

Bake for about 6 minutes, or until golden and crisp.

MAKES 40

Caraway-seed cake

125 g softened butter

½ cup castor sugar

2 eggs, beaten

125 g self-raising flour

½ teaspoon baking powder

50 g ground almonds

2 heaped teaspoons
   caraway seeds

¼ cup yoghurt

1½ tablespoons toasted
   rolled oats

icing sugar, for dusting

Preheat oven to 180°C. Lightly grease a 20-cm round cake tin and line the base with non-stick baking paper.

Cream the butter and sugar until light and fluffy. Slowly add the eggs until well combined.

Sift the flour and baking powder into another bowl. Stir in the ground almonds and caraway seeds. Fold into the butter mixture and stir in the yoghurt.

Spoon into the prepared tin, sprinkle with oats and dust with icing sugar.

Bake for 45–60 minutes or until the cake is cooked through. Cool in the tin for 10 minutes before turning out onto a wire rack to cool completely.

Cardamom muffins

1½ cups self-raising flour

pinch of salt

1 teaspoon ground
  cardamom

¼ cup castor sugar

1 egg

50 g butter, melted

⅓ cup sour cream

Preheat oven to 200°C. Grease muffin tins.

Sift flour, salt and cardamom and stir in sugar.

Beat together egg, melted butter and sour cream.

Pour egg mixture onto dry ingredients and mix until just combined.

Three-quarters fill prepared muffin tins and bake for 15–20 minutes.

MAKES 12

Carol's very moist carrot cake

2 cups plain flour

2 teaspoons bicarbonate
of soda

2 teaspoons baking powder

2 teaspoons ground
cinnamon

1 teaspoon salt

2 cups castor sugar

1 cup chopped walnuts

1½ cups vegetable oil

4 eggs

3 cups grated carrot

cream cheese icing
(page 682)

chopped walnuts, for
decorating

Preheat oven to 175°C. Line a 23-cm square cake tin with non-stick baking paper.

Sift the flour into a large mixing bowl with the bicarbonate of soda, baking powder, cinnamon and salt. Stir in the sugar and chopped walnuts.

In another bowl, mix the oil and eggs until well combined. Stir in the grated carrot.

Pour the wet mixture into the dry ingredients and mix to form a smooth batter.

Pour into the prepared tin and bake for 60–80 minutes or until cooked through. Cool for 5 minutes before turning out onto a wire rack.

When completely cold, use a spatula to cover the top and sides of the cake with cream cheese icing and decorate with chopped walnuts.

Carrot, bacon & parsley muffins

2 cups plain flour

1 tablespoon baking powder

1 cup grated tasty cheese

1 onion, grated

1 cup grated carrot

handful chopped parsley

2 tablespoons bacon bits

1 egg

1 large tablespoon butter, melted

1 cup milk

Preheat oven to 200°C. Grease muffin tins.

Sift together flour and baking powder.

Add cheese, onion, carrot, parsley and bacon bits.

Beat egg in a separate bowl, then add melted butter and milk. Mix into cheese mixture until just combined.

Three-quarters fill prepared muffin tins and bake for 15–20 minutes.

MAKES 16

Carrot cake muffins

1¾ cups plain flour

⅔ cup soft brown sugar, firmly packed

1 teaspoon baking powder

½ teaspoon bicarbonate of soda

½ teaspoon salt

1 teaspoon ground cinnamon

pinch of ground mace

½ cup crushed pineapple in juice

½ cup vegetable oil

1 egg, lightly beaten

1 teaspoon vanilla extract

2 cups grated carrot

½ cup raisins

Preheat oven to 200°C. Grease muffin tins.

In a large bowl, mix sifted flour, brown sugar, baking powder, bicarbonate of soda, salt, cinnamon and mace.

In a separate bowl, mix pineapple, oil, egg and vanilla until blended.

Make a well in the centre of the dry ingredients, then add pineapple mixture and stir to just combine.

Stir in carrot and raisins.

Spoon batter into prepared muffin tins and bake for 15–20 minutes.

MAKES 14−16

Carrot & ginger muffins

2 cups plain flour

1 tablespoon baking powder

¼ teaspoon ground ginger

¼ cup soft brown sugar

¾ cup grated carrot

¼ cup crystallised ginger

1 egg

¾ cup milk

50 g butter, melted

Preheat oven to 200°C. Grease muffin tins.

Sift together flour, baking powder and ground ginger. Stir in sugar, carrot and crystallised ginger.

Combine egg and milk in a separate bowl, and add melted butter.

Make a well in the centre of the dry ingredients and pour in egg mixture. Stir quickly until just combined.

Three-quarters fill muffin tins and bake for 20 minutes.

MAKES 16

Cath's poppy seed slice

240 g butter

1 cup white sugar

2 eggs, beaten

⅓ cup poppy seeds

juice and grated zest
    of 1 lemon

1 tablespoon wholemeal
    plain flour

1½ cups plain flour

1 tablespoon custard powder
    or cornflour

1 teaspoon baking powder

½ cup chopped walnuts,
    toasted

½ cup sultanas

icing sugar, for dusting

Preheat oven to 180°C. Lightly grease and line a 19-cm × 29-cm slice tin or small roasting pan.

Melt butter in a large saucepan. Add sugar and dissolve over low heat. Remove from heat and cool for a few minutes so eggs don't scramble when added. Stir in eggs, then poppy seeds, lemon zest and juice. (For a lighter slice, grind the poppy seeds first.)

In a separate bowl sift together the flours, custard powder or cornflour and baking powder. Stir into the egg mixture, followed by the nuts and sultanas. Mix well.

Pour mixture into the prepared tray. Bake for 45 minutes. Let cool a little, but cut into squares while still warm.

When cold, dust with icing sugar.

MAKES 36

Cheese & bacon muffins

1 cup plain flour

½ teaspoon salt

1 teaspoon baking powder

1½ cups bran

¼ cup castor sugar

½ teaspoon bicarbonate
of soda

1½ cups milk

1 tablespoon butter, melted

1 egg, lightly beaten

1 tablespoon golden syrup

3 rashers bacon, cooked
and chopped

1 cup grated tasty cheese

Preheat oven to 200°C. Grease muffin tins.

Sift together flour, salt and baking powder. Stir in bran and sugar, and make a well in the centre.

Dissolve bicarbonate of soda in milk.

Combine milk, melted butter, egg and golden syrup.

Add chopped bacon and cheese to dry ingredients, then pour in milk mixture. Stir until just combined.

Three-quarters fill prepared muffin tins and bake for 10–15 minutes.

MAKES 14–16

Cheese & chive muffins

1 cup self-raising flour

1 egg

¾ cup water

½ teaspoon salt

1½ cups grated tasty cheese

1 tablespoon chopped
  fresh chives

coarse sea salt, for
  sprinkling (optional)

Preheat oven to 190°C. Grease muffin tins.

Sift flour into a large bowl, then mix in all other ingredients until just combined.

Spoon mixture into muffin tins and sprinkle with sea salt.

Bake for 15 minutes.

MAKES 12

Cheese–cream sandwiches

1½ cups plain flour

½ teaspoon turmeric

2 teaspoons curry powder

¼ teaspoon freshly ground
    black pepper

¼ teaspoon salt

125 g cold butter, cut into
    small pieces

¼ cup finely grated
    cheddar cheese

1 egg yolk

3 teaspoons cold water

paprika, for sprinkling

FILLING

60 g cream cheese

¼ cup finely grated
    cheddar cheese

2 tablespoons finely grated
    parmesan cheese

freshly ground black pepper

Preheat oven to 180°C. Lightly grease baking trays.

Sift together flour, turmeric, curry powder, pepper and salt. Using your fingertips, rub in the butter until the mixture is crumbly. Add cheese and mix to just combine.

Add egg yolk and water and mix to a firm dough. Turn out onto floured surface and knead lightly. Roll out dough to 3 mm in thickness. Cut into rounds with a 4-cm biscuit cutter.

Place rounds onto baking trays. Bake for 8–10 minutes or until light golden.

For the filling, beat cream cheese until soft and smooth. Add cheddar and parmesan and season to taste with pepper. Beat again until soft and spreadable.

When biscuits are cold, sandwich together with the cheese cream. Sprinkle tops with paprika.

MAKES 20

Cheese muffins

2 cups plain flour

3 teaspoons baking powder

¼ teaspoon salt

½ teaspoon mustard powder

freshly ground black pepper

2 cups grated tasty cheese

2 eggs

1 cup milk

Preheat oven to 200°C. Grease muffin tins.

Sift together flour, baking powder, salt, mustard and freshly ground pepper.

Add grated cheese.

Lightly beat eggs and milk together. Add to dry ingredients and mix lightly until just combined.

Three-quarters fill prepared muffin tins and bake for 10–15 minutes or until golden brown.

MAKES 16

Cheese straws

⅓ cup plain flour

pinch of salt

pinch of cayenne pepper

60 g cold butter, cut into
    small pieces

½ cup grated tasty cheese

1 egg yolk

1 teaspoon lemon juice

Preheat oven to 180°C. Lightly grease baking trays.

Sift together flour, salt and cayenne pepper. Rub in the butter with your fingertips until crumbly.

Add grated cheese, then mix in the egg yolk and lemon juice to form a pliable dough.

Roll dough out thinly on a lightly floured surface and cut into thin strips. (Use a fluted pastry cutter to create a ruffled edge.) Place on trays and bake for 6 minutes, or until golden brown.

Serve cheese straws on their own, or with dip.

MAKES 24–36

Cheese & tomato layer muffins

2 cups self-raising flour

½ teaspoon salt

1 egg

¾ cup water

1½ cups grated cheddar
cheese

¾ cup tomato pasta sauce

Preheat oven to 200°C. Grease muffin tins.

Combine sifted flour with salt, egg, water and cheese.

Half-fill prepared muffin tins with mixture.

Put up to 2 teaspoons of sauce into the middle of each muffin. Take care that sauce stays mostly in the centre. (If there is too much sauce, muffins will come apart when removed from tins.)

Cover each muffin with remaining mixture until tins are three-quarters full. Bake for 12–15 minutes.

MAKES 16

Cheese, vegetable & bacon muffins

5 cups plain flour

1½ cups mixed vegetables

½ cup finely chopped bacon

2 cups grated tasty cheese

50 g butter, melted

5 teaspoons baking powder

salt

1 onion, finely chopped
(or use chives)

3 eggs, beaten

1 teaspoon vegetable
stock powder

milk, to mix

Preheat oven to 200°C. Grease muffin tins.

Sift flour into a large bowl. Add remaining ingredients and mix with enough milk to make a soft dough.

Spoon into prepared muffin tins.

Bake for about 20 minutes.

Quantities can be halved.

MAKES 36

Cheese & zucchini slice

3 large zucchini,
   finely grated

1 medium onion, finely
   chopped

1 cup grated tasty cheese

¾ cup self-raising flour

salt and freshly ground
   black pepper

½ cup vegetable oil

4 eggs, beaten

Preheat oven to 180°C. Lightly grease and line a 19-cm × 29-cm slice tin.

Squeeze the grated zucchini to remove any excess liquid.

In a large bowl, combine the zucchini with the onion, cheese, sifted flour, salt and pepper.

Mix the oil with the beaten eggs, then add to the other ingredients and stir to combine.

Pour into tin and bake for 45–50 minutes or until firm to touch and golden brown.

Cut into squares or fingers when cold.

MAKES 24

Cherry coconut crisps

125 g softened butter

1½ tablespoons icing sugar

½ teaspoon vanilla extract

1 egg yolk

1 cup plain flour

pinch of salt

2 tablespoons desiccated coconut (or use coconut flakes)

¼ cup glacé cherries, chopped

Cream the butter and sifted icing sugar until light and fluffy. Add the vanilla and egg yolk and beat well.

Sift together the flour and salt and stir into the creamed mixture, followed by the coconut and cherries.

Roll mixture into a long log about 5 cm in diameter. Wrap tightly in foil and chill in the refrigerator until cold.

Preheat oven to 180°C. Lightly grease baking trays.

Cut refrigerated dough into thin slices, place on baking trays and bake for 12–15 minutes or until golden.

(This biscuit dough can be stored in the refrigerator for up to 2 weeks, or frozen for 2 months.)

MAKES 36

Cherry muffins

330 g plain flour

1 cup castor sugar

2 teaspoons baking powder

¼ teaspoon salt

2 eggs, beaten

½ cup milk

120 g butter or margarine, melted

1 teaspoon almond essence

2 cups fresh or tinned pitted red cherries

TOPPING

1–2 tablespoons sugar

¼ teaspoon ground nutmeg

1–2 tablespoons sliced almonds

Preheat oven to 190°C. Grease muffin tins.

In a mixing bowl, stir together sifted flour, sugar, baking powder and salt. Make a well in the centre and set aside.

In another bowl, combine eggs, milk, butter or margarine and almond essence.

Add to flour mixture all at once and stir until just moistened. If using tinned cherries, drain and discard liquid. Gently fold cherries into mixture.

Spoon mixture into muffin tins.

Combine topping ingredients and sprinkle over batter.

Bake for 20–25 minutes.

MAKES 16–18

Cherry & pineapple ring

175 g softened butter

175 g castor sugar

2 eggs, beaten

1½ cups self-raising flour

¼ cup milk

65 g glacé cherries,
    quartered

25 g glacé pineapple,
    chopped

glacé pineapple pieces and
    whole glacé cherries, for
    decorating

glacé icing (page 679)

Preheat oven to 180°C. Lightly grease a 20-cm ring tin and line the base with non-stick baking paper.

Cream butter and sugar. Add eggs a little at a time, beating well after each addition and adding 1 tablespoon sifted flour with last amount of egg. Fold remaining sifted flour into mixture, then add milk, cherries and pineapple.

Pour into prepared tin and bake for 55–60 minutes. Turn out onto a wire rack.

When cool, ice with glacé icing. Decorate with glacé pineapple and cherries, trickling any remaining icing over fruit and down sides of cake.

Cherry & walnut cake

175 g softened butter

175 g castor sugar

3 eggs, beaten

2 tablespoons milk

½ cup chopped walnuts

few drops lemon essence

50 g glacé cherries, halved

1½ cups plain flour

1 teaspoon baking powder

lemon butter icing
   (page 677)

desiccated coconut and glacé
   cherries, for decorating

Preheat oven to 180°C. Lightly grease and flour a 20-cm cake tin.

Cream butter and sugar. Add eggs, milk, chopped walnuts, lemon essence, glacé cherries, and sifted flour and baking powder. Mix until well combined.

Pour mixture into prepared tin and bake for 60–90 minutes, or until a skewer inserted into the centre of the cake comes out clean.

Ice with lemon butter icing, sprinkle with coconut and decorate with glacé cherries.

Cherry & walnut muffins

2 cups plain flour

⅓ cup castor sugar

3 teaspoons baking powder

¼ cup chopped glacé
cherries

⅓ cup chopped walnuts

1 egg

1 cup milk

60 g butter, melted

1 teaspoon vanilla extract

Preheat oven to 200°C. Grease muffin tins.

Sift together flour, sugar and baking powder, then add cherries and walnuts.

In a separate bowl, beat together egg, milk, melted butter and vanilla.

Add to dry ingredients and mix gently until just combined.

Three-quarters fill prepared muffin tins and bake for 15–20 minutes.

MAKES 16

Chilled summer berry pudding

1 kg mixed fresh or frozen
    berries (pitted cherries,
    raspberries, blueberries,
    blackberries, strawberries,
    mulberries)

1 cup castor sugar

100 ml fresh orange juice

10–12 thin slices of white,
    day-old bread, crusts
    removed

Combine the fruit, sugar and orange juice in a saucepan. Cook over a gentle heat for 4–5 minutes or until the sugar has dissolved and the fruit juices start to flow. Remove and cool a little.

Line a 1.7-litre pudding basin with the sliced bread, cutting it to neatly fit the sides and base. Spoon in about two-thirds of the fruit and leave for 30 minutes. Spoon in the remaining fruit and cover the top with bread slices so that the fruit is completely enclosed. Place a piece of cling wrap or non-stick baking paper over the top and then place a plate on top of the pudding to weigh it down. Refrigerate overnight.

Remove the plate and loosen the sides with a palette knife before turning the pudding out onto a deep-sided serving plate, to catch any excess fruit juices.

Serve in slices with ice-cream or cream.

SERVES 8

Chilli corn muffins

1 finely chopped fresh chilli or 1 teaspoon chilli powder

1 small onion, finely chopped

¼ cup vegetable oil

1½ cups All-Bran

1½ cups skim milk

3 egg whites

1⅔ cups self-raising flour

1 × 325-g tin corn kernels, drained

½ cup grated tasty cheese

Preheat oven to 190°C. Grease muffin tins.

Sauté chilli and onion in 1 tablespoon of the oil until onion is tender. Cool.

Place All-Bran and milk in a large bowl and stand for 5 minutes to soften.

Stir in chilli mixture, remaining oil and 2 egg whites. Add sifted flour, corn and half the cheese.

Beat remaining egg white until stiff peaks form, then fold into mixture.

Three-quarters fill muffin tins and sprinkle each muffin with a little of the remaining cheese.

Bake for 25–30 minutes.

MAKES 12–16

Choc-chip cake

200 g softened butter

200 g castor sugar

3 eggs, lightly beaten

275 g self-raising flour

150 g dark chocolate chips,
   or roughly chopped dark
   cooking chocolate

50 g ground almonds

2 tablespoons milk

2 tablespoons chopped
   almonds

Preheat oven to 180°C. Lightly grease a 20-cm round springform cake tin and line the base with non-stick baking paper.

Cream the butter and sugar until light and fluffy. Add the eggs a little at a time, alternating with a tablespoon of sifted flour. Beat well to make a light batter.

Fold in the remaining flour, chocolate, ground almonds and milk.

Pour the mixture into the prepared tin and sprinkle the chopped almonds over the top.

Bake for 90 minutes or until a skewer inserted into the centre of the cake comes out clean. Cool in the tin for 5 minutes before turning out onto a wire rack.

Choc-chip macadamia muffins

50 g softened butter

½ cup castor sugar

1 egg

1 cup milk

2 cups plain flour

2 teaspoons baking powder

160 g white chocolate,
  chopped

1 cup chopped macadamias

Preheat oven to 190°C. Grease muffin tins.

Cream butter and sugar until light and fluffy.

Stir in egg and milk.

Mix in sifted flour, baking powder, chocolate and nuts
until just combined.

Three-quarters fill muffin tins and bake for 20 minutes.

MAKES 16

Chocolate big chip muffins

2 cups plain flour

⅓ cup soft brown sugar, firmly packed

⅓ cup castor sugar

2 teaspoons baking powder

½ teaspoon salt

⅔ cup milk

2 eggs

125 g butter, melted and cooled slightly

1 teaspoon vanilla extract

2 cups large chocolate chips or chunks

½ cup chopped pecans

chocolate glacé icing (page 680)

small chocolate chips and chopped pecans, for decorating

Preheat oven to 200°C. Grease muffin tins.

In a large bowl mix together sifted flour, sugars, baking powder and salt.

In a separate bowl mix together milk, eggs, butter and vanilla.

Make a well in the centre of the dry ingredients and add milk mixture. Stir to combine, then fold in chocolate chips and pecans.

Spoon batter into prepared muffin tins and bake for 15–20 minutes.

Serve topped with chocolate icing and sprinkled with chocolate chips and pecans.

MAKES 16

Chocolate bourbon muffins

¾ cup plain flour

½ teaspoon bicarbonate
of soda

¼ teaspoon salt

125 g softened butter

½ cup castor sugar

50 g dark cooking chocolate,
chopped

1 egg

1 tablespoon bourbon

1 teaspoon vanilla extract

½ cup chocolate chips

½ cup chopped pecans

icing sugar or cocoa,
for dusting

Preheat oven to 200°C. Grease muffin tins.

Sift together flour, bicarbonate of soda and salt.

In a separate bowl cream butter and sugar until light and fluffy.

Melt chocolate in a double boiler over simmering water, or on MEDIUM in the microwave. Cool slightly, then beat into creamed mixture along with egg, bourbon and vanilla.

Add dry ingredients and combine, then fold in chocolate chips and pecans.

Spoon batter into prepared muffin tins and bake for 15–20 minutes.

Serve dusted with icing sugar or cocoa.

MAKES 8–12

Chocolate caramel muffins

2 cups plain flour

2 teaspoons baking powder

1 tablespoon cocoa

1 egg

75 g softened butter

150 g dark cooking chocolate
   melted in 1 cup boiling
   water

½ cup castor sugar

FILLING

200 ml condensed milk

1½ teaspoons butter

1 tablespoon golden syrup

Preheat oven to 180°C. Grease muffin tins.

Sift together flour, baking powder and cocoa. Add remaining muffin ingredients and mix until just combined.

Three-quarters fill prepared muffin tins and bake for 15–20 minutes. Leave to cool.

To make filling, boil all ingredients, stirring every 30 seconds, until thickened into caramel. Take care as this mixture changes quickly.

Remove muffins from tins, make a diagonal cut into each and fill with caramel.

MAKES 16

Chocolate cherry brandy muffins

2 cups plain flour

2 teaspoons baking powder

1 tablespoon cocoa

1 egg

150 g dark cooking
   chocolate, melted in
   1 cup boiling water

75 g softened butter

½ cup castor sugar

1 cup glacé cherries mixed
   with ¼ cup brandy

Preheat oven to 180°C. Grease muffin tins.

Sift together flour, baking powder and cocoa.
Add remaining ingredients and mix well until just
combined.

Three-quarters fill prepared muffin tins and bake
for 15–20 minutes.

MAKES 16

Chocolate cherry clafoutis

450 g black cherries, pitted

⅓ cup brandy or rum

½ cup plain flour

2 tablespoons cocoa

pinch of salt

50 g icing sugar

25 g butter, melted

1¼ cups milk

3 eggs, lightly beaten

icing sugar, for dusting

Soak the cherries in the brandy or rum for 20 minutes.

Preheat oven to 220°C. Generously grease a 1-litre ovenproof dish.

Make the batter in a food processor by first sifting the flour, cocoa, salt and icing sugar together and adding them to the processor. With the motor running, pour in the melted butter, milk and eggs and blend to a smooth batter.

Pour about half a cup of the batter into the base of the prepared dish and bake for 10 minutes or until just set.

Drain any liquid from the cherries and mix it into the reserved batter. Spoon the cherries over the base of the baking dish and then pour remaining batter over the fruit.

Bake for 40–45 minutes or until risen and set. Leave to cool for 5 minutes. Dust generously with icing sugar.

Serve warm with cream or ice-cream.

SERVES 4

Chocolate cherry slice

BASE

1 cup icing sugar

2 tablespoons cocoa

2 cups Rice Bubbles

125 g butter, melted

TOPPING

2 cups desiccated coconut

½ cup icing sugar

125 g glacé cherries,
   chopped

2 egg whites

Grease and line a 19-cm × 29-cm slice tin.

For the base, sift together icing sugar and cocoa, then stir in Rice Bubbles. Add melted butter and mix until well combined.

Press mixture into the tin. Refrigerate until set.

For the topping, combine coconut, sifted icing sugar and cherries in a bowl. Add unbeaten egg whites and mix well.

Spread topping evenly over the base. Refrigerate several hours or overnight. Cut into bars or squares to serve.

MAKES 24 | NO BAKE

Chocolate chip cookies

125 g softened butter

½ cup soft brown sugar

¼ cup white sugar

1 teaspoon vanilla extract

1 egg

1 cup plain flour

½ teaspoon bicarbonate
of soda

pinch of salt

¾ cup chocolate chips

Cream butter and sugars until light and fluffy. Add vanilla and egg and beat until combined.

Sift together flour, bicarbonate of soda and salt and stir into creamed mixture. Add chocolate chips and mix well.

Roll mixture into a log about 5 cm in diameter, then wrap in cling wrap and freeze for 1–2 hours.

Preheat oven to 190°C. Lightly grease baking trays.

Remove from freezer and thaw for 10 minutes before cutting into 1-cm slices. Place slices onto baking trays and bake for 10–12 minutes, or until golden brown.

MAKES 36

Chocolate diamonds

60 g dark cooking chocolate, chopped

120 g butter

1 cup castor sugar

2 eggs

1 teaspoon vanilla extract

½ cup plain flour

¾ cup chopped walnuts

Preheat oven to 200°C. Grease a 25-cm × 30-cm Swiss roll tin and dust with flour.

Melt chocolate and butter together in a double boiler over simmering water, or on MEDIUM in the microwave. Add sugar and mix until it dissolves. Remove from heat and allow to cool a little.

Add eggs and vanilla, beating well. Then fold in the sifted flour.

Spread mixture into the tin, sprinkle with nuts and bake for about 12 minutes. Cool for 5 minutes, then cut into diamond shapes.

MAKES 36

Chocolate fruit slice

175 g dark chocolate
(*not* cooking chocolate),
chopped

1 × 175-g packet mixed
dried fruit

50 g glacé cherries

1 cup desiccated coconut

¼ cup castor sugar

40 g butter, melted

1 egg, beaten

Preheat oven to 180°C. Grease and line a 19-cm square cake tin.

Melt chocolate in a double boiler over simmering water, or on MEDIUM in the microwave, then spread it evenly over the base of the tin. Chill in the refrigerator until set.

Mix remaining ingredients together until well combined. Spread over chocolate base.

Bake for 20–25 minutes until golden brown.

Cool in the tin at room temperature, then chill at least 1 hour, until completely cold.

Cut into fingers and turn out of tin.

MAKES 36 | GLUTEN FREE

Chocolate fudge cake

125 g butter

¾ cup soft brown sugar

1 tablespoon cocoa

1 egg, lightly beaten

2 tablespoons desiccated
   coconut

½ cup chopped walnuts, or
   sunflower or sesame seeds

¼ cup chopped pitted
   morella cherries

½ cup sultanas

½ teaspoon vanilla extract

2 cups crushed Marie
   biscuits or other sweet
   biscuits

chocolate glacé icing
   (page 680)

Lightly grease a 20-cm × 30-cm tin and line the base
with non-stick baking paper.

In a large saucepan melt butter, sugar and cocoa.
Remove from heat and add egg and remaining
ingredients. Combine well.

Press into prepared tin and refrigerate until firm.

Ice with chocolate icing. Store in refrigerator.

NO BAKE

Chocolate fudge slice

180 g dark cooking
   chocolate, chopped

1 × 395-g tin condensed
   milk

2 teaspoons cocoa

1 teaspoon vanilla extract

300 g sweet gluten-free
   biscuits (such as sweet rice
   biscuits), crushed

⅓ cup slivered almonds or
   chopped nuts

1 cup mixed dried fruit

½ cup desiccated coconut

Grease and line a 19-cm × 29-cm slice tin.

Combine chocolate, condensed milk and sifted cocoa in a large microwave-safe bowl and microwave on MEDIUM for about 2 minutes, stirring occasionally, until chocolate has melted.

Add vanilla, biscuit crumbs, nuts and fruit to chocolate mixture and mix to combine.

Press mixture firmly into tin. Smooth the top and sprinkle with coconut. Cover and refrigerate until firm. Cut into bars to serve.

MAKES 36 | GLUTEN FREE | NO BAKE

Chocolate ginger rounds

1 cup gluten-free flour mix
  (page 6)

2 tablespoons cocoa

25 g ground almonds

⅓ cup white sugar

1 egg, beaten

75 g butter, melted

2 tablespoons crystallised
  ginger, finely chopped

Preheat oven to 180°C. Lightly grease baking trays.

Sift together flour and cocoa. Add ground almonds and sugar and mix to combine. Add egg, butter and ginger and mix together until a soft dough forms.

Roll dough into walnut-sized balls and place on trays. Flatten slightly with a fork.

Bake for 12–15 minutes.

MAKES 36 | GLUTEN FREE

Chocolate jam slice

BASE

125 g softened butter

½ cup castor sugar

1 egg, beaten

½ teaspoon vanilla extract

2 cups self-raising flour

raspberry jam (or other
fruit jam), for spreading

TOPPING

1 cup desiccated coconut

1 egg

½ cup white sugar

3 tablespoons cocoa

Preheat oven to 180°C. Lightly grease and line
a 19-cm × 29-cm slice tin.

For the base, cream butter and sugar until light and
fluffy. Beat in egg and vanilla extract. Add sifted flour
and mix to a fairly stiff dough.

Press mixture into tin. Spread evenly with jam.

For coconut topping, beat all ingredients together.
Spread over the jam.

Bake for 15–20 minutes. Cut into squares when cool.

MAKES 36

Chocolate molasses slice

1 cup plain flour

½ teaspoon baking powder

¼ teaspoon bicarbonate
   of soda

pinch of salt

1 cup walnuts, chopped

125 g softened butter

½ cup white sugar

½ cup molasses

1 egg

50 g dark cooking chocolate,
   chopped

Preheat oven to 180°C. Lightly grease and line a 19-cm × 29-cm slice tin.

Sift together flour, baking powder, bicarbonate of soda and salt. Mix in walnuts.

In a separate bowl, cream the butter and sugar until light and creamy. Then beat in molasses and egg.

Melt chocolate in a double boiler over simmering water, or on MEDIUM in the microwave. Add melted chocolate to the creamed mixture and mix. Stir into the dry ingredients and mix well.

Pour into prepared tin and bake for 30 minutes or until firm. Cool in the tin for 5 minutes, then cut into squares and cool on a wire rack.

MAKES 24

Chocolate mousse cake

225 g dark cooking
   chocolate, chopped

125 g unsalted butter

7 eggs, separated

½ cup castor sugar

¼ cup brandy

pinch of salt

icing sugar, for dusting

Preheat oven to 160°C. Lightly grease a 23-cm springform cake tin and line the base with non-stick baking paper.

Melt the chocolate and butter in a double boiler over simmering water or on MEDIUM in the microwave. Allow to cool a little.

Cream the egg yolks and sugar until pale and thick (3–4 minutes). Stir in the cooled chocolate mixture and brandy.

In another bowl, whip the egg whites with a pinch of salt until stiff peaks form. Take two large spoonfuls of the egg-white mixture and carefully mix this through the chocolate mixture. Tip the chocolate mixture into the remaining egg-white mixture and fold through.

Spoon into the prepared tin and bake for 30–35 minutes or until cooked.

Cool in the tin on a wire rack. The cake will fall in the centre a little. When cold, remove from the tin and turn out onto a plate. Dust with icing sugar to serve.

Chocolate muffins

150 g fine polenta

⅓ cup self-raising flour

2 tablespoons cocoa

1 tablespoon baking powder

pinch of salt

⅓ cup soft brown sugar

60 g butter, melted

⅔ cup sour cream

1 egg

2 tablespoons strong
   black coffee

50 g dark cooking chocolate,
   cut into 12 pieces

cocoa, for dusting

Preheat oven to 200°C. Grease muffin tins.

Sift polenta, flour, cocoa, baking powder and salt into a large bowl.

Add brown sugar, then stir in butter, sour cream, egg and coffee. Mix to combine.

Spoon half the batter into prepared muffin tins.

Place a piece of chocolate in each muffin, then cover with remaining batter.

Bake for 20 minutes.

Dust with cocoa before serving.

MAKES 12

Chocolate pudding cake

1½ cups water

1 cup raisins

250 g butter

1 cup castor sugar

½ teaspoon ground
   cinnamon

½ teaspoon ground ginger

½ teaspoon mixed spice

3 tablespoons cocoa

pinch of salt

1 teaspoon bicarbonate
   of soda dissolved in
   ¼ cup boiling water

2 cups plain flour

cream, butterscotch sauce
   (page 682) or pouring
   custard (page 683)

Preheat oven to 180°C. Lightly grease a 23-cm round or oval cake tin and line the base with non-stick baking paper.

Combine the water, raisins, butter, sugar, spices, cocoa and salt in a saucepan. Gently heat until boiling and then turn down to a simmer and cook for 5 minutes. Remove from the heat and allow to cool. Stir in the bicarbonate of soda mixture. Fold in the sifted flour to make a smooth cake batter.

Pour into the prepared tin and bake for 35–40 minutes or until firm and cooked through. Cool in the tin before turning out onto a wire rack.

Serve warm with cream, butterscotch sauce or pouring custard.

Chocolate raspberry muffins

1 × 425-g tin raspberries
  in syrup

2 cups self-raising flour

½ cup castor sugar

½ cup chocolate chips

1 egg

60 g butter, melted and
  cooled slightly

¾ cup buttermilk

FILLING

1 × 300-ml carton cream

2 tablespoons cocoa

2 tablespoons icing sugar

2 tablespoons raspberry jam

Preheat oven to 190°C. Grease muffin tins.

Put undrained raspberries in a saucepan and bring
to the boil. Simmer for 12 minutes, then allow to cool.

In a large bowl mix together sifted flour, sugar and
chocolate chips.

In a separate bowl mix together egg, butter and
buttermilk.

Make a well in the centre of the dry ingredients and add
buttermilk mixture. Stir to combine, then fold in raspberry
mixture.

Spoon into prepared muffin tins and bake for 15 minutes.

To make filling, whip cream, cocoa and icing sugar
together until thick, then fold in jam.

To serve, split each muffin and add filling.

MAKES 16

Chocolate rice biscuits

100 g softened butter

½ cup castor sugar

1½ cups rice flour

2 tablespoons cocoa

1 egg, beaten

Preheat oven to 180°C. Lightly grease baking trays.

Cream butter and sugar until light and fluffy. Stir in sifted flour and cocoa. Add the egg and mix well to combine.

Roll mixture into small balls and place on baking trays. Flatten slightly with a fork.

Bake for 12–18 minutes until brown.

VARIATIONS
For coffee biscuits, replace cocoa with 1 teaspoon instant coffee granules. For lemon or orange biscuits, replace cocoa with 1 tablespoon lemon or orange juice. For vanilla biscuits, replace cocoa with ½ teaspoon vanilla extract.

MAKES 30 | GLUTEN FREE

Chocolate, ricotta & hazelnut cheesecake

BASE

50 g finely chopped
   hazelnuts

100 g sweet biscuit crumbs

75 g butter, melted

FILLING

2 eggs, separated

35 g castor sugar

¾ cup ricotta

20 g ground hazelnuts

75 ml cream

1 tablespoon cocoa

1 teaspoon dark rum

icing sugar, for dusting

Preheat oven to 170°C. Lightly grease a 20-cm springform cake tin and line the base with non-stick baking paper.

Combine the base ingredients and press into prepared cake tin.

Whisk the egg yolks and sugar until thick and creamy. Beat in the ricotta, ground hazelnuts, cream and cocoa. Stir in the dark rum.

Whip the egg whites until stiff and carefully fold through the chocolate mixture. Pour into the tin and bake for 60 minutes or until lightly risen and just firm to touch.

Cool a little before removing from the tin. Dust liberally with icing sugar before serving.

Chocolate rocks

100 g dark cooking
    chocolate, chopped

80 g butter

1 cup plain flour

2 tablespoons cocoa

¼ teaspoon bicarbonate
    of soda

1 cup castor sugar

1 egg, beaten

icing sugar, for coating

Melt the chocolate and butter in a saucepan over low heat, or in the microwave on MEDIUM.

Sift together the flour, cocoa and bicarbonate of soda. Add to the chocolate mixture along with the sugar and egg. Mix well.

Chill in the refrigerator for at least 20 minutes.

Preheat oven to 180°C. Line baking trays with baking paper.

When dough is firm enough to handle, roll into small balls. Roll each ball in icing sugar, then place on the trays (leaving room for spreading). Bake for 15 minutes.

Cool on the trays before transferring to a wire rack.

MAKES 24

Chocolate & walnut caramel custard pudding

1 cup castor sugar

⅓ cup water

30 g dark cooking chocolate

¾ cup toasted walnuts

1 × 400-g tin condensed milk

1¾ cups milk

2 eggs, plus 2 egg yolks

grated chocolate, for decorating

Preheat oven to 175°C. Lightly grease eight 125-ml custard cups.

Combine the sugar and water in a small saucepan over low heat, stirring continually until the sugar dissolves. Increase the heat and boil until the sugar syrup starts to turn a golden brown. Immediately remove from the heat and spoon the caramel evenly into the eight custard cups.

Process the chocolate and walnuts in a food processor for 1–2 minutes. Transfer to a mixing bowl. Heat the condensed milk and milk in a saucepan until boiling. Pour over the chocolate and nuts. Stir until smooth. Cool slightly, then stir in the eggs and egg yolks.

Spoon the chocolate mixture evenly into the cups. Place the cups in a bain-marie (see page 3). Bake for 45 minutes or until the puddings are just set. Take cups out of the bain-marie. Cool on a wire rack. Run a knife around the edge of the puddings and turn out onto serving plates.

Decorate with grated chocolate.

SERVES 8

Chocolate yoghurt cake

130 g dark cooking
  chocolate, chopped

¼ cup water

½ cup yoghurt

50 g softened butter

½ cup castor sugar

¼ cup soft brown sugar

2 small eggs

1 cup plain flour

1 teaspoon bicarbonate
  of soda

½ teaspoon salt

1 teaspoon vanilla extract

TOPPING

70 g dark cooking chocolate,
  chopped

¼ cup yoghurt

Preheat oven to 180°C. Lightly grease and flour a 23-cm ring tin.

Melt chocolate with water in a double boiler over simmering water or on MEDIUM in the microwave. Allow to cool and add yoghurt.

Cream butter and sugars, then beat in eggs. Sift flour, bicarbonate of soda and salt. Add vanilla extract and sifted ingredients to creamed mixture alternately with yoghurt mixture.

Pour into prepared tin and bake for 35 minutes. Cool.

Prepare topping by melting chocolate in a double boiler or in the microwave, then stirring in yoghurt. Spread over cake.

Christmas morning cranberry muffins

1 cup cranberries

½ cup castor sugar

1½ cups plain flour

2 teaspoons baking powder

1 teaspoon salt

½ teaspoon ground cinnamon

¼ teaspoon ground allspice

¼ teaspoon ground nutmeg

1 egg, beaten

¼ teaspoon finely grated orange zest

¾ cup orange juice

75 g butter, melted and cooled slightly

¼ cup chopped nuts

Preheat oven to 190°C. Grease muffin tins.

Chop cranberries coarsely and sprinkle with half the sugar. Set aside.

In a large bowl mix together remaining sugar, sifted flour, baking powder, salt and spices.

In a separate bowl mix together egg, orange zest, orange juice and butter.

Make a well in the centre of the dry ingredients and add orange mixture. Stir to moisten, then fold in cranberries and chopped nuts.

Spoon batter into prepared muffin tins and bake for 15–20 minutes.

MAKES 12

Christmas muffins

2½ cups castor sugar

4 cups plain flour

1 tablespoon ground
cinnamon

1 tablespoon bicarbonate
of soda

1 teaspoon salt

1 cup raisins, soaked in
brandy and drained

1 cup desiccated coconut

4 cups grated carrot

2 cups grated apple

1 cup pecans or walnuts,
roughly chopped

6 eggs

2 cups vegetable oil

1 teaspoon vanilla extract

icing sugar, for dusting

Preheat oven to 190°C. Grease deep muffin tins.

Sift dry ingredients into a large bowl.

Mix raisins into flour with your hands.

Add coconut, carrot, apple and nuts, and stir well.

Add eggs, oil and vanilla. Stir until combined.

Spoon into muffin tins and bake for 20 minutes.

Serve dusted with icing sugar.

Quantities can be halved.

MAKES 32

Christmassy mince slice

1 cup plain flour

½ cup rice flour

⅓ cup castor sugar

125 g cold butter, cut into small pieces

2 eggs, separated

400 g fruit mince

2 tablespoons castor sugar mixed with 1 teaspoon ground cinnamon, for sprinkling

Preheat oven to 180°C. Lightly grease and line a 20-cm × 30-cm lamington tin.

In a food processor, blend the sifted flours, sugar and butter until crumbly. With the motor running, add the egg yolks and blend until a soft dough forms.

Remove dough and knead gently on a lightly floured surface. Press two-thirds of the dough into the tin. Spread fruit mince evenly over the base and then crumble remaining dough over the top.

Beat egg whites until frothy and drizzle over the top. Sprinkle with the cinnamon sugar.

Bake for 20 minutes until golden brown. Cool before cutting into squares.

MAKES 24

Cinnamon macaroons

2 cups white sugar

1 tablespoon ground
  cinnamon

7 egg whites

2 cups ground almonds

2 teaspoons finely grated
  lemon zest

2 cups castor sugar

Preheat oven to 160°C. Lightly grease and line baking trays.

Mix together white sugar and cinnamon.

In a separate bowl, beat egg whites until frothy. Add ¼ cup of the sugar mix at a time, beating all the while. Once all the sugar has been added, continue beating for about 10 minutes, until the mixture is very thick.

Fold ground almonds and lemon zest into the mixture, then fold in the castor sugar.

Drop spoonfuls of mixture onto prepared baking trays, leaving space for spreading. Bake for 25 minutes or until lightly browned.

MAKES 48 | GLUTEN FREE

Cinnamon orange squares

2 cups plain flour

1 teaspoon ground
   cinnamon

1 teaspoon bicarbonate
   of soda

grated zest and juice
   of 1 large orange

125 g butter

3 tablespoons orange
   marmalade

⅓ cup golden syrup

⅓ cup soft brown sugar

½ cup milk

1 egg, beaten

Preheat oven to 180°C. Lightly grease and line a
19-cm × 29-cm slice tin.

Sift together flour, cinnamon and bicarbonate of soda.
Then stir in orange zest.

In a saucepan, heat the butter, marmalade, golden
syrup, sugar and milk until the butter melts. Add the
orange juice.

Stir the liquid mixture into the dry ingredients,
then add the egg and beat until smooth.

Pour into prepared tin and bake for 40 minutes.
Cool in the tray, then transfer to a wire rack.
Cut into squares when cold.

MAKES 20

Cinnamon sugar bars

2 tablespoons softened
  butter

⅔ cup castor sugar

1 cup self-raising flour

pinch of salt

1 teaspoon baking powder

1 teaspoon ground
  cinnamon

½ cup milk

1 egg, beaten

2 tablespoons castor sugar
  mixed with 1 teaspoon
  ground cinnamon, for
  sprinkling

Preheat oven to 180°C. Lightly grease and line
a 20-cm × 20-cm lamington tin.

Cream the butter and sugar until light and fluffy.

In a separate bowl, sift together the flour, salt, baking
powder and cinnamon. Mix into the creamed mixture.
Mix the milk and egg together and beat into the mixture.

Spread mixture into tin and bake for 15 minutes.
Sprinkle generously with cinnamon sugar then return to
the oven for another 10 minutes. Cut into bars to serve.

MAKES 18

Cinnamon sugar muffins

2 teaspoons ground
 cinnamon

⅔ cup castor sugar

2 cups self-raising flour

¾ cup water

1 egg

2 tablespoons golden syrup

Preheat oven to 200°C. Grease muffin tins.

Mix cinnamon and sugar together. Reserve one-third for topping and two-thirds for muffin centres.

Mix sifted flour with remaining ingredients until just combined.

One-third fill prepared muffin tins with mixture and sprinkle with two-thirds of the cinnamon sugar.

Fill tins with remaining mixture and sprinkle tops with the rest of the cinnamon sugar.

Bake for 15 minutes.

MAKES 16

Classic sponge pudding with strawberry jam sauce

100 g softened butter

100 g castor sugar

2 eggs, beaten

175 g self-raising flour

1 teaspoon vanilla extract

3–4 tablespoons milk

SAUCE

⅓ cup strawberry jam

2 tablespoons castor sugar

juice of 1 lemon

2 tablespoons water

Preheat oven to 190°C. Lightly butter a 900-ml pudding basin or four 200-ml ramekins.

Cream the butter and sugar until light and fluffy. Slowly add the eggs. Fold in the sifted flour, vanilla and milk to make a soft batter that drops off the spoon easily.

Pour into the prepared pudding basin (or ramekins) and place in a bain-marie (see page 3). Cover tightly with a double thickness of greased foil, pleated in the centre to allow for expansion of the mixture.

Bake for 60–90 minutes. (Reduce the cooking time to 35–45 minutes for the individual puddings.) Remove and turn out.

To make the strawberry jam sauce, place all the ingredients in a saucepan and stir over a gentle heat until smooth. Bring to the boil and cook for 2 minutes. Strain into a jug, and serve with the pudding.

SERVES 4

Cocoa slice

1 cup self-raising flour

1 tablespoon cocoa

1 cup desiccated coconut

1 cup crushed Corn Flakes

½ cup white sugar

125 g butter, melted

chocolate glacé icing
   (page 680)

Preheat oven to 180°C. Lightly grease and line a 19-cm × 29-cm slice tin.

Sift together flour and cocoa. Stir in coconut, Corn Flakes and sugar. Mix in melted butter.

Press into tin and bake for 20–25 minutes.

While still hot, spread with chocolate icing and cut into squares. Remove from tin when cold.

MAKES 36

Coconut apricot crunch

250 g white vegetable shortening, chopped

250 g dried apricots, finely chopped

125 g hazelnuts, finely chopped

3 cups Corn Flakes

1¼ cups desiccated coconut

¾ cup white sugar

¼ cup full-cream milk powder

Grease and line a 19-cm × 29-cm slice tin.

Heat shortening gently until just melted. Add to remaining ingredients and stir until well combined.

Press mixture into tin. Refrigerate for at least 2 hours, then cut into bars.

MAKES 24 | NO BAKE

Coconut cake with caramel rum sauce

1 cup castor sugar

120 g softened butter

1 teaspoon vanilla extract

2 eggs

1 cup self-raising flour

¾ cup sour cream

¾ cup shredded coconut

¼ cup coconut cream

SAUCE

½ cup white sugar

2 tablespoons water

1 tablespoon dark rum

40 g butter

½ cup cream

Preheat oven to 175°C. Lightly grease a 19-cm square cake tin and line the base with non-stick baking paper.

Cream the sugar, butter and vanilla extract until light and fluffy. Add the eggs, one at a time. Fold in the sifted flour. Stir in the sour cream, shredded coconut and coconut cream. Mix to a smooth batter.

Pour into the prepared tin and bake for 45–55 minutes or until lightly browned and cooked through. Cool in the tin on a wire rack.

To make the caramel rum sauce, slowly heat the sugar and water in a heavy-based saucepan, stirring until the sugar is melted. Increase the heat and cook until the syrup starts to caramelise, turning a light golden colour. Remove from the heat and stir in the dark rum, butter and cream. Whisk over a low heat until the sauce is smooth. Cool. Pour over cake to serve.

Coconut fancies

1¼ cups desiccated coconut

½ cup gluten-free puffed
   rice cereal

1 × 395-g tin condensed
   milk

Preheat oven to 180°C. Grease and line baking trays.

Mix all ingredients together.

Spoon mixture onto trays. Cook biscuits for
25–30 minutes or until lightly browned.

Cool on the baking trays.

MAKES 24 | GLUTEN FREE

Coconut ice slice

BASE

115 g softened butter

¾ cup white sugar

1 egg, beaten

1 cup self-raising flour

¾ cup desiccated coconut

TOPPING

75 g butter, melted

3 cups icing sugar

1½ cups desiccated coconut

¼ cup milk

1½ teaspoons vanilla extract

Preheat oven to 180°C. Lightly grease and line a 19-cm × 29-cm slice tin.

For the base, cream the butter and sugar together until light and fluffy. Add egg, then sifted flour and coconut. Mix well.

Pour into tin and bake for 30 minutes.

For the topping, mix all ingredients together until well combined. Spread over the base while still hot. Cool, then cut into squares.

MAKES 36

Coconut pineapple muffins

2 cups plain flour

1 tablespoon baking powder

½ teaspoon salt

½ cup castor sugar

½ cup desiccated coconut

1 egg

¼ cup vegetable oil

⅓ cup milk

1 teaspoon vanilla extract

1 × 225-g tin crushed
   pineapple, drained

½ cup slivered almonds

Preheat oven to 200°C. Grease muffin tins.

In a large bowl mix together sifted flour, baking powder, salt, sugar and coconut.

In a separate bowl mix together egg, oil, milk, vanilla and pineapple.

Add wet ingredients to dry ingredients and stir until just moistened.

Spoon batter into prepared muffin tins and sprinkle over slivered almonds.

Bake for 20 minutes.

MAKES 16

Coconut pudding with passionfruit sauce

4 eggs

finely grated zest and juice
    of 2 lemons

1 cup castor sugar

1½ cups buttermilk

1 cup desiccated coconut

SAUCE

⅔ cup passionfruit pulp

¼ cup castor sugar

zest and juice of 1 orange

Preheat oven to 160°C. Lightly grease a 1-litre ovenproof dish.

Combine the eggs, lemon zest and juice, castor sugar, buttermilk and desiccated coconut.

Pour into the prepared dish and bake for 45–60 minutes or until firm and lightly golden. Cool completely.

To make passionfruit sauce, heat all ingredients in a small saucepan, stirring until the sugar has melted. Bring to the boil and cook for 1 minute. Remove and strain into a bowl. Allow to cool.

Pour sauce over pudding to serve.

SERVES 6

Coconut rough slice

BASE

1 cup self-raising flour

3 teaspoons cocoa

pinch of salt

⅓ cup castor sugar

¼ cup desiccated coconut

115 g butter, melted

TOPPING

⅓ cup condensed milk

1 tablespoon cocoa

1 cup icing sugar

30 g butter, melted

1 cup desiccated coconut

1 teaspoon vanilla extract

icing sugar, for dusting

Preheat oven to 160°C. Lightly grease and line a 19-cm × 29-cm slice tin.

For the base, sift together flour, cocoa and salt. Add sugar, coconut and melted butter and stir until well combined.

Press into prepared tin (it will be quite thin, as this slice rises during cooking). Bake for 25 minutes. Set aside to cool a little.

For the topping, mix all ingredients together until well combined. Spread over slice.

When cool, dust with icing sugar and cut into long fingers.

MAKES 24

Coffee layer slice

1 cup plain flour

1 teaspoon ground
cinnamon

1 teaspoon mixed spice

⅓ cup soft brown sugar,
firmly packed

125 g cold butter, cut into
small pieces

BASE

125 g softened butter

¼ cup castor sugar

1 cup plain flour

¼ cup self-raising flour

FILLING

1 × 395-g tin condensed
milk

30 g butter

2 tablespoons golden syrup

3 teaspoons instant coffee
granules

⅓ cup finely chopped nuts
(almonds, walnuts, etc.)

Preheat oven to 180°C. Lightly grease and line a
25-cm × 30-cm Swiss roll tin.

For the topping, sift together flour, spices and sugar.
Rub in butter with your fingertips until crumbly. Mix to
a firm dough. Refrigerate for 30 minutes while making
the base.

For the base, cream butter and sugar until light and
fluffy. Add sifted flours and mix to a firm dough.
Press evenly over base of tin and bake for 15 minutes.
Set aside to cool. (Leave oven on.)

For the filling, combine condensed milk, butter, golden
syrup and coffee in a saucepan. Stir over medium heat
until it just begins to bubble, then cook for a further
3 minutes or until thick.

Remove from heat, stir in the nuts and spread over the
base. Crumble or grate the chilled topping over the filling
until evenly covered.

Bake for a further 20 minutes, or until the topping is firm.
Cool in the tin for 15 minutes before cutting into squares.
Leave in the tin to cool completely.

MAKES 40

Corn & bacon muffins

1 egg

2 cups plain flour

½ teaspoon salt

1 tablespoon baking powder

1 cup creamed corn

1 cup grated tasty cheese

2 rashers bacon, cooked
  and chopped

Preheat oven to 200°C. Grease muffin tins.

Make egg up to ¾ cup with water.

In a separate bowl, sift together flour, salt and baking powder. Add egg mix and remaining ingredients and mix until just combined.

Spoon into prepared muffin tins and bake for 15–20 minutes.

MAKES 16

Corn muffins with sun-dried tomatoes

½ cup plain flour

2 teaspoons castor sugar

1½ teaspoon baking powder

¼ teaspoon salt

60 g polenta

1 small egg

100 ml milk

1 tablespoon corn oil

25 g sun-dried tomatoes in oil, drained and finely chopped

Preheat oven to 220°C. Grease muffin tins.

Sift together flour, sugar, baking powder and salt. Add polenta.

Beat egg with milk and oil and gently mix into flour mixture.

Fold chopped sun-dried tomatoes into batter.

Spoon mixture into prepared muffin tins and bake for 12 minutes.

VARIATION
You could vary the flavour by adding chopped chilli, olives, garlic, etc. to the muffin mix in place of sun-dried tomatoes.

MAKES 12

Corn & tomato muffins

¾ cup polenta

½ cup plain flour

1 tablespoon white sugar

3 teaspoons baking powder

¼ teaspoon salt

⅔ cup skim milk

1 egg white, lightly beaten

½ cup seeded and diced
plum tomatoes

1 tablespoon finely chopped
fresh basil

1 tablespoon finely chopped
fresh oregano

Preheat oven to 200°C. Grease muffin tins.

In a medium bowl, combine polenta, sifted flour, sugar, baking powder and salt.

In a small bowl, combine milk, egg white, tomato and herbs. Pour into flour mixture, stirring until just combined.

Spoon into muffin tins and bake for 20 minutes.

MAKES 12

Cottage cheese & cheddar muffins

1 cup self-raising flour

1 teaspoon salt

1 egg

¾ cup water

1 cup cottage cheese

1 cup grated tasty cheese

2 tablespoons grated
   parmesan cheese

Preheat oven to 190°C. Grease muffin tins.

Sift flour and salt, then mix in all ingredients except
parmesan until just combined.

Spoon into muffin tins and sprinkle with parmesan.

Bake for 12–15 minutes.

MAKES 12

Cottage cheese muffins

2 cups plain flour

½ teaspoon salt

1 teaspoon mustard powder

2½ teaspoons baking powder

25 g cold butter, cut into small pieces

1 egg

¾ cup milk

250 g cottage cheese

¼ cup chopped fresh parsley

1 small onion, finely chopped

¼ cup grated tasty cheese

¼ teaspoon paprika

Preheat oven to 200°C. Grease muffin tins.

Sift together flour, salt, mustard and baking powder. Rub in butter.

Beat together egg and milk, then add cottage cheese, parsley and onion. Mix well.

Stir liquid mixture into dry ingredients until just combined.

Three-quarters fill muffin tins, then sprinkle over mixed grated cheese and paprika.

Bake for 20 minutes.

Serve warm.

MAKES 16

Cranberry & apple muffins

1½ cups plain flour

1 teaspoon bicarbonate
 of soda

1 teaspoon ground
 cinnamon

¼ teaspoon salt

2 egg whites

¾ cup soft brown sugar,
 firmly packed

¼ cup apple sauce

1 teaspoon vanilla extract

¾ cup diced apple

¾ cup cranberries, chopped

Preheat oven to 180°C. Grease muffin tins and dust with flour.

In a mixing bowl, sift together flour, bicarbonate of soda, cinnamon and salt.

In a separate bowl, whip egg whites until stiff. Stir in brown sugar, apple sauce, vanilla, apple and cranberries.

Mix dry ingredients with wet ingredients until just combined.

Fill muffin tins three-quarters full.

Bake for 20–25 minutes, or until lightly browned.

MAKES 12–16

Cream cheese & lemon muffins

110 g cream cheese, cut into
    small pieces

1½ cups plain flour

finely grated zest of 1 lemon

1 egg

130 ml vegetable oil

½ cup milk

⅔ cup castor sugar

1½ teaspoons baking powder

½ teaspoon salt

TOPPING

2 tablespoons freshly
    squeezed lemon juice

1 tablespoon castor sugar

Preheat oven to 190°C. Grease muffin tins.

Mix cream cheese with 2 tablespoons of the flour.
Add lemon zest.

Add sifted flour and remaining ingredients. Mix until
just combined.

Spoon into prepared muffin tins and bake in the oven
for 20–25 minutes.

To make topping, mix ingredients together to form
lemon sugar. Sprinkle over warm muffins.

MAKES 12–16

Cut-and-come-again cake

1½ cups self-raising flour

pinch of salt

½ teaspoon mixed spice

125 g cold butter, cut into
    small pieces

125 g castor sugar

125 g chopped raisins

125 g currants

¼ cup mixed peel

1 egg

¼ cup milk

icing sugar, for dusting

Preheat oven to 180°C. Lightly grease and flour a 20-cm × 10-cm loaf tin.

Sift together flour, salt and spice, then rub in butter. Add sugar, raisins, currants and peel.

Beat egg and milk and add to other ingredients, mixing well.

Pour into prepared tin and bake for 60–90 minutes, or until a skewer inserted into the centre of the cake comes out clean.

Dust with icing sugar or ice as required.

Date muffins

40 g softened butter

¼ cup soft brown sugar

2 eggs

1 cup milk

2 cups plain flour

1 teaspoon baking powder

pinch of salt

1 cup finely chopped dates

Preheat oven to 200°C. Grease muffin tins.

Cream butter and sugar until light and fluffy.

Add eggs and milk, then sifted flour, baking powder and salt.

Fold in finely chopped dates. Stir to just combine.

Three-quarters fill prepared muffin tins and bake for 12–15 minutes.

MAKES 16

Date & orange muffins

1 orange, peeled and
    quartered

½ cup orange juice

1 egg

100 g butter, melted

1½ cups plain flour

1 teaspoon baking powder

¼ teaspoon salt

1 teaspoon bicarbonate
    of soda

¾ cup castor sugar

½ cup chopped dates

Preheat oven to 190°C. Grease muffin tins.

Place orange in food processor and process to pulp.

Add orange juice, egg and melted butter, and combine.

In a large bowl, sift flour, baking powder, salt,
bicarbonate of soda and sugar.

Add mixture from processor to dry ingredients.
Add chopped dates and mix until just combined.

Three-quarters fill muffin tins and bake for 15 minutes
or until a skewer inserted comes out clean.

MAKES 12

Date & walnut muffins

1 teaspoon bicarbonate
  of soda

1 cup chopped dates

¾ cup boiling water

2 eggs

1 cup soft brown sugar

1 teaspoon vanilla extract

1½ cups plain flour

½ teaspoon salt

2 teaspoons baking powder

½ cup roughly chopped
  walnuts

Preheat oven to 180°C. Grease muffin tins.

Sprinkle bicarbonate of soda over dates, pour over
boiling water and leave to cool.

Whisk together eggs, sugar and vanilla and mix into
cooled date mix.

Add sifted flour, salt and baking powder, and nuts
and mix until just combined.

Spoon into muffin tins and bake for 18–20 minutes.

MAKES 12

Double chocolate muffins

¼ cup cocoa

¼ cup boiling water

3 cups self-raising flour

¾ cup castor sugar

1 cup chocolate chips

1 egg, beaten

1½ cups evaporated milk

125 g butter, melted and
   cooled slightly

icing sugar or cocoa,
   for dusting

Preheat oven to 190°C. Grease muffin tins.

Mix sifted cocoa and boiling water together to make a smooth paste. Allow to cool.

Sift flour and sugar into a large bowl and add chocolate chips.

In a separate bowl mix together cocoa mixture, egg, evaporated milk and butter.

Make a well in the centre of the dry ingredients and add milk mixture. Stir until just combined.

Spoon batter into prepared muffin tins and bake for 20 minutes.

Serve dusted with icing sugar or cocoa.

MAKES 24

Double-dip Mars bar slice

BASE

4 × 65-g Mars bars

125 g butter

4 cups Rice Bubbles

TOPPING

200 g milk chocolate,
  chopped

30 g butter

Grease and line a 19-cm square cake tin.

For the base, melt together the Mars bars and butter in a heavy-bottomed saucepan over low heat. Add Rice Bubbles and mix well.

Press into tin. Refrigerate about 3 hours, until set.

For the topping, melt the chocolate and butter in a double boiler over simmering water or heat on MEDIUM in the microwave, then stir until smooth. Spread over the base, leave to set, then cut into squares.

MAKES 24 | NO BAKE

Doughnut-flavoured muffins

1¾ cups plain flour

1½ teaspoons baking powder

½ teaspoon salt

¼ teaspoon ground
   cinnamon

½ teaspoon ground nutmeg

⅓ cup vegetable oil

¾ cup castor sugar

1 egg

¾ cup milk

TOPPING

120 g butter, melted

¾ cup castor sugar mixed
   with 1 teaspoon ground
   cinnamon

Preheat oven to 190°C. Grease muffin tins.

In a large bowl sift together flour, baking powder, salt
and spices.

In a separate bowl mix together oil, sugar, egg and milk.
Add oil mixture to dry ingredients and stir to combine.

Spoon batter into prepared muffin tins and bake for
20 minutes.

Remove from tins while still warm and brush with melted
butter, then sprinkle with cinnamon sugar.

VARIATION
Half-fill muffin tins with batter. Add 1 teaspoon raspberry
jam to each muffin and cover with remaining batter.

MAKES 12

Easy cherry & ricotta strudel

2 cups ricotta

2 eggs, lightly beaten

½ cup pitted tinned
   cherries, well drained

50 g softened cream cheese

½ cup dried breadcrumbs

3 tablespoons castor sugar

4 sheets filo pastry

50 g butter, melted

icing sugar, for dusting

Preheat oven to 200°C. Grease a baking tray.

Combine the ricotta, eggs, cherries, cream cheese, dried breadcrumbs and sugar. Chill until ready to use.

Place a sheet of non-stick baking paper on your work surface. Lay down the first sheet of filo pastry, shortest side towards you, and brush lightly with melted butter. Lay a second sheet of filo pastry over the top and brush with butter. Repeat with the third and fourth sheets.

Spoon the filling in a thick sausage along the short side of the pastry sheets, leaving a border at the end. Fold the long sides in over the filling. Carefully roll up the filo from the short side to form a log-shaped packet.

Slide onto baking tray. Sprinkle with icing sugar and bake for 15 minutes.

Reduce the oven temperature to 180°C and bake for a further 15–20 minutes or until the pastry is light brown and crisp.

Cool a little before cutting into slices with a serrated knife. Dust with icing sugar before serving.

SERVES 6

Espresso coffee & walnut cake

¾ cup icing sugar

4 eggs, separated

1 tablespoon fresh
   breadcrumbs

1 tablespoon finely ground
   espresso coffee beans

1 tablespoon cocoa

1½ cups walnuts, roughly
   chopped

icing sugar, for dusting

Preheat oven to 180°C. Lightly grease a 20-cm round springform cake tin and line the base with non-stick baking paper.

Using an electric mixer beat the sifted icing sugar and egg yolks until pale and thick. Stir in the breadcrumbs, ground coffee beans, cocoa and chopped walnuts.

In another bowl, whip the egg whites until stiff peaks form. Fold two large spoonfuls of the coffee batter into the egg whites. Tip the egg-white mixture into the remaining coffee batter and fold carefully with a metal spoon.

Pour the batter into the prepared cake tin and bake for 55–60 minutes or until a skewer inserted into the centre of the cake comes out clean. Cool in the tin before carefully turning out onto a serving plate.

Dust with icing sugar and serve with whipped cream.

Extra-fibre muffins

1¼ cups plain flour

½ cup castor sugar

1 tablespoon baking powder

2 cups All-Bran

1¼ cups skim milk

1 egg

¼ cup apple sauce

Preheat oven to 200°C. Grease muffin tins.

Sift together flour, sugar and baking powder.

In a large mixing bowl combine All-Bran and milk. Let stand 5 minutes or until All-Bran softens.

Add egg and apple sauce to All-Bran. Mix well.

Add flour mixture, stirring until just combined.

Three-quarters fill muffin tins and bake for 20 minutes, or until lightly brown.

MAKES 12–16

Fairy cakes

125 g softened butter

⅔ cup castor sugar

2 eggs

1 cup plain flour

2 teaspoons baking powder

1½ tablespoons milk

Preheat oven to 190°C. Lay out 24 fairy cake (cupcake) papers on a baking tray.

Cream butter and sugar until light and fluffy.
Add eggs one at a time, beating well after each addition.
Sift flour and baking powder into mixture and add milk.
Mix thoroughly but do not beat.

Place a large teaspoonful of mixture into each paper case. Bake for 15–20 minutes or until cooked.

Allow to cool before decorating with your favourite icing (see pages 677–82).

MAKES 24

Family chocolate cake

125 g softened butter

⅔ cup castor sugar

½ cup icing sugar

1¼ cups self-raising flour

½ cup cocoa

1 teaspoon bicarbonate
   of soda

pinch of salt

2 eggs

1 cup milk

1 teaspoon vanilla extract

chocolate butter icing
   (page 678)

Preheat oven to 180°C. Lightly grease and flour
a 23-cm cake tin.

Cream butter with castor sugar and icing sugar.

Sift flour, cocoa, bicarbonate of soda and salt into
a separate bowl. Add flour mixture to creamed mixture,
along with eggs, milk and vanilla extract, and beat well.

Spoon into prepared tin and bake for 40–55 minutes,
or until a skewer inserted into the centre of the cake
comes out clean.

Ice with chocolate butter icing when cold.

Favourite blueberry muffins

2 cups plain flour

1 tablespoon baking powder

2 teaspoons custard powder

1 cup castor sugar

¾ cup blueberries
   (or blackcurrants)

2 eggs

¾ cup milk

¾ cup vegetable oil

icing sugar, for dusting

Preheat oven to 190°C. Grease muffin tins.

Sift flour, baking powder and custard powder into a bowl. Add sugar and blueberries.

In a separate bowl mix together eggs, milk and oil.

Add milk mixture to dry ingredients and combine.

Spoon batter into prepared muffin tins and bake for 15–20 minutes.

Serve dusted with icing sugar.

MAKES 16

Fig, ginger & pecan loaf

185 g softened butter

¾ cup castor sugar

3 eggs, lightly beaten

150 g sultanas

150 g glacé figs

150 g glacé ginger

½ cup plain flour

½ cup self-raising flour

⅔ cup pecan nuts, roughly
  chopped

Preheat oven to 160°C. Grease a 23-cm × 12-cm loaf tin and line the base with non-stick baking paper.

Cream the butter and sugar until light and fluffy. Slowly add the eggs until combined. Stir in the sultanas, figs and ginger.

Sift the flours into another bowl and mix in the nuts. Fold into the cake batter.

Spoon into the prepared tin and bake for 75 minutes or until a skewer inserted comes out clean. Cool in the tin for 20 minutes before turning out onto a wire rack.

Florentine bars

185 g dark cooking
    chocolate, chopped

¾ cup sultanas

2 cups Corn Flakes, crushed

½ cup mixed nuts, crushed

60 g glacé cherries, chopped

⅔ cup condensed milk

Grease and line a 19-cm × 29-cm slice tin.

Melt chocolate in a double boiler over simmering water, or on MEDIUM in the microwave.

Spread evenly over base of tin. Refrigerate until set.

Preheat oven to 180°C.

Combine sultanas, Corn Flakes, nuts, cherries and condensed milk in a bowl. Mix well. Spread evenly over chocolate base.

Bake for 15–20 minutes. Cool at room temperature, then chill until set before cutting into bars.

MAKES 36

Florentines

1 cup soft brown sugar,
 lightly packed

125 g butter

½ cup golden syrup

1 cup self-raising flour

⅓ cup hazelnuts, chopped

⅓ cup blanched almonds,
 chopped

1 tablespoon mixed peel

1 tablespoon glacé cherries,
 chopped

125 g dark cooking
 chocolate, chopped

Preheat oven to 160°C. Line baking trays with baking paper.

Gently heat the sugar, butter and golden syrup in a saucepan until butter has melted and sugar has dissolved. Remove from heat and add to sifted flour, nuts, peel and cherries. Mix thoroughly.

Drop spoonfuls of mixture onto prepared trays, spaced well apart to allow for spreading. Bake for 12–15 minutes, until lightly golden brown.

Cool on the trays for a few minutes before transferring to wire racks.

When the biscuits are cold, melt chocolate in a double boiler over simmering water, or on MEDIUM in the microwave. Spread melted chocolate over the flat side of each Florentine. (For a different look, dip one half of each biscuit in the melted chocolate.)

MAKES 18

Fran's dairy-free chocolate cake

3 cups plain flour

½ teaspoon salt

1 teaspoon baking powder

1 teaspoon bicarbonate
   of soda

⅔ cup cocoa or carob
   powder

2 cups castor sugar

2 tablespoons vinegar

2 cups chilled water

⅔ cup vegetable oil

1 teaspoon vanilla extract

chocolate butter icing
   (page 678)

Preheat oven to 180°C. Lightly grease and flour
a 23-cm cake tin.

Sift flour, salt, baking powder, bicarbonate of soda
and cocoa into a large bowl. Add remaining ingredients
and mix well.

Pour into prepared tin and bake for 40–45 minutes.
Ice with chocolate butter icing.

DAIRY FREE

Fresh berry slice

BASE

¼ cup softened butter

¾ cup white sugar

1 egg

2 cups self-raising flour

pinch of salt

raspberry jam, for spreading

½ cup fresh raspberries,
   blueberries or blackberries

TOPPING

1 cup white sugar

1 cup desiccated coconut

1 egg

Preheat oven to 180°C. Lightly grease and line a 19-cm × 29-cm slice tin.

For the base, cream butter and sugar until light and fluffy. Mix in egg, sifted flour and salt.

Press mixture into tin, spread thickly with jam and sprinkle with fresh berries.

For the topping, mix all ingredients together and spread evenly over berries.

Bake for about 20 minutes. Cool before slicing.

MAKES 24

Fresh fruit muffins

2 cups plain flour

1 tablespoon baking powder

½ teaspoon salt

½ cup castor sugar

100 g butter, melted and
  cooled slightly

1 cup milk

1 egg

1–1½ cups chopped
  fresh fruit

1 cup chopped walnuts

1 tablespoon sugar mixed
  with ½ teaspoon ground
  cinnamon

Preheat oven to 200°C. Grease muffin tins.

In a large bowl sift together flour, baking powder, salt
and sugar.

In a separate bowl mix together butter, milk and egg.

Add milk mixture to dry ingredients, followed by fruit
and walnuts. Stir to combine.

Spoon into prepared muffin tins and sprinkle with
cinnamon sugar.

Bake for 15 minutes.

Split muffins and serve with butter.

VARIATION
Serve with whipped cream, or with yoghurt mixed
with the appropriate fruit.

MAKES 16

Fresh plum tart with crumble topping

1¼ cups castor sugar

pinch of salt

125 g cold butter, cut into
   small pieces

1¼ cups plain flour

½ teaspoon ground
   cinnamon

¼ teaspoon baking powder

2 eggs

½ cup sour cream

½ teaspoon vanilla extract

12 dark plums, pitted and
   each cut into eight

icing sugar, for dusting

pouring custard (page 683)
   or cream

Preheat oven to 180°C. Lightly grease a 20-cm tart tin.

Combine 1 cup of the sugar with the salt, butter and sifted flour in a food processor and pulse until the mixture resembles coarse breadcrumbs. Divide the mixture into two.

Add the cinnamon and baking powder to one mixture. Lightly beat 1 egg and stir into the mixture to form a sticky ball. Press into the base of the tart tin and cook for 10 minutes or until just set.

Meanwhile, whisk the other egg with the remaining castor sugar, sour cream and vanilla extract.

Remove the base from the oven (leave oven on). Arrange the plums over the base, then pour over egg custard mixture. Take the remaining flour-and-butter mixture and sprinkle it over the top.

Return to the oven and bake for 20–30 minutes or until lightly browned. Cool a little.

Dust with icing sugar and serve with pouring custard or cream.

SERVES 6

Fresh raspberry muffins

2 cups plain flour

¾ teaspoon bicarbonate
of soda

¾ teaspoon ground
cinnamon

¼ teaspoon freshly grated
nutmeg

¼ teaspoon ground ginger

¼ teaspoon salt

1 cup castor sugar

2 eggs

2 teaspoons vanilla extract

½ cup vegetable oil

80 g butter, melted and
cooled slightly

1 cup fresh raspberries

Preheat oven to 200°C. Grease muffin tins.

Sift flour, bicarbonate of soda, cinnamon, nutmeg,
ginger and salt into a large mixing bowl.

Whisk sugar and eggs in a small bowl until light.
Blend in vanilla, oil and butter.

Make a large well in the centre of the dry ingredients,
pour in egg-sugar mixture and combine the two mixtures
quickly until batter is formed.

Gently fold in raspberries.

Spoon batter into prepared muffin tins, filling them
two-thirds full.

Bake for 20–22 minutes.

MAKES 16

Frilled Easter biscuits

115 g softened butter

⅓ cup castor sugar, plus extra for sprinkling

1 egg, separated

1¾ cups plain flour

½ teaspoon mixed spice

½ teaspoon ground cinnamon

⅓ cup currants

1 tablespoon mixed peel, finely chopped

1–2 tablespoons milk

Preheat oven to 180°C. Lightly grease baking trays.

Cream the butter and sugar until light and fluffy, then beat in the egg yolk.

Sift together flour and spices, then fold into the egg mixture. Stir in the currants and peel. Add enough milk to form a fairly soft dough.

Turn dough onto a lightly floured surface, knead gently, then roll out to 5 mm thick. Cut into rounds using a fluted biscuit cutter. Gather any leftover dough, roll out again and use to make more biscuits.

Place on prepared trays and bake for 10 minutes. Remove but leave oven on.

Beat the egg white until frothy, then brush over the biscuits. Sprinkle with castor sugar and bake for another 10 minutes, or until golden.

MAKES 16

Fruit salad cake

3 cups plain flour

1 teaspoon salt

1 teaspoon bicarbonate
  of soda

1 teaspoon garam masala
  or ground cinnamon

2 cups castor sugar

3 eggs, beaten

1½ cups safflower or
  corn oil

1½ teaspoons vanilla extract

1 × 250-g tin crushed
  pineapple, undrained

2 cups chopped very ripe
  banana

FILLING

50 g softened butter

250 g cream cheese

1 teaspoon vanilla extract

1½ cups icing sugar

pawpaw or mango, diced
  or thinly sliced

Preheat oven to 180°C. Lightly grease and flour three 18-cm sponge tins.

Sift flour, salt, bicarbonate of soda and spice into a large bowl. Stir in sugar. Add eggs and oil, stirring well. Do not beat. Stir in vanilla extract, pineapple and banana.

Spoon the batter into the three prepared tins and bake for 25–30 minutes, or until a skewer inserted into the centre comes out clean. Allow to cool in tins for 10 minutes before removing.

To make cream cheese filling, beat together butter, cream cheese, vanilla and sifted icing sugar. Spread filling on top of all three cakes. Layer the cakes, spreading small pieces of pawpaw or mango on top of the filling between layers.

Fruit salad muffins

2 cups self-raising flour

½ cup castor sugar

2 eggs

1 × 440-g tin fruit salad
in juice, drained
(juice reserved)

100 g butter, melted

Preheat oven to 180°C. Grease muffin tins.

Sift flour into a large mixing bowl, then add sugar.
Stir in eggs, fruit, butter and ¾ cup reserved juice.
Mix until just combined.

Spoon into muffin tins and bake for 15–20 minutes.

MAKES 16

Fruity bran muffins

1¼ cups All-Bran, plus
    extra for sprinkling

¾ cup skim milk

1 egg

¼ cup vegetable oil

¼ cup raw sugar

1¾ cups self-raising flour

1 teaspoon ground
    cinnamon

⅔ cup mixed dried fruit

1 egg white

Preheat oven to 190°C. Grease muffin tins.

Place All-Bran and milk in a bowl and let stand for
5 minutes to soften.

Beat egg, oil and sugar together and add to All-Bran.

Sift flour and add to All-Bran with cinnamon and mixed
fruit. Mix until just combined.

Beat egg white until stiff peaks form, then fold into
mixture.

Three-quarters fill muffin tins and sprinkle each muffin
with some extra All-Bran.

Bake for 25–30 minutes or until a skewer inserted
comes out clean.

MAKES 16

Fruity cereal bars

1 cup wholemeal self-raising
 flour

1 cup breakfast cereal with
 dried fruit

½ cup soft brown sugar

125 g butter, melted

TOPPING

1½ cups breakfast cereal
 with dried fruit

2 eggs, beaten

1 teaspoon vanilla extract

¾ cup soft brown sugar

½ cup unsalted raw peanuts

Preheat oven to 180°C. Lightly grease and line
a 19-cm × 29-cm slice tin.

For the base, sift flour and mix with remaining
ingredients until well combined.

Press mixture into tin and bake for 15 minutes.
Leave oven on.

For the topping, mix all ingredients together until
well combined. Spread over base.

Bake for a further 30–35 minutes. Cool in the tin
before cutting into slices.

MAKES 24

Fruity Christmas pudding

150 g raisins

150 g sultanas

80 g currants

50 g mixed peel

50 g dried apple, chopped

25 g prunes, pitted and
  roughly chopped

25 g dates, pitted and
  roughly chopped

50 ml rum

30 ml dark ale

125 g butter

100 g soft brown sugar

40 g finely grated carrot

20 g plain flour

40 g finely chopped almonds

1 tablespoon dark treacle

½ teaspoon mixed spice

¼ teaspoon ground nutmeg

1 egg

1¼ cups fresh breadcrumbs

1¼ cups dried breadcrumbs

ice-cream or pouring
  custard (page 683),
  to serve

Combine the dried fruit in a large bowl and pour the rum and dark ale over the top. Leave to soak for a day.

Melt the butter and brown sugar over low heat. Pour over the fruit and stir in the remaining ingredients. Mix well with a spoon or use your hands.

Divide the mixture in half and form into two balls. Place each pudding into a baking bag and tie with string, leaving room for the pudding to swell a little.

Suspend in a pot of simmering water and cook, covered, for 2½ hours. Remove and leave to cool.

To reheat, cook in the bag for 40 minutes or until the pudding is heated through.

Serve warm with ice-cream, or pouring custard with a splash of rum added.

MAKES TWO 600-g PUDDINGS

Fruity muffins

75 g butter, melted

1 egg, beaten

1 cup milk

1–1½ cups diced fresh fruit
(peaches, pineapple,
blueberries, apricots,
strawberries)

2 cups plain flour

1 tablespoon baking powder

½ teaspoon salt

½ cup castor sugar

1 tablespoon sugar mixed
with ½ teaspoon ground
cinnamon

Preheat oven to 220°C. Grease muffin tins.

Beat together butter, egg and milk.

Add with fruit to sifted dry ingredients. Don't over mix.

Spoon into muffin tins and sprinkle with cinnamon sugar.

Bake for 15–20 minutes.

MAKES 16–20

Fruit yoghurt muffins

2 cups plain flour

1 tablespoon baking powder

½ cup castor sugar

1 egg

¾ cup water

150 g fruit-flavoured
    yoghurt

50 g butter, melted

Preheat oven to 180°C. Grease muffin tins.

Sift together flour and baking powder. Mix in remaining ingredients until just combined.

Three-quarters fill prepared muffin tins and bake for 15–20 minutes.

MAKES 16

Fruity yoghurt cake

1 cup castor sugar

125 g softened butter

2 eggs

2 cups plain flour

1 teaspoon baking powder

1 teaspoon bicarbonate
of soda

pinch of salt

1 cup natural yoghurt

1 teaspoon vanilla extract

2 teaspoons ground
cinnamon

½ cup raisins

½ cup chopped walnuts

icing sugar, for dusting

Preheat oven to 180°C. Lightly grease and flour
a 23-cm square tin.

Cream three-quarters of the sugar with the butter
until light and fluffy. Add eggs one at a time, beating
well after each addition.

Sift together flour, baking powder, bicarbonate of soda
and salt. Stir into creamed mixture alternately with
yoghurt until just blended. Stir in vanilla extract.

Pour 2 cups of mixture into prepared tin.

Combine remaining sugar with cinnamon, raisins
and walnuts, and sprinkle ½ cup over mixture in tin.

Stir remaining nut mixture into batter in bowl.
Spread over mixture in tin.

Bake for 45 minutes, or until a skewer inserted into
the centre of the cake comes out clean. Dust with
icing sugar to serve.

Fudge-filled peanut butter muffins

½ cup chocolate chips

1 tablespoon unsalted butter

1⅔ cups plain flour

1 tablespoon baking powder

½ cup soft brown sugar,
    firmly packed

¼ teaspoon salt

¾ cup milk

½ cup peanut butter

⅓ cup vegetable oil

1 egg, beaten

1 teaspoon vanilla extract

½ cup chopped salted
    peanuts

Preheat oven to 200°C. Grease muffin tins.

In a small saucepan heat chocolate chips and butter over low heat until melted. Set aside.

In a large bowl sift together flour, baking powder, sugar and salt.

In a separate bowl mix together milk, peanut butter, oil, egg and vanilla until well combined.

Make a well in the centre of the dry ingredients and add milk mixture. Stir to combine.

Spoon half the batter into prepared muffin tins. Put a spoonful of melted chocolate mixture on top, making sure it does not touch the sides. Cover with remaining batter.

Sprinkle over chopped peanuts and bake in the oven for 15–20 minutes.

MAKES 12

Fudgy fruit slice

¾ cup dates, chopped

¼ cup dried apricots,
chopped

¼ cup preserved ginger,
chopped

½ cup soft brown sugar

125 g butter

4 cups Rice Bubbles

desiccated coconut, for
coating

Grease and line a 19-cm square cake tin.

In a heavy-bottomed saucepan, heat the dates, apricots, ginger, sugar and butter. Simmer about 15 minutes, until the fruit is soft and fudgy. (Do not cook for too long, as the mixture may burn or start to set.)

Add Rice Bubbles and mix well. Press into tin.

Refrigerate for at least 2 hours, until set, then cut into cubes and coat in coconut.

MAKES 16 | NO BAKE

Georgian baklava

PASTRY

250 g cold butter, cut into
   small pieces

1¾ cups plain flour

½ teaspoon bicarbonate
   of soda

1 egg yolk

1 cup sour cream

FILLING

½ cup walnuts, finely
   ground

1 cup white sugar

½ teaspoon vanilla extract

2 egg whites

1 egg yolk, beaten

For the pastry, blend the butter with the sifted flour and bicarbonate of soda in a food processor until crumbly. Add the egg yolk and sour cream and blend to make a soft dough. Wrap dough in cling wrap and refrigerate for at least 2 hours.

Preheat oven to 180°C. Lightly grease a 19-cm square cake tin and dust with flour.

For the filling, combine the ground walnuts with the sugar and vanilla. In a separate bowl beat the egg whites until stiff peaks form. Gently fold egg whites into the nut mixture.

Divide the dough into three pieces, and roll each out to the size of the tin. Use the first pastry sheet to line the base of the tin. Spread with half the filling, leaving a 2-cm border all the way around. Place the second sheet of pastry on top.

Cover with the remaining filling and top with the last piece of dough. Tuck the edges of the dough under to seal. Press down firmly with your hands.

Using a sharp knife, score the top of the slice into diamonds. Brush with egg yolk.

Bake for 45–50 minutes or until golden brown. Cut into diamonds to serve.

MAKES 48

Ginger almond cake

1 egg

175 g butter, melted

230 g plain flour

¼ teaspoon salt

210 g white sugar

125 g glacé ginger, chopped

50 g whole blanched
 almonds

white sugar, for sprinkling

Preheat oven to 180°C. Lightly grease and flour a 20-cm round tin.

Beat the egg and, reserving a little to glaze the top, add to butter. Add sifted flour and salt, sugar and ginger pieces, and mix well.

Pour into prepared tin. Place almonds on top, brush with remainder of beaten egg and sprinkle with sugar.

Bake for 45 minutes.

Ginger & apple upside-down cake

3 tablespoons soft brown
  sugar

2 Granny Smith apples,
  peeled, cored and thinly
  sliced

4 cups plain flour

1 tablespoon ground ginger

225 g cold butter, cut into
  small pieces

2 cups castor sugar

4 tablespoons golden syrup

2 teaspoons bicarbonate
  of soda

1½ cups milk

2 tablespoons lemon juice

Preheat oven to 170°C. Lightly grease and line a
deep 20-cm round cake tin.

Sprinkle the lined tin with the brown sugar and arrange
apple slices to cover bottom of tin.

Sift flour and ginger into a large bowl and rub in butter.
Add sugar, golden syrup, and bicarbonate of soda
dissolved in milk. Mix well. Add lemon juice.

Pour mixture over apple slices in cake tin. Bake for
60–75 minutes.

Turn cake out onto a plate with apples on top.
Carefully remove baking paper.

Ginger biscuits

1¼ cup gluten-free flour mix (page 6)

1½ teaspoons bicarbonate of soda

½ teaspoon cream of tartar

2 teaspoons ground ginger

½ cup white sugar

¼ cup olive oil

2 tablespoons golden syrup

1 egg, beaten

Preheat oven to 190°C. Lightly grease baking trays.

Sift together flour, bicarbonate of soda, cream of tartar and ginger. Stir in sugar.

Warm the oil and golden syrup together over low heat until blended. Allow to cool slightly, then add to the dry ingredients. Add the beaten egg and mix until a firm dough forms.

Roll dough into walnut-sized balls and place on trays, leaving plenty of space for spreading.

Bake for 15–20 minutes or until brown.

VARIATION

For gluten-free gingerbread men substitute treacle for the golden syrup and reduce bicarbonate of soda to ½ teaspoon. Roll out the dough to 5 mm thick or less, then cut out gingerbread men shapes with a biscuit cutter.

MAKES 36 | GLUTEN FREE

Gingerbread lemon-iced muffins

1¼ cups plain flour

½ cup wholemeal plain
flour

½ cup soft brown sugar,
firmly packed

1 teaspoon bicarbonate
of soda

¼ teaspoon salt

2 teaspoons ground ginger

1 teaspoon ground
cinnamon

pinch of ground cloves

pinch of ground nutmeg

¾ cup buttermilk

½ cup vegetable oil

2 eggs, beaten

¼ cup molasses

1 cup currants

lemon glacé icing
(page 679)

Preheat oven to 200°C. Grease muffin tins.

In a large bowl sift together flours, sugar, bicarbonate
of soda, salt and spices.

In a separate bowl mix together buttermilk, oil, eggs
and molasses.

Make a well in the centre of the dry ingredients and add
buttermilk mixture. Stir to combine, then fold in currants.

Spoon batter into prepared muffin tins and bake for
15–20 minutes.

Drizzle lemon icing over muffins.

MAKES 16

Gingerbread men

125 g butter

2 tablespoons golden syrup

¾ cup white sugar

1 egg, beaten

2 cups self-raising flour

pinch of salt

2 teaspoons ground ginger

currants, cherries,
    liquorice, chocolate chips,
    etc., for decorating

Preheat oven to 150°C. Lightly grease baking trays.

Melt butter and golden syrup over low heat, then remove from heat and stir in sugar and egg.

Add the sifted flour, salt and ginger and mix well.

Turn dough onto a lightly floured surface and knead gently until it forms a ball. Roll out thinly. Use biscuit cutters to cut out gingerbread men (or other shapes). Gather any leftover dough, roll out again and use to make more biscuits.

Place on baking trays and add dried fruit, chocolate and lollies to make eyes, mouth, buttons, etc. Bake for about 10 minutes, until golden brown.

MAKES 18

Gingerbread & rhubarb pudding

110 g softened butter

½ cup soft brown sugar, firmly packed

2 eggs, lightly beaten

⅔ cup treacle

1 teaspoon ground ginger

1½ cups plain flour

1 teaspoon bicarbonate of soda

⅓ cup milk

450 g rhubarb, trimmed and cut into small chunks

icing sugar, for dusting

Preheat oven to 180°C. Grease a 1.5-litre ovenproof dish.

Cream the butter and sugar until light and fluffy. Slowly add the eggs. Pour in the treacle and mix well.

Sift the ginger and flour and stir into the batter. Dissolve the bicarbonate of soda in the milk and stir in.

Spoon one-third of the mixture into the prepared dish and scatter over the rhubarb. Spoon the rest of the batter over the top.

Bake for 45 minutes. Then reduce the oven temperature to 160°C. Loosely cover the top of the pudding with foil and bake for a further 30 minutes.

Dust with icing sugar before serving with ice-cream or whipped cream.

SERVES 6−8

Gingerbread ring

⅓ cup treacle

¾ cup soft brown sugar

125 g butter

1⅓ cups plain flour

2 teaspoons ground ginger

1½ teaspoons ground
   cinnamon

½ cup milk

1 teaspoon bicarbonate
   of soda

1 large egg, beaten

icing sugar, for dusting

Preheat oven to 140°C. Lightly grease and flour
a 22-cm ring cake tin.

Heat treacle, sugar and butter together, but do not boil.
Add to sifted flour and spices.

Warm milk in small saucepan and add bicarbonate
of soda. Add to mixture with beaten egg.

Pour into prepared tin and bake for 75 minutes.
Dust with icing sugar to serve.

Like all gingerbread, this cake should be stored for a
little while before eating to allow the flavour to mature.

Gingerbread squares

3 cups plain flour

1 teaspoon bicarbonate
of soda

3 teaspoons ground ginger

pinch of salt

2 tablespoons cold butter,
cut into small pieces

2 tablespoons soft brown
sugar

¾ cup golden syrup

1 egg, beaten

1 cup milk

lemon glacé icing
(page 679)

Preheat oven to 180°C. Lightly grease and line a
20-cm × 30-cm lamington tin.

Sift together the flour, bicarbonate of soda, ginger and
salt. Rub in the butter with your fingertips until crumbly,
then mix in sugar.

Heat golden syrup until just warm, then mix with egg and
milk. Add to the dry ingredients and mix until smooth.

Pour into prepared tin and bake for 30–35 minutes or
until risen and set.

Once cool, top with lemon icing. Cut into squares to
serve.

MAKES 24

Ginger & date slice

1 cup dates, chopped

250 g butter

⅓ cup castor sugar

60 g preserved ginger,
    finely chopped

3 cups Corn Flakes

125 g dark cooking
    chocolate, chopped

Grease and line a 19-cm × 29-cm slice tin.

Combine dates, butter, sugar and ginger in a saucepan
and stir over low heat until well mixed and mushy.
Add Corn Flakes and mix well.

Press mixture into tin and refrigerate until cold and firm.

Melt chocolate in a double boiler over simmering water,
or on MEDIUM in the microwave, then spread over slice.
Chill for about 5 minutes to allow the chocolate to set a
little, then mark out squares by scoring lines in the top
with a sharp knife.

Return to refrigerator and chill until completely set.
Cut into squares along the scored lines.

MAKES 36 | NO BAKE

Ginger muffins

1 cup milk

50 g butter

1 tablespoon golden syrup

1 teaspoon bicarbonate
  of soda

1 egg, lightly beaten

1 cup oat bran

½ cup castor sugar

2 tablespoons chopped
  crystallised ginger

1 teaspoon ground ginger

1 cup plain flour

½ cup rolled oats

½ teaspoon salt

Preheat oven to 200°C. Grease muffin tins.

Heat milk, butter and golden syrup over low heat until butter melts. Add bicarbonate of soda and egg.

In a mixing bowl, combine oat bran, sugar, crystallised and ground ginger, sifted flour, rolled oats and salt.

Add milk mixture and mix until just combined.

Three-quarters fill prepared muffin tins and bake for 10–15 minutes.

MAKES 12

Ginger nuts

125 g butter

1 cup white sugar

1 tablespoon golden syrup

1 egg, beaten

2 cups self-raising flour

½ teaspoon bicarbonate
   of soda

2 teaspoons ground ginger

1 teaspoon mixed spice

Preheat oven to 220°C. Lightly grease baking trays.

Gently heat butter, sugar and golden syrup until butter has melted and sugar has dissolved. Remove from heat, cool slightly, then add egg.

Add sifted dry ingredients and mix thoroughly.

Roll dough into walnut-sized balls. Place on baking trays, leaving space for spreading. Chill for 15 minutes.

Bake for 5 minutes, then reduce heat to 180°C and bake for a further 7–10 minutes.

Cool on trays until nearly cold before transferring to wire racks to cool completely.

MAKES 36

Ginger pear muffins

2 cups plain flour

½ cup soft brown sugar,
firmly packed

1 teaspoon bicarbonate
of soda

½ teaspoon salt

2 teaspoons ground ginger

1 teaspoon ground
cinnamon

pinch of ground nutmeg

pinch of ground cloves

1 cup natural yoghurt

½ cup vegetable oil

3 tablespoons molasses

1 egg, beaten

1½ cups diced pear

½ cup raisins

¼ cup chopped walnuts

Preheat oven to 200°C. Grease muffin tins.

In a large bowl sift together flour, brown sugar, bicarbonate of soda, salt and spices.

In a separate bowl mix together yoghurt, oil, molasses and egg.

Make a well in the centre of the dry ingredients and add yoghurt mixture. Stir to combine, then fold in pear, raisins and walnuts.

Spoon batter into prepared muffin tins and bake for 20 minutes. Serve warm with butter.

VARIATION
Top with ginger icing, made by mixing 1½ cups sifted icing sugar, 1 teaspoon ground ginger, 1 tablespoon butter and enough boiling water to make desired consistency.

MAKES 16

Ginger pineapple muffins

1 cup plain flour

1 cup wholemeal plain flour

1 tablespoon baking powder

2 teaspoons ground ginger

½ cup soft brown sugar

2 eggs

1 cup milk

100 g butter, melted

1 × 440-g tin crushed
   pineapple, drained

½ cup bran

Preheat oven to 180°C. Grease muffin tins.

Sift together flours, baking powder, ginger and sugar. Mix in remaining ingredients until just combined.

Three-quarters fill prepared muffin tins and bake for 15–20 minutes.

VARIATION
Up to half the milk can be replaced by the liquid from the pineapple if it is in juice. Don't use if it is syrup.

MAKES 16

Ginger slice

BASE

125 g softened butter

½ cup white sugar

2 cups plain flour

1 teaspoon baking powder

1 teaspoon ground ginger

TOPPING

80 g butter

½ cup icing sugar

1 tablespoon golden syrup

2 teaspoons ground ginger

Preheat oven to 180°C. Lightly grease a 23-cm square slab tin.

For the base, cream butter and sugar until light and fluffy. In a separate bowl sift together flour, baking powder and ginger. Fold into creamed mixture to form a dough.

Turn onto a lightly floured surface and knead dough well. Press into prepared tin.

Bake for 20–25 minutes or until firm to touch and lightly golden brown.

For the topping, heat all ingredients in a saucepan and stir until smooth. Pour over slice while still hot. Cool for 5 minutes before cutting into squares.

MAKES 24

Ginger & sour cream cake

1½ cups self-raising flour

1½ teaspoons ground ginger

1½ cups soft brown sugar

3 eggs, lightly beaten

180 g butter, melted

½ cup sour cream

Preheat oven to 180°C. Lightly grease a 23-cm round springform cake tin and line the base with non-stick baking paper.

Sift the flour and ginger into a mixing bowl and stir in the sugar. Stir in the eggs and melted butter. Combine to make a smooth batter.

Spoon into the prepared tin and spread the sour cream over the top.

Bake for 45 minutes or until lightly browned on top.

Cool for 10 minutes in the tin on a wire rack. Turn out onto the rack and cool completely before serving.

Ginger sticks

4 eggs, separated

⅓ cup castor sugar, plus
extra for sprinkling

1 tablespoon ground ginger

1⅔ cup gluten-free flour
mix (page 6)

icing sugar, for dusting

Preheat oven to 180°C. Lightly grease baking trays.

Mix the egg yolks with the sugar and ginger to form
a smooth paste.

Beat egg whites until stiff peaks form. Fold a spoonful
into the egg-yolk mixture, then gradually fold in remaining
egg white, alternately with flour.

Put mixture into a piping bag and pipe 5-cm long sticks
onto the baking trays.

Sprinkle with castor sugar and bake for 8–10 minutes
or until light brown.

Dust with icing sugar to serve.

MAKES 30 | GLUTEN FREE

Glacé-cherry macaroons

2 egg whites

100 g ground almonds

¾ cup castor sugar

2 tablespoons white sugar

glacé cherries, for
   decorating

Preheat oven to 180°C. Lightly grease baking trays.

Beat egg whites until thick. Gently fold in remaining ingredients (except cherries).

Pipe or spoon the mixture onto prepared trays, leaving plenty of space for spreading. Top each biscuit with a glacé cherry.

Bake for 10–15 minutes, until light brown – remove from the oven as soon as they start to change colour, as they burn easily.

MAKES 24 | GLUTEN FREE

Gluten-free amaretti

1 cup ground almonds

1 cup castor sugar

2 egg whites

½ teaspoon vanilla extract

few drops almond essence

blanched almonds, split in
  half, for decorating

Preheat oven to 180°C. Lightly grease baking trays and dust with flour.

Combine ground almonds and sugar. Add egg whites, vanilla extract and almond essence. Beat with an electric mixer on medium speed for 3 minutes, until light and fluffy.

Spoon mixture into a piping bag fitted with a 1-cm round tip and pipe biscuits onto baking trays. Use a circular motion, starting from the centre, to make biscuits 4 cm in diameter.

Top each biscuit with half an almond, and bake for 12 minutes or until tops are lightly browned.

MAKES 20 | GLUTEN FREE

Goat's cheese & pesto muffins

2 cups plain flour

½ teaspoon salt

1 tablespoon baking powder

½ cup pesto

¾ cup water

1 egg

100 g goat's cheese,
   crumbled or cubed

1 cup grated cheddar cheese

Preheat oven to 200°C. Grease muffin tins.

Sift together flour, salt and baking powder.

Stir pesto into water, then mix with egg.

Add pesto mixture to flour along with cheeses and
mix until just combined.

Spoon into muffin tins and bake for 12–15 minutes.

MAKES 16

Golden medley muffins

BOWL 1

1 cup plain flour

1 cup wholemeal plain flour

2 teaspoons bicarbonate
of soda

2 teaspoons ground
cinnamon

½ teaspoon allspice

¼ teaspoon ground
cardamom

½ teaspoon salt

½ cup rolled oats

BOWL 2

1 cup raisins

1 cup grated apple

½ cup grated zucchini

½ cup grated carrot

½ cup desiccated coconut

½ cup finely chopped
pecans

BOWL 3

½ cup vegetable oil

1 cup honey

2 eggs, beaten

1 teaspoon vanilla extract

Preheat oven to 180°C. Grease muffin tins.

For Bowl 1, sift together all ingedients except oats.
Stir in oats.

For Bowl 2, mix together fruit, vegetables, coconut
and pecans.

For Bowl 3, combine all wet ingredients.

Add contents of Bowl 3 to Bowl 1. Mix until moist.

Fold in contents of Bowl 2.

Three-quarters fill prepared muffin tins. Sprinkle extra
pecans or oats on top if desired.

Bake 25–30 minutes.

MAKES 16–20

Golden slice

BASE

125 g softened butter

½ cup white sugar

1 teaspoon vanilla extract

1 cup plain flour

1 cup desiccated coconut

FILLING

1 × 395-g tin condensed milk

60 g butter

2 tablespoons golden syrup

TOPPING

60 g butter

1 tablespoon golden syrup

1 cup desiccated coconut

½ cup sweet biscuit crumbs or rolled oats

Preheat oven to 180°C. Lightly grease and line a 20-cm × 30-cm lamington tin.

For the base, cream butter, sugar and vanilla until light and creamy. Add sifted flour and coconut. Mix well.

Press mixture evenly into tin. Bake for 20 minutes, then remove and cool slightly. (Leave oven on.)

Meanwhile, make the caramel filling by combining all ingredients in a saucepan and stirring over a low heat until the butter melts. Turn up heat slightly and simmer gently for about 5 minutes, stirring continuously. Remove from the heat as soon as it reaches a light caramel colour. Spread over the base.

For the topping, stir butter and golden syrup in a saucepan over low heat until the butter has melted. Add the coconut and biscuit crumbs or oats and mix well. Sprinkle topping evenly over filling.

Return to oven and bake for another 15–20 minutes or until golden brown. Cool before cutting into squares.

MAKES 36

Granola squares

3½ cups rolled oats

½ cup desiccated coconut

160 g butter, melted

4 tablespoons honey

1 egg, beaten

1 cup currants

1 cup nuts (e.g. walnuts, almonds, hazelnuts), chopped

½ cup soft brown sugar

½ teaspoon vanilla extract

pinch of salt

Preheat oven to 180°C. Grease a 25-cm × 30-cm Swiss roll tin.

Toast oats on an ungreased baking tray for about 20 minutes or until golden.

Combine oats with all other ingredients and mix well.

Press mixture firmly into tin. Bake for 20–25 minutes, until golden brown. Cool before cutting into squares.

MAKES 36

Greek hazelnut & yoghurt cake

3 eggs, separated

²⁄₃ cup soft brown sugar

3 tablespoons Greek-style yoghurt

grated zest of 1 lemon

1¼ cups ground roasted hazelnuts

Preheat the oven to 180°C. Lightly grease and line a 16.5-cm × 22-cm oval tin or a 23-cm round springform cake tin.

Whisk the egg yolks with the sugar until thick and creamy. Stir in the yoghurt, lemon zest and ground hazelnuts.

In another bowl, whip the egg whites until stiff peaks form. Carefully fold the whipped egg whites through the hazelnut mixture.

Spoon into the prepared tin and bake for 35 minutes or until a skewer inserted comes out clean.

Cool in the tin on a wire rack. Turn out onto a plate to serve.

Serve with fresh fruit slices.

GLUTEN FREE

Ham & cheese muffins

1 egg, beaten

1 cup plain flour

1 tablespoon baking powder

1 cup grated tasty cheese

½ cup crumbled blue cheese

1 cup chopped ham

Preheat oven to 200°C. Grease muffin tins.

Make egg up to 1 cup with water and mix with sifted flour and remaining ingredients until just combined.

Three-quarters fill prepared muffin tins and bake for 12–15 minutes.

MAKES 12

Ham & cheese slice

BASE

2 cups self-raising flour

½ teaspoon salt

75 g cold butter, cut into
  small pieces

½ cup milk

¼ cup mayonnaise

FILLING

2 tablespoons Dijon or
  wholegrain mustard

225 g ham, shredded

1 cup chopped onion

125 g grated tasty cheese,
  plus extra for sprinkling

salt and freshly ground
  black pepper

2 tablespoons chopped fresh
  parsley

milk, for brushing

Preheat oven to 220°C. Lightly grease and line a
20-cm × 30-cm lamington tin.

For the base, sift together flour and salt, then rub in
butter with your fingertips until crumbly. Combine milk
and mayonnaise and add to the dry ingredients, mixing
until a soft dough forms.

Divide dough in half. Roll out the first portion on a lightly
floured surface to fit the base of the prepared tin.

For the filling, spread mustard thinly over the base and
sprinkle over the ham. In a bowl, combine the onion,
cheese, salt and pepper and parsley. Spread evenly
over the ham.

Roll out remaining pastry and use to cover the filling.
Brush top with milk and sprinkle with extra cheese.

Bake for 20 minutes. Cut into squares while still warm.

MAKES 16

Hazelnut crescents

250 g softened butter

½ cup icing sugar, plus
extra for dusting

1 teaspoon vanilla extract

1 egg yolk

2½ cups self-raising flour

¾ cup ground hazelnuts

Preheat oven to 180°C. Line baking trays with baking paper.

Cream butter and sifted icing sugar until light and fluffy. Add vanilla and egg yolk and beat until well combined.

Fold in sifted flour and ground hazelnuts until just combined. If the dough is too firm, add 2 teaspoons of iced water.

Take tablespoons of the dough and shape into 8-cm crescents. Place crescents 2 cm apart on prepared trays.

Cook for about 12 minutes, or until lightly browned. Allow crescents to cool on trays. Serve heavily dusted with icing sugar.

MAKES 36

Hazelnut praline muffins

½ cup chopped hazelnuts

1¼ cups castor sugar

⅓ cup vegetable oil

1 egg

¾ cup milk

1¾ cups plain flour

1½ teaspoons baking powder

Preheat oven to 190°C. Grease muffin tins.

Gently boil hazelnuts and ½ cup of the sugar until mixture turns golden brown.

Pour onto greased tinfoil and leave to set.

Break praline into small pieces and crush with rolling pin or in a food processor.

Whisk oil with remaining sugar, egg and milk, then add sifted flour, baking powder and praline, mixing until just combined.

Spoon into muffin tins and bake for 20 minutes.

MAKES 12

Hazelnut, ricotta & chocolate cake

225 g softened butter

250 g castor sugar

6 eggs, separated

60 g plain flour

½ cup grated dark cooking
  chocolate

350 g ground roasted
  hazelnuts

400 g ricotta

1 teaspoon vanilla extract

Preheat oven to 160°C. Lightly grease a 23-cm round cake tin and line the base with non-stick baking paper.

Cream the butter and sugar until light and fluffy. Add the egg yolks one at a time.

Combine the sifted flour, chocolate and ground hazelnuts and fold into the batter. Stir in the ricotta and vanilla extract.

Whisk the egg whites until soft peaks form and then fold into the batter.

Bake for 45–50 minutes or until a skewer inserted into the centre of the cake comes out clean. Cool in the tin before turning out.

Hazelnut spiced muffins

2 cups plain flour

2 teaspoons baking powder

½ teaspoon salt

1 teaspoon ground
cinnamon

pinch of ground cloves

125 g softened butter

½ cup soft brown sugar,
firmly packed

¼ cup castor sugar

1 egg, beaten

1 teaspoon grated lemon zest

½ teaspoon vanilla extract

1 cup milk

¾ cup ground or very finely
chopped hazelnuts

¼ cup raspberry jam

1 tablespoon castor sugar
mixed with 1 teaspoon
ground cinnamon

Preheat oven to 200°C. Grease muffin tins.

In a large bowl sift together flour, baking powder, salt,
cinnamon and cloves.

In a separate bowl cream butter and sugars until light
and fluffy, then beat in egg, lemon zest, vanilla and milk.

Make a well in the centre of the dry ingredients and add
butter mixture. Stir to combine, then fold in hazelnuts.

Spoon half the batter into prepared muffin tins.

Put a spoonful of raspberry jam on top of each, then
cover with remaining batter.

Bake for 15–20 minutes.

Sprinkle with cinnamon sugar to serve.

MAKES 16

Health biscuits

125 g softened butter

¼ cup castor sugar

2 tablespoons honey

1 egg

1 cup wholemeal plain flour

½ cup self-raising flour

½ cup plain flour

¼ cup bran, plus extra
   for sprinkling

pinch of salt

Preheat oven to 180°C. Lightly grease baking trays.

Cream butter and sugar until very light and creamy.
Add honey and egg and beat until well combined.

Add sifted flours, bran and salt and mix well.

Turn dough onto a lightly floured surface and knead
gently. Roll dough out to 3 mm in thickness and sprinkle
with a little extra bran. Run a rolling pin lightly over it to
press the bran into the dough.

Using a 6-cm biscuit cutter, cut pastry into rounds.
Gather any leftover dough, roll out again and use to
make more biscuits. Place rounds on baking trays.
Prick biscuits all over with a fork.

Bake for 12–15 minutes or until light golden brown.
Cool for 5 minutes on the tray before transferring
to wire racks.

MAKES 24

Herby cheese crackers

180 g softened butter

½ cup grated cheddar
 cheese

⅓ cup crumbled blue cheese

1 cup wholemeal plain flour

1 small clove garlic, crushed

1 teaspoon finely chopped
 fresh parsley

1 teaspoon finely chopped
 fresh chives

1 teaspoon finely chopped
 fresh oregano

Cream butter and cheeses until smooth. Add sifted flour, garlic and herbs and mix well. If necessary, add a little cold water to make the dough hold together.

Roll dough into a log 4 cm in diameter and chill for at least 30 minutes.

Preheat oven to 190°C. Lightly grease baking trays.

Slice dough into rounds and place on baking trays. Bake for 8–10 minutes.

MAKES 40

High protein muffins

2½ cups bran flakes

1½ cups raisins

1¾ cups milk

1 cup wholemeal plain flour

1 cup soy flour

1 tablespoon baking powder

1½ teaspoons ground
nutmeg

¾ teaspoon salt

1 cup toasted wheatgerm

4 eggs, lightly beaten

⅔ cup honey

⅔ cup vegetable oil

¼ cup dark molasses

Preheat oven to 180°C. Grease muffin tins.

Combine bran flakes, raisins and milk in a large bowl.

In a separate bowl, sift together wholemeal flour, soy flour, baking powder, nutmeg and salt. Stir in wheatgerm. Set aside.

Combine eggs, honey, oil and molasses in a small bowl and blend well.

Add egg mixture to soaked bran flakes. Mix well.

Add dry ingredients to bran mixture, stirring to just moisten.

Spoon batter into prepared muffin tins, filling about three-quarters full.

Bake for 25 minutes or until golden brown.

MAKES 16–20

Hodge podge

125 g butter

½ cup white sugar

1 tablespoon golden syrup

1 egg, lightly beaten

1½ cups plain flour

½ cup self-raising flour

1 teaspoon ground nutmeg

2 cups mixed dried fruit
with glacé cherries

¼ cup raw almonds,
coarsely chopped

Preheat oven to 170°C. Lightly grease and line a deep 19-cm × 29-cm slice tin.

Heat butter, sugar and golden syrup in a saucepan until butter has melted and sugar has almost dissolved. Remove from heat and cool for a few minutes so egg doesn't scramble when added. Mix in egg.

Sift together flours and nutmeg, then stir in fruit and nuts. Mix in the liquid mixture.

Press into the slice tin. Bake for about 30 minutes or until a skewer inserted into the centre comes out clean and the slice is nicely browned.

MAKES 20

Homemade water crackers

1 cup plain flour

½ teaspoon baking powder

pinch of salt

30 g cold butter, cut into
　small pieces

sea salt, for sprinkling

Preheat oven to 200°C. Lightly grease baking trays.

Sift together flour, baking powder and salt. Rub butter into the flour with your fingertips until crumbly. Stir in just enough water to bring the ingredients together into a firm dough.

Roll out dough to about 5 mm in thickness. Cut into small rounds with a biscuit cutter. Gather any leftover dough, roll out again and use to make more biscuits.

Take the rounds and roll out again until they are very thin and oval in shape. Place on baking trays and lightly prick all over with a fork.

Brush crackers with water and sprinkle with sea salt.

Bake for 10 minutes until golden and slightly puffed.

VARIATIONS
Substitute the sea salt with freshly ground black pepper, sesame seeds, mixed dried herbs or cumin seeds.

MAKES 30

Honey bran muffins

1¼ cups wholemeal plain
    flour

2 teaspoons baking powder

½ teaspoon bicarbonate
    of soda

1¼ cups wheat bran

1¼ cups buttermilk

¼ cup honey

1 egg

2 tablespoons vegetable oil

Preheat oven to 190°C. Grease muffin tins.

In a large mixing bowl, sift together flour, baking powder and bicarbonate of soda. Stir in bran and mix thoroughly.

In a small bowl, beat together buttermilk, honey, egg and vegetable oil.

Pour wet ingredients over dry ingredients and stir until just moistened.

Spoon batter into prepared muffin tins.

Bake for 15–20 minutes, or until lightly browned and muffins spring back to the touch. Cool slightly before serving.

MAKES 12–16

Honeybunch hearts

185 g softened butter

½ cup castor sugar

½ cup honey

1 egg

2½ cups plain flour

½ teaspoon mixed spice

½ teaspoon ground
   cinnamon

100 g dark cooking
   chocolate, chopped

In a food processor, blend the butter, sugar and honey until smooth. Add the egg and blend until combined.

Add sifted flour and spices and process until a smooth dough forms. Wrap dough in cling wrap and chill in the refrigerator for 30 minutes.

Preheat oven to 180°C. Line baking trays with baking paper.

Roll out dough between 2 sheets of non-stick baking paper until 3 mm thick. Using a heart-shaped biscuit cutter, cut out biscuits. Gather any leftover dough, roll out again and use to make more biscuits.

Place hearts on prepared baking trays and bake for 12–15 minutes, or until golden and crisp. Cool on a wire rack.

When the biscuits are cold, melt chocolate in a double boiler over simmering water, or on MEDIUM in the microwave. Dip one half of each biscuit in the melted chocolate.

MAKES 16

Honey & date muffins

75 g butter

½ cup honey

1½ cups chopped dates

2 eggs

¼ cup milk

1½ cups plain flour

2 teaspoons baking powder

Preheat oven to 200°C. Grease muffin tins.

Heat butter and honey only long enough to melt butter. Stir in chopped dates.

Beat eggs with milk. In a separate bowl, sift flour and baking powder.

Make a well in the centre of the flour and add honey and egg mixtures. Mix until dry ingredients are just moistened.

Three-quarters fill prepared muffin tins and bake for 15–20 minutes or until cooked.

MAKES 12

Honey joys

40 g butter

2 tablespoons castor sugar

1 tablespoon honey

5 cups Corn Flakes

Preheat oven to 150°C. Lay out paper patty cases on baking trays.

Melt butter, sugar and honey over low heat. Remove from heat and mix in Corn Flakes.

Place spoonfuls into paper patty cases and bake for about 20 minutes. Set aside until cool and set.

MAKES 36

Hot cross muffins

2 cups plain flour

¾ cup castor sugar

2 teaspoons baking powder

½ teaspoon salt

¼ teaspoon ground
cinnamon

pinch of ground allspice

1 cup milk

125 g butter, melted and
cooled slightly

1 egg, beaten

1 teaspoon vanilla extract

½ teaspoon finely grated
orange zest

¼ teaspoon finely grated
lemon zest

1 cup currants

GLAZE

⅓ cup icing sugar

1½ teaspoons lemon juice

Preheat oven to 190°C. Grease muffin tins.

In a large bowl sift together flour, sugar, baking powder, salt, cinnamon and allspice.

In a separate bowl mix together milk, butter, egg, vanilla, orange zest and lemon zest.

Make a well in the centre of the dry ingredients and add milk mixture. Stir to just combine, then fold in currants.

Spoon batter into prepared muffin tins and bake for 15–20 minutes.

For glaze, combine sifted icing sugar and lemon juice. Drizzle glaze in a cross on top of each muffin.

MAKES 16

Individual baked alaskas

BASE

125 g butter

90 g dark cooking chocolate, chopped

2 eggs

⅔ cup castor sugar

¾ cup chopped pecan nuts

1 cup plain flour

¼ cup milk

MERINGUE

2 egg whites

¼ teaspoon cream of tartar

¼ cup castor sugar

FILLING

4 large scoops of chocolate ice-cream

Preheat oven to 180°C. Lightly grease a 30-cm × 20-cm shallow baking dish and line with non-stick baking paper.

For the brownie base, melt the butter and chocolate in a saucepan over low heat, stirring occasionally. Remove from heat and cool a little.

Using an electric mixer, whisk the eggs and sugar together until pale and thick. Combine the nuts and sifted flour and add to the egg mixture, along with the melted chocolate and butter. Stir to combine and then stir in the milk.

Pour into the prepared dish and bake for 25–30 minutes, or until cooked through. Cool in the tin for 15 minutes and then place on a wire rack.

To make the meringue mixture, place the 2 egg whites in a bowl with the cream of tartar and whisk with an electric beater until soft peaks form. Add in the castor sugar one spoonful at a time as you continue whisking, until the meringue mixture is shiny.

Preheat oven to 220°C. Line a baking tray with baking paper.

Scoop four large scoops of chocolate ice-cream onto a baking tray and place in the freezer until ready to use.

Cut four even-sized pieces of brownie base to fit under the ice-cream scoops and place onto prepared baking tray. (Cut the remaining brownie base into small squares and store for future use.) >

Remove the ice-cream from the freezer and place each scoop on top of a square of brownie base. Using a spatula, spread the meringue carefully all over the ice-cream and brownie, making sure there is no ice-cream or base showing.

Bake for 3–4 minutes or until the meringue is lightly browned. Serve immediately.

SERVES 4

Individual bread puddings

6 slices of day-old white
   bread, torn into small
   pieces

300 ml milk

1 large apple, peeled, cored
   and grated

1 cup mixed dried fruit,
   finely chopped (pears,
   apples, sultanas, raisins)

80 g mixed peel

2 tablespoons soft brown
   sugar

2 tablespoons dark orange
   marmalade

60 g self-raising flour

2 eggs, beaten

1 teaspoon lemon juice

1 teaspoon ground
   cinnamon

1 teaspoon mixed spice

60 g butter, melted

icing sugar, for dusting

pouring custard (page 683)

Preheat oven to 150°C. Lightly grease six ramekins.

Combine the bread and milk in a large bowl and leave to soak until soft (about 20 minutes). Beat well with a fork to form a smooth puree.

Add the apple, mixed dried fruit and peel. Stir in the sugar, marmalade, sifted flour, eggs, lemon juice and spices. Add half of the melted butter and stir well.

Spoon the pudding mixture into the six ramekin dishes and drizzle the remaining butter over the top.

Bake for 45–60 minutes or until lightly browned and firm to the touch. Cool a little.

Dust with icing sugar and serve with pouring custard.

SERVES 6

Irish coffee muffins

2 cups plain flour

1 teaspoon baking powder

½ teaspoon salt

½ cup castor sugar

1 egg, beaten

80 g butter, melted

½ cup heavy cream

¼ cup Irish whiskey

¼ cup coffee liqueur

Preheat oven to 200°C. Grease muffin tins.

Sift together flour, baking powder and salt. Add sugar.

Stir in remaining ingredients, until dry ingredients are moistened.

Three-quarters fill prepared muffin tins, and bake for approximately 20 minutes.

MAKES 16

Italian polenta, raisin & ricotta cake

150 g raisins

¼ cup brandy

200 g coarse polenta

1⅓ cups self-raising flour

1 heaped teaspoon baking
   powder

250 g castor sugar

1 cup ricotta

100 g butter, melted

¾ cup warm water

Preheat oven to 170°C. Lightly grease a 20-cm × 10-cm cake tin and line the base with non-stick baking paper.

Place the raisins in a saucepan with the brandy and heat gently for 3–4 minutes until plumped up. Set aside to cool.

Combine the polenta, sifted flour and baking powder. Stir in the sugar, ricotta, melted butter and water. Beat, using an electric mixer, until well combined. Stir in the raisins and brandy.

Spoon the mixture into the prepared cake tin. Bake for 60–90 minutes or until a skewer inserted into the centre of the cake comes out clean.

Cool in the tin for 20 minutes, then turn out and cool on a wire rack.

Serve with whipped cream or mascarpone.

Italian rice tart

1⅓ cups plain flour

75 g cold butter, cut into
small pieces

1 egg, lightly beaten with
2 tablespoons chilled
water

1 litre milk

¾ cup castor sugar

1 teaspoon vanilla extract

½ cup short-grain rice

grated zest of 1 lemon

30 g pine nuts

20 g currants

50 g fresh or frozen
blackberries

icing sugar, for dusting

strawberries or raspberries,
to serve

Lightly grease a 23-cm flan dish.

Sift the flour into a food processor, add the butter and
blend until the mixture resembles fine breadcrumbs.
Pour in the egg and water and process until just
combined. Add a little more chilled water if necessary.
Remove and knead lightly.

Roll out the pastry and use it to line the prepared dish.
Chill in the fridge while you make the rice filling.

Preheat oven to 180°C.

In a saucepan, bring the milk to the boil with the sugar
and vanilla extract. Add the rice and cook for 20 minutes
at a simmer. Remove and pour into a mixing bowl. Stir in
the lemon zest, pine nuts, currants and blackberries.
Leave to cool.

Pour into the prepared pastry base and bake for
30 minutes or until set and lightly browned on top.
Cool completely before cutting.

Dust the top with icing sugar and serve with a purée
of strawberries or raspberries.

Jamaica slice

25 g butter

200 g dark cooking
   chocolate, chopped

½ cup castor sugar

1 cup raisins, chopped

2 eggs, lightly beaten

1½ cups plain flour

1 tablespoon rum

icing sugar or cocoa,
   for dusting

Preheat oven to 160°C. Lightly grease and line a
20-cm × 30-cm lamington tin.

Combine butter, chocolate, sugar and raisins in a
saucepan and heat gently until the chocolate has melted.
Remove from heat and cool for a few minutes so eggs
don't scramble when added.

Stir in eggs, sifted flour and rum and mix well.

Spread mixture into the prepared tin and bake for about
30 minutes, or until just firm to the touch.

Cool in the tray, dust with icing sugar or cocoa and cut
into slices.

MAKES 40

Jam bars

185 g softened butter

1 egg

1 teaspoon vanilla extract

2 cups plain flour

½ teaspoon baking powder

⅔ cup castor sugar

raspberry or apricot jam
  (or other fruit jam),
  for filling

Preheat oven to 180°C.

Cream butter until fluffy, then beat in egg and vanilla.

Stir in sifted flour, baking powder and sugar, to form a dough.

Turn on to a lightly floured surface. Divide into four pieces and shape each into a log about 2-cm in diameter.

Arrange logs on ungreased baking trays, about 10 cm apart to allow for spreading. Using a knife handle, make a depression about 5-mm deep lengthwise along the centre of each roll. Fill with jam.

Bake for 15–20 minutes.

Remove from the oven and cut each log diagonally into bars while still warm. Transfer to a wire rack to cool.

MAKES 24

Jam fancies

1 cup plain flour

pinch of salt

½ cup castor sugar

125 g butter, cut into small
pieces

125 g cream cheese, cut into
small pieces

raspberry jam, for spreading

Sift together flour and salt, then mix in sugar. Add butter
and cream cheese and blend thoroughly to form a very
soft dough.

Shape dough into a ball, wrap in cling wrap and
refrigerate for 1 hour.

Preheat oven to 200°C. Lightly grease baking trays
and dust with flour.

Roll dough out to 3 mm in thickness and cut into rounds
with a 5-cm biscuit cutter. Remove the centres from half
the rounds using a 2.5-cm cutter. Gather centres and
any leftover dough, roll out again and use to make more
rounds and rings.

Place biscuits on baking trays, leaving space for
spreading. Bake for 10–12 minutes, or until golden
brown.

When cool, spread rounds with raspberry jam and place
a ring on top.

MAKES 36

Jam-filled muffins

1½ cups plain flour

2 teaspoons baking powder

½ teaspoon bicarbonate
of soda

½ teaspoon salt

¼ cup castor sugar

60 g butter

1 cup plain yoghurt

¼ cup milk

1 egg

½ teaspoon vanilla extract

jam, for filling

icing sugar, for dusting

Preheat oven to 180°C. Grease muffin tins.

Sift together flour, baking powder, bicarbonate of soda and salt. Stir in sugar.

Melt butter in a saucepan over low heat. Take off heat and stir in yoghurt and milk.

Beat in egg and vanilla.

Add butter mixture to dry ingredients and stir until moistened.

Spoon half the batter into prepared muffin tins. Place about 1 teaspoon of jam into the centre of each muffin and then top with remaining batter.

Bake for 15–20 minutes.

Dust with icing sugar to serve.

MAKES 12

Jolly cake

175 g softened butter

¾ cup soft brown sugar, firmly packed

grated zest of 1 lemon

3 eggs, beaten

1¼ cups self-raising flour

⅓ cup whisky

FILLING

¾ cup icing sugar

50 g softened butter

1 tablespoon lemon juice

2 tablespoons thick honey

Preheat oven to 190°C. Lightly grease and line two 18-cm sandwich tins.

Cream butter, sugar and lemon zest until light and fluffy. Gradually beat in eggs, keeping mixture stiff. Fold in half the sifted flour, then add the whisky and lastly the remaining flour.

Spoon into prepared tins. Bake for 20–25 minutes. Allow to cool on a wire rack.

To make lemon buttercream filling, beat sifted icing sugar with all other ingredients. Sandwich cake together with half the buttercream and swirl the rest over the top.

Katie's flapjacks

1 cup soft brown sugar

170 g butter

1 dessertspoon golden syrup

2 cups rolled oats

Preheat oven to 170°C. Lightly grease and line a 19-cm × 29-cm slice tin.

Combine the sugar, butter and golden syrup in a saucepan over medium heat. Stir until butter has melted and sugar has dissolved, then mix in the oats.

Press into the tin and bake for about 20 minutes or until golden brown. Cool before cutting into thick fingers.

MAKES 16

Khaki cake

1 cup milk

1 tablespoon golden syrup

½ teaspoon bicarbonate
of soda

125 g softened butter

¾ cup castor sugar

1 egg

1½ cups plain flour

pinch of salt

1 teaspoon baking powder

1 tablespoon cocoa

⅓ cup sultanas or currants

1 teaspoon vanilla extract

chocolate glacé icing
(page 680)

desiccated coconut, for
decorating

Preheat oven to 180°C. Lightly grease and flour a
23-cm ring tin.

Warm milk and golden syrup together. Add bicarbonate
of soda and allow to cool.

Cream butter and sugar, add egg and beat well.
Sift together flour, salt and baking powder and add to
creamed mixture with cooled milk mixture. Beat well.

Pour half the mixture into the prepared tin. To remaining
mixture add cocoa, sultanas and vanilla extract. Pour
into tin.

Bake for 45–60 minutes.

Ice with chocolate icing and sprinkle with coconut.

Kiss cakes

125 g softened butter

1 cup castor sugar

2 eggs

1 cup self-raising flour

1 cup cornflour

raspberry jam, for spreading

icing sugar, for dusting

Preheat oven to 190°C. Lightly grease baking trays.

Cream butter and sugar until light and fluffy. Beat in eggs one at a time. Mix in sifted flour and cornflour.

Drop teaspoonfuls onto prepared trays and bake for 8–10 minutes, or until pale golden brown.

When cold, sandwich together with raspberry jam and dust generously with icing sugar.

MAKES 24

Kiwifruit muffins

50 g butter, melted

¾ cup milk

2 eggs, beaten

2 cups plain flour

2 teaspoons baking powder

½ cup soft brown sugar

1 cup chopped kiwifruit

Preheat oven to 200°C. Grease muffin tins.

Mix butter with milk and eggs.

Sift together flour, baking powder and sugar. Add butter mixture and kiwifruit and mix until just combined.

Spoon into prepared muffin tins and bake for 20–25 minutes.

MAKES 16

Kylie's chocolate–iced slice

1 cup plain flour

1 teaspoon baking powder

2 tablespoons cocoa

½ cup white sugar

¾ cup desiccated coconut

125 g butter, melted

TOPPING

1 cup icing sugar

2 teaspoons cocoa

¾ cup desiccated coconut,
    plus extra for sprinkling

40 g butter, melted

¼ teaspoon vanilla extract

Preheat oven to 180°C. Lightly grease and line a
19-cm × 29-cm slice tin.

For the base, sift together flour, baking powder and
cocoa, then mix in sugar and coconut. Stir in melted
butter and mix until well combined.

Press mixture into tin. Bake for about 15 minutes.

For the topping, sift together sugar and cocoa, then
stir in coconut. Mix to a paste with butter and vanilla.

When slice is cool, ice with topping and sprinkle with
extra coconut.

MAKES 24

Korzhiki (Russian shortbread)

2 cups plain flour

pinch of salt

½ teaspoon baking powder

½ cup sour cream

2 eggs

3 tablespoons castor sugar

40 g softened butter, diced

Preheat oven to 220°C. Lightly grease baking trays.

Sift together the flour, salt and baking powder. Make a well in the centre, add the sour cream, 1 egg, sugar and butter, and stir until a moist dough forms.

Roll out on a lightly floured surface until about 5 mm in thickness. Cut into rounds using a biscuit cutter. Gather any leftover dough, roll out again and use to make more biscuits. Prick biscuits all over with a fork and brush with the remaining egg.

Bake for 10–15 minutes or until lightly browned.

MAKES 36

Lebkuchen

1 cup castor sugar

2 eggs

¾ tablespoon finely grated
   lemon zest

2 cups ground almonds

⅓ cup mixed peel, finely
   chopped

½ teaspoon ground nutmeg

½ teaspoon ground
   cinnamon

½ teaspoon ground cloves

½ teaspoon ground
   cardamom

lemon glacé icing
   (page 679)

Preheat oven to 180°C. Lightly grease baking trays.

Beat together sugar, eggs and zest until very light
and fluffy.

Add remaining ingredients and mix to a firm dough.

Drop dessertspoonfuls of mixture onto prepared trays,
leaving about 5 cm between biscuits for spreading.
Bake for 10 minutes or until golden.

When the biscuits are cold, spread with lemon icing.

MAKES 40 | GLUTEN FREE

Lemon banana muffins

110 g softened unsalted
  butter

1¼ cups castor sugar

2 large eggs

1 cup mashed banana

2 tablespoons lemon juice

1 teaspoon vanilla extract

2 cups plain flour

1 teaspoon bicarbonate
  of soda

pinch of salt

¾ cup buttermilk (or use
  yoghurt or milk)

Preheat oven to 180°C. Grease muffin tins.

Cream the butter and sugar until light and fluffy.
Beat in eggs, one at a time.

Whip in banana, lemon juice and vanilla.

In a separate bowl, sift together flour, bicarbonate
of soda and salt. Stir into banana mixture alternately
with the buttermilk.

Bake for 20 minutes.

MAKES 16

Lemon coconut muffins

1 cup All-Bran

1½ cups skim milk

1 egg, lightly beaten

2 tablespoons vegetable oil

grated zest and juice of
  1 lemon

1½ cups self-raising flour

¼ cup castor sugar

½ cup desiccated coconut,
  plus extra for sprinkling

Preheat oven to 190°C. Grease muffin tins.

Place All-Bran and milk in a large bowl and let stand for 5 minutes until softened.

Stir in egg, oil, lemon zest and juice.

Combine sifted flour, sugar and coconut and stir into All-Bran mixture. Mix carefully to just combine.

Three-quarters fill prepared muffin tins and sprinkle with extra coconut.

Bake for 25–30 minutes.

MAKES 12

Lemon delicious pudding

60 g softened unsalted butter

⅓ cup castor sugar

85 g self-raising flour

grated zest of 2 lemons

juice of 1 lemon

2 eggs, separated

300 ml milk

Preheat oven to 180°C. Lightly grease a 1-litre ovenproof dish.

Cream butter and sugar until light and fluffy. Sift in the flour, and add the lemon zest and juice.

Whisk the egg yolks and milk and mix into the pudding batter until well combined.

Whip the egg whites until stiff peaks form and carefully fold into the pudding mixture.

Spoon mixture into the prepared dish and place in a bain-marie (see page 3). Bake for 30–35 minutes or until the sponge on top is golden.

Serve immediately.

SERVES 6

Lemon fluff slice

BASE

1 cup plain flour

1 cup self-raising flour

125 g cold butter, cut into
small pieces

½ cup white sugar

½ teaspoon vanilla extract

1 egg, beaten

FILLING

1½ cups white sugar

2 cups water

finely grated zest and juice
of 2 lemons

¼ cup custard powder

¼ cup cornflour

2 tablespoons butter, melted

TOPPING

1 cup white sugar

1 cup water

2 dessertspoons gelatine

pinch of cream of tartar

desiccated coconut, for
sprinkling

Preheat oven to 180°C. Lightly grease and line a
19-cm × 29-cm slice tin.

For the base, sift flours together, then rub in butter using
your fingertips until crumbly. Add sugar and vanilla, then
mix to a dough with the egg.

Press mixture into tin and bake until golden. Cool.

For the lemon filling, place sugar, water, lemon juice and
zest in a saucepan. Bring to the boil.

In a small bowl or cup, blend sifted custard powder and
cornflour to a paste with a little cold water. Stir into the
lemon mixture to thicken, then add butter and mix well.
Pour filling over cooked biscuit base and leave to cool.

For the marshmallow topping, bring sugar, water and
gelatine to the boil in a saucepan. Add cream of tartar
and simmer for 8 minutes. Allow to cool, then beat until
thick and fluffy.

Pour topping over lemon filling. Toast coconut in a dry
frying pan, then sprinkle over slice. Cut into squares or
fingers when completely set.

MAKES 36

Lemon jumbles

2¾ cups plain flour

1 teaspoon cream of tartar

½ teaspoon bicarbonate
of soda

pinch of salt

250 g softened butter

1 cup white sugar

1 egg

1 tablespoon finely grated
lemon zest

1 tablespoon lemon juice

1 teaspoon almond essence

GLAZE

2 cups icing sugar

40 g butter, melted

¼ cup lemon juice

yellow food colouring
(optional)

Preheat oven to 180°C. Lightly grease baking trays.

Sift together the flour, cream of tartar, bicarbonate of
soda and salt.

In a separate bowl, cream the butter, sugar, egg, lemon
zest, lemon juice and almond essence until light and well
blended.

Stir in the flour mixture and combine well.

Shape the dough into a ball, divide into four pieces, then
roll out each piece into a flat round. Cut each round into
12 wedges.

Roll each wedge into a 10-cm long rope, of even width.
Bring the ends together and press firmly to create a ring.

Place rings on baking trays, leaving space between for
spreading.

Bake for 8–12 minutes or until slightly golden at the
edges. Transfer immediately to a wire rack to cool.

To make the glaze, beat sifted icing sugar with other
ingredients until smooth. If necessary, add extra lemon
juice to produce a thin glaze.

Dip the top of each ring into the glaze and shake off
excess. Let stand 1 hour or until glaze is completely
set. If desired, add a little yellow food colouring to any
leftover icing, then pipe or drizzle zigzag lines across
the glazed areas.

MAKES 48

Lemon meringue pie

100 g cold butter, cut into
   small pieces

1½ cups plain flour

1 teaspoon grated lemon zest

⅓ cup icing sugar

1 egg, lightly beaten

2–3 tablespoons chilled
   water

FILLING

½ cup cornflour

1 cup castor sugar

½ cup lemon juice

1¼ cups water

3 egg yolks

60 g butter

MERINGUE

3 egg whites

½ cup castor sugar

Using a food processor, pulse the butter and sifted flour until the mixture resembles fine breadcrumbs. Add the lemon zest and icing sugar and pulse for 1 minute.

Combine the egg and water and, with the motor running, slowly pour enough liquid into the food processor for the mixture to come together. Remove and roll into a ball. Wrap dough in cling wrap and chill for 30 minutes.

Preheat oven to 220°C. Lightly grease a 24-cm flan dish.

On a floured board, roll out the pastry to fit the flan dish. Blind-bake pastry (see page 3) for 10–15 minutes or until lightly browned. Remove from the oven and reduce oven temperature to 180°C.

To make filling, combine the sifted cornflour and castor sugar in a saucepan and slowly stir in the lemon juice and water. Stir over a low heat until the mixture comes to the boil. Continue stirring until the mixture thickens. Remove from the heat and whisk in egg yolks and butter. Cool, covered with baking paper, until ready to use.

To make meringue, whisk egg whites until soft peaks form. Slowly add castor sugar while whisking, until the egg whites are stiff and glossy.

Spoon the filling into the pastry shell and spread evenly. Spoon the meringue over the top. Bake on a preheated baking tray for 10–15 minutes or until the meringue is lightly browned.

SERVES 8

Lemon poppy seed muffins

150 g softened butter

¾ cup castor sugar

1½ cups plain flour

1 egg, beaten

grated zest and juice of
    2 lemons

125 ml sour cream

1 teaspoon baking powder

1 teaspoon bicarbonate
    of soda

3 tablespoons poppy seeds

lemon glacé icing
    (page 679)

Preheat oven to 160°C. Line muffin tins with paper cases.

Cream butter and sugar, then stir in sifted flour and
remaining ingredients until just combined.

Spoon into paper cases and bake for 15–20 minutes.

When cool, top with lemon icing.

MAKES 12

Lemon poppy seed traybake

120 g softened butter

½ cup castor sugar

1¼ cups self-raising flour

1½ teaspoons baking powder

finely grated zest and juice
  of 1 lemon

1 tablespoon poppy seeds

2 tablespoons milk

2 eggs, lightly beaten

½ cup castor sugar

Preheat oven to 180°C. Lightly grease a 30-cm × 20-cm lamington tin and line with non-stick baking paper.

Cream the butter and sugar until light and fluffy. Sift the flour and baking powder together and fold into the butter mixture. Add the lemon zest, poppy seeds, milk and eggs. Mix to a smooth batter.

Pour into the prepared tin and smooth the top.

Bake for 20–25 minutes or until the cake is golden brown and pulls away from the sides of the tin. Dissolve castor sugar in lemon juice, then brush over the warm cake.

Allow to cool a little and then turn out onto a wire rack to cool completely. Cut into squares.

Lemon seed cake

1⅓ cups plain flour

3 tablespoons cornflour

¼ teaspoon baking powder

175 g butter

¾ cup castor sugar

grated zest of ½ lemon

3 eggs, lightly beaten

1 tablespoon hot water

2 teaspoons caraway seeds

Preheat oven to 160°C. Lightly grease and flour a traditional bundt tin.

Sift together flour, cornflour and baking powder.

Cream butter and sugar until light and fluffy, then stir in grated lemon zest. Beat in eggs, adding a little sifted flour mixture to prevent curdling. Fold in remaining flour.

Pour hot water over caraway seeds and add to cake mixture.

Pour into prepared tin and bake for 50 minutes, or until well risen and golden.

Lemon semolina cake with orange glaze

¾ cup self-raising flour

1 teaspoon baking powder

1½ cups semolina

1 cup castor sugar

¾ cup natural yoghurt

½ cup buttermilk

½ cup canola oil

3 eggs

grated zest and juice
    of 1 lemon

GLAZE

½ cup orange marmalade

⅓ cup orange juice

candied citrus zest,
    for decorating

Preheat oven to 170°C. Lightly grease a 15-cm round deep cake tin and line the base with non-stick baking paper.

Sift the flour, baking powder, semolina and sugar into a mixing bowl.

In another bowl, combine the yoghurt, buttermilk, oil, eggs, and lemon zest and juice.

Make a well in the centre of the flour mixture and pour in the wet mixture. Stir to make a runny batter.

Pour into the prepared tin and bake for 55–70 minutes or until lightly browned on top and cooked through. Cool in the tin for 5 minutes before turning out onto a wire rack.

To make orange glaze, heat the marmalade and orange juice in a saucepan and stir until melted. Pour over the cooled cake and allow to set.

Decorate with candied citrus zest. Serve with yoghurt mixed with a little honey.

Lemon sultana muffins

1 cup sultanas

2 tablespoons honey

grated zest and juice
  of 2 lemons

2 cups plain flour

¼ cup milk

1 cup natural yoghurt

50 g butter, melted

1 egg

2 teaspoons baking powder

⅓ cup castor sugar

Preheat oven to 190°C. Grease muffin tins.

Combine sultanas, honey and lemon zest and juice in a saucepan. Bring to the boil, then allow to cool.

Add sifted flour and remaining ingredients and mix until just combined.

Spoon into muffin tins and bake for 12–15 minutes.

MAKES 16

Lemon tea muffins

1 cup plain flour

½ cup castor sugar

1 teaspoon baking powder

1 teaspoon salt

½ cup freshly squeezed
   lemon juice

2 eggs

finely grated zest of 1 lemon

60 g butter, melted and
   cooled slightly

TOPPING

60 g butter, melted

1 tablespoon freshly
   squeezed lemon juice

½ cup castor sugar

Preheat oven to 190°C. Grease muffin tins.

In a large bowl sift together flour, sugar, baking powder
and salt.

In a separate bowl mix lemon juice, eggs, lemon zest
and melted butter.

Stir wet ingredients into dry ingredients until combined.

Spoon batter into prepared muffin tins and bake
for 15–20 minutes.

Remove from tins while still warm and brush with
topping made from melted butter and lemon juice
mixed together. Then sprinkle with sugar.

MAKES 12

Lemon three-layer slice

BASE

180 g butter, melted

250 g sweet biscuits, crushed

FILLING

1 × 395-g tin condensed
    milk

½ cup lemon juice

2 teaspoons gelatine

¾ cup boiling water

TOPPING

1 teaspoon gelatine

1 packet lemon-flavoured
    jelly crystals

1 cup boiling water

Lightly grease a 20-cm × 30-cm lamington tin.

For the base, mix butter and biscuits together, then press evenly into tin. Chill until cold.

For the lemon filling, mix condensed milk with lemon juice. Dissolve gelatine in boiling water, cool, then stir into condensed milk mixture. Spread filling over the biscuit base. Chill again until cold.

For the topping, dissolve gelatine and jelly crystals in boiling water, then set aside to cool. When slightly gluggy (a bit like egg whites), pour over the slice.

Return to the refrigerator and chill until jelly topping has set completely, then cut into squares.

MAKES 24 | NO BAKE

Lemony sponge biscuits

3 eggs, separated

⅓ cup white sugar, plus
extra for dusting

3 tablespoons ground
almonds

⅓ cup rice flour

2 tablespoons potato flour

finely grated zest of 1 lemon

Preheat oven to 160°C. Grease and line baking trays.

Beat egg yolks with sugar to form a stiff paste. Mix in
the ground almonds, sifted flours and lemon zest.

In a separate bowl, beat egg whites until stiff peaks
form, then gently fold into the almond mixture.

Drop spoonfuls of mixture onto prepared trays and
dust with sugar.

Bake for 8–10 minutes. Turn out onto a wire rack and
return to the oven, at its very lowest setting, for 1 hour.

MAKES 36 | GLUTEN FREE

Lemony Swiss roll

LEMON CURD

finely grated zest and juice
    of 2 lemons

⅓ cup castor sugar

1 tablespoon cornflour

4 egg yolks

CAKE

4 large eggs, separated

⅔ cup castor sugar

½ cup lemon juice

grated zest of 2 lemons

50 g ground almonds

FILLING

½ cup cream

4 tablespoons lemon curd
    (above)

2 tablespoons toasted flaked
    almonds

icing sugar, for dusting

To make lemon curd, combine the lemon juice, sugar and cornflour in a saucepan. Slowly bring to the boil and stir until mixture thickens. Remove from the heat and whisk in the egg yolks and lemon zest. Return to a gentle heat and cook for 2–3 minutes. Remove and allow to cool. (Makes about 1 cup.) This will be used to make the filling.

Preheat oven to 190°C. Lightly grease and line a 30-cm × 25-cm Swiss roll tin.

To make cake mixture, whisk the egg yolks and sugar until thick and creamy. Stir in the lemon juice and zest and the ground almonds. In another bowl, whip the egg whites until stiff. Carefully fold into the cake batter. Pour into the prepared tin.

Bake for 20–25 minutes or until set and lightly browned. Cool in the tin for 5–8 minutes. Carefully turn the cake out onto a double thickness of greaseproof paper and remove the baking paper. Cover with a tea towel until cool.

To make the filling, whip the cream until thick and fold in the lemon curd and flaked almonds. Spread over the cake and roll up carefully. Place on a serving platter 'seam' side down, and dust liberally with icing sugar.

Lemony treacle tart

PASTRY

150 g cold butter, cut into
   small pieces

2 cups plain flour

1 teaspoon grated lemon zest

⅓ cup icing sugar

1 egg, lightly beaten

2–3 tablespoons chilled
   water

FILLING

2 cups fresh breadcrumbs

3 eggs, lightly beaten

finely grated zest and juice
   of 1 lemon

350 ml golden syrup

150 ml cream

150 ml milk

Using a food processor, pulse the butter and sifted flour until the mixture resembles fine breadcrumbs. Add the lemon zest and icing sugar and pulse for 1 minute.

Combine the egg and water and, with the motor running, slowly pour liquid into the food processor until the mixture comes together. Remove and roll into a ball. Wrap in cling wrap and chill for 30 minutes.

Preheat oven to 180°C. Lightly grease a deep 23-cm loose-based tart tin.

On a floured board, roll out the pastry to fit the tart tin. Trim any excess pastry. Blind-bake pastry (see page 3) for 10–15 minutes or until lightly golden. Remove from the oven. Reduce oven temperature to 170°C.

Sprinkle the breadcrumbs over the prepared pastry shell. Combine all other filling ingredients in the food processor and blend until smooth. Pour over the breadcrumbs and bake for 35 minutes or until the filling is golden and puffed up.

Cool in the tin before turning out and serving.

SERVES 8

Little Christmas cakes

875 g sultanas

375 g raisins

125 g currants

125 g mixed peel

200 g glacé cherries

¾ cup sherry

1 tablespoon orange
   marmalade

375 g softened butter

1½ cups soft brown sugar

6 eggs

3 cups plain flour

3 teaspoons mixed spice

Mix the fruit together with the sherry and marmalade and leave to soak overnight.

Preheat oven to 145°C. Lightly grease and line four 12-cm deep square cake tins with a double thickness of non-stick baking paper.

Cream the butter and sugar until light and fluffy. Add the eggs one at a time until well combined. Sift the flour and mixed spice together and stir into the fruit mixture.

Fold the butter mixture and fruit mixture together until well combined.

Spoon the batter evenly into the cake tins, smooth the top and push the mixture into the corners.

Bake for 2 hours (rotating the cakes every 30 minutes). Cool in the tins for 30 minutes before turning out onto a wire rack to cool completely.

Tie festive ribbon around the cakes, making a large, attractive bow on the top. Store in an airtight container until ready to eat or give away as Christmas presents.

MAKES 4

Little orange sponge puddings with rhubarb sauce

40 g softened butter

¾ cup castor sugar

grated zest of 2 oranges

¼ teaspoon salt

3 eggs, separated

½ cup orange juice

½ cup milk

3 tablespoons plain flour

SAUCE

4 stalks rhubarb, trimmed
    and cut into small chunks

¼ cup soft brown sugar

2 tablespoons orange juice

Preheat oven to 180°C. Lightly grease six 125-ml ramekin dishes or tea cups and sprinkle a little castor sugar inside to coat the sides and base.

Cream the butter and a third of the sugar until light and fluffy. Add the orange zest, salt and egg yolks and beat well. Mix in the orange juice, milk and sifted flour.

In another bowl, whisk the egg whites until soft peaks form and then gradually whisk in remaining sugar.

Gently fold the egg whites into the egg-yolk mixture.

Spoon into the prepared dishes and place in a bain-marie (see page 3). Bake for 35 minutes or until puffed up. Place ramekins on a wire rack to cool.

To make the rhubarb sauce, gently heat the rhubarb with the brown sugar and orange juice in a saucepan for 8–10 minutes. Cool to room temperature.

Once puddings are cool, turn them out onto individual plates and serve with a spoonful of rhubarb sauce.

MAKES 6

Little self-saucing chocolate puddings

110 g dark cooking
  chocolate, chopped

115 g butter

4 eggs

½ cup castor sugar

60 g plain flour

3 tablespoons ground
  almonds

pouring custard (page 683)
  or raspberries, to serve

Preheat oven to 160°C. Grease eight 125-ml ramekin dishes or pudding bowls.

Melt the chocolate and butter in a small saucepan over a gentle heat. Leave to cool.

Using an electric mixer, beat the eggs and sugar until pale and thick (3–4 minutes). Combine the sifted flour and ground almonds and carefully fold into the egg mixture.

Gently fold through the chocolate mixture.

Spoon into the prepared dishes and bake for 15–20 minutes or until just cooked but still a little soft in the middle.

Serve warm, turned out onto individual plates, with pouring custard or puréed raspberries.

MAKES 8

Little sticky date puddings with hot butterscotch sauce

1¼ cups chopped pitted
   dates

1¼ cups water

1 teaspoon bicarbonate
   of soda

60 g softened butter

¾ cup castor sugar

2 eggs, lightly beaten

1 cup self-raising flour

SAUCE

½ cup cream

100 g butter

½ cup soft brown sugar

Preheat oven to 180°C. Lightly grease a six-cup jumbo muffin tin.

Place the dates and water in a saucepan and bring to the boil, simmering for about 5 minutes or until the dates are softened. Remove from the heat and stir in the bicarbonate of soda.

Cream the butter and sugar until light and fluffy. Add the eggs a little at a time, beating after each addition, to make a smooth batter. Fold in the sifted flour and then stir in the date-and-water mixture until well combined.

Spoon into the prepared muffin tin and bake for 20 minutes or until firm and springy to touch.

To make the butterscotch sauce, combine all the ingredients in a saucepan and stir over a low heat until the butter is melted. Simmer for 10 minutes or until thickened.

Turn the puddings out and serve warm with hot butterscotch sauce poured over the top.

MAKES 6

Low-fat fruit muffins

1¾ cups plain flour

2 teaspoons baking powder

2 teaspoons bicarbonate
of soda

1 egg

1½ tablespoons vegetable oil

¾ cup golden syrup

¾ cup bran

1 cup unsweetened stewed
apple or other fruit

2 cups berries (blueberries,
raspberries, blackberries)

Preheat oven to 200°C. Grease muffin tins.

Sift together flour, baking powder and bicarbonate of
soda. Add remaining ingredients and mix together until
just combined.

Spoon into muffin tins and bake for 25 minutes.

VARIATION

Replace stewed fruit with tinned pie apple or pie fruit,
such as apple and rhubarb.

MAKES 12–16

Lucy's ginger slice

1 cup self-raising flour

1 cup desiccated coconut

¾ cup white sugar

1 cup mixed dried fruit

¼ cup preserved ginger,
   finely chopped

250 g butter, melted

1 egg, lightly beaten

¼ teaspoon vanilla extract

sesame seeds or desiccated
   coconut, for sprinkling

Preheat oven to 180°C. Lightly grease and line a
19-cm × 29-cm slice tin.

Mix together sifted flour, coconut, sugar, dried fruit
and ginger. Add butter, egg and vanilla and mix well.

Press mixture into tin and sprinkle top with sesame
seeds or coconut. Bake for 20 minutes.

Cool completely before cutting into squares.

MAKES 24

Macadamia meringue squares

100 g softened butter

½ cup castor sugar

2 eggs

½ teaspoon vanilla extract

1½ cups plain flour

pinch of salt

1 teaspoon baking powder

100 g macadamia nuts,
   chopped

¾ cup soft brown sugar

Preheat oven to 180°C. Lightly grease and line a 19-cm × 29-cm slice tin.

Cream butter and castor sugar until light and fluffy.

Separate the eggs, keeping the two whites separate. In a small bowl, beat the egg yolks and 1 egg white. Add to the creamed mixture, along with the vanilla extract, and beat well.

Mix in sifted flour, salt and baking powder.

Press into the tin and sprinkle with the nuts.

Beat the remaining egg white until stiff peaks form, then fold in sifted soft brown sugar. Spread meringue over the top of the slice and bake for 20–25 minutes.

When cool, cut into squares.

MAKES 24

Madeira cake

175 g softened butter

¾ cup castor sugar

grated zest of 1 lemon

1½ cups plain flour

1 teaspoon baking powder

3 eggs, lightly beaten

2 tablespoons milk

3 slices candied citrus peel,
  cut into small pieces

Preheat oven to 180°C. Lightly grease and line a 20-cm × 10-cm loaf tin.

Cream the butter, sugar and lemon zest until light and fluffy. Sift flour with baking powder.

Slowly add the eggs to the butter mixture, alternating with a tablespoon of flour. Fold in remaining flour and then the milk.

Pour into the prepared tin and bake for 60 minutes.

Sprinkle with the citrus peel and return to the oven. Bake for a further 30 minutes or until lightly browned, risen and cooked through.

Cool in the tin for 15 minutes before carefully turning out onto a wire rack to cool completely.

Maggie's garden muffins

1½ cups plain flour

1 cup wholemeal plain flour

1 tablespoon baking powder

½ teaspoon salt

1 egg, plus 2 egg whites

⅔ cup skim milk

⅓ cup virgin olive oil

1 cup grated zucchini

3 tablespoons finely
    chopped fresh basil

1 teaspoon crushed garlic

⅓ cup freshly grated
    Romano cheese

½ cup pine nuts

Preheat oven to 220°C. Grease muffin tins.

Sift flours, baking powder and salt into a large bowl.

In a small bowl, whisk together egg, egg whites, milk and oil until well blended.

Add egg mixture to dry ingredients and mix gently.

Stir in zucchini, basil, garlic, cheese and pine nuts and mix until just combined.

Three-quarters fill prepared muffin tins and bake for about 20 minutes.

MAKES 12–16

Maple nut muffins

1 cup wholemeal plain
  flour

1 cup plain flour

2½ teaspoons baking
  powder

¼ teaspoon bicarbonate
  of soda

½ teaspoon salt

½ cup castor sugar

½ cup chopped nuts

1 egg

½ cup milk

¼ cup maple syrup

¼ cup vegetable oil

½ cup sour cream

Preheat oven to 200°C. Grease muffin tins.

In a large bowl sift together flours, baking powder, bicarbonate of soda and salt. Stir in sugar and nuts.

In a separate bowl mix together egg, milk, maple syrup, oil and sour cream.

Add milk mixture to dry ingredients and stir until just moistened.

Spoon batter into prepared muffin tins and bake for 20 minutes.

MAKES 16

Marble cake

50 g dark cooking chocolate, chopped

175 g softened butter

¾ cup castor sugar

3 eggs, lightly beaten

⅓ cup milk

175 g self-raising flour

½ teaspoon baking powder

Preheat oven to 180°C. Lightly grease a 20-cm round cake tin and line the base with non-stick baking paper.

Melt chocolate in a double boiler over simmering water, or on MEDIUM in the microwave. Keep warm.

Cream the butter and sugar until light and fluffy. Add the eggs a little at a time until well combined. Add milk and stir until combined. Stir in the sifted flour and baking powder.

Remove half of the mixture and stir in the melted chocolate until well combined.

Drop spoonfuls of the cake mixtures into the prepared tin, alternating between light and dark mixtures and starting with the light mixture.

Bake for 60–75 minutes or until a skewer inserted into the centre of the cake comes out clean.

Cool in the tin for 10 minutes before turning out onto a wire rack to cool completely.

Marbled muffins

¼ cup milk

1 egg

50 g butter, melted

1 cup natural yoghurt

1 teaspoon vanilla extract

2 cups plain flour

2 teaspoons baking powder

⅓ cup castor sugar

1 teaspoon red food
colouring

2 tablespoons cocoa mixed
with 2 tablespoons milk

50 g dark cooking chocolate,
grated (optional)

Preheat oven to 190°C. Grease muffin tins.

Mix together milk, egg, butter, yoghurt and vanilla.

Add sifted flour, baking powder and sugar and mix
until just combined.

Put 1 tablespoon of mixture into each muffin cup.

Divide remaining mixture between two bowls.
To one bowl add food colouring, to the other add
cocoa mixture and grated chocolate (if using).

Put spoonfuls of each mixture into muffin cups
and give a quick swirl with a knife.

Bake for 15–20 minutes.

MAKES 16

Maria's easy-peasy biscuits

2½ cups self-raising flour

¾ cup white sugar

1 tablespoon berry jam
   (or other fruit jam)

250 g butter, melted

Preheat oven to 180°C. Lightly grease baking trays.

Combine sifted flour, sugar and jam in a bowl.
Mix in melted butter.

Place teaspoonfuls of mixture onto the prepared trays,
leaving plenty of space between each for spreading.

Bake for 12–15 minutes or until lightly coloured.

MAKES 30

Marshmallow fingers

BASE

1 cup self-raising flour

1 dessertspoon cocoa

3 Weet-Bix biscuits, crushed

½ cup white sugar

½ cup desiccated coconut

115 g butter, melted

TOPPING

1 cup white sugar

1 dessertspoon gelatine

¾ cup water

few drops food colouring
   (optional)

Preheat oven to 180°C. Lightly grease and line a 19-cm × 29-cm slice tin.

For the base, sift together flour and cocoa, then stir in Weet-Bix, sugar and coconut. Add butter and mix until well combined.

Press into the tin. Bake for 12–15 minutes.

For the marshmallow topping, combine all ingredients (except colouring) in a saucepan and boil for 3 minutes. Cool, then add food colouring (if using). Beat until very thick, then spread over slice.

Slice into fingers once set.

MAKES 16

Marshmallow maraschino slice

½ cup chopped almonds

1 cup desiccated coconut

75 g butter

250 g pink marshmallows

¾ cup sultanas

¼ cup drained maraschino
   cherries, halved

4 cups Corn Flakes

125 g dark cooking
   chocolate, chopped

Lightly grease a 19-cm × 29-cm slice tin.

In a dry frying pan, lightly toast the almonds and
coconut until golden.

Melt the butter and marshmallows over a low heat.
Mix in toasted almonds and coconut, sultanas, cherries
and Corn Flakes.

Press mixture into prepared tin and chill until set.

Melt chocolate in a double boiler over simmering water,
or on MEDIUM in the microwave, then spread over slice.

Cut into small squares when set.

MAKES 36 | NO BAKE

Mary's chocolate cake

250 g softened butter

3 cups plain flour

2 cups castor sugar

¾ cup cocoa

2 teaspoons bicarbonate of soda

1 teaspoon salt

2 cups milk

3 eggs

1 tablespoon vinegar

1½ teaspoons vanilla extract

1 tablespoon coffee liqueur (optional)

chocolate butter icing (page 678) or whipped cream, to serve

Preheat oven to 180°C. Lightly grease and line two 20-cm round cake tins or grease and flour a traditional bundt tin.

To butter add sifted dry ingredients and milk, then beat for 2 minutes with an electric mixer. Add eggs, vinegar, vanilla and coffee liqueur (if using) and beat well.

Pour into prepared tins. Bake for 45–60 minutes, depending on the size of the tin/s used.

Ice cakes with chocolate icing. Alternatively, cut cakes in half or layers, sprinkle with coffee liqueur, fill with whipped cream and dust with icing sugar.

Marzipan marvels

240 g softened butter

1 cup soft brown sugar

1 egg

2½ cups plain flour

4 tablespoons cocoa

200 g marzipan

115 g white cooking
chocolate, chopped

Preheat oven to 180°C. Lightly grease baking trays.

Cream the butter and sugar until light and fluffy.
Add the egg and beat well.

Stir in the sifted flour and cocoa, then knead with your
hands to form a soft dough.

On a lightly floured surface, roll dough out to 5 mm in
thickness. Cut into rounds using a 5 cm biscuit cutter.
Gather any leftover dough, roll out again and cut more
rounds, until you have 72 in total.

Roll marzipan into 36 small balls. Place half the biscuit
rounds on the prepared trays, place a marzipan ball in
the centre of each, then top each with a second biscuit
round. Use a fork to press around the edges to seal.

Bake for 10–12 minutes, until well-risen.

When the biscuits are cold, melt white chocolate in a
double boiler over simmering water or on MEDIUM in the
microwave. Drizzle melted chocolate over each biscuit.

MAKES 36

May's date cake

1 cup chopped pitted dates

1 teaspoon bicarbonate
 of soda

1 cup boiling water

125 g softened butter

½ cup castor sugar

pinch of salt

¼ teaspoon vanilla extract

2 eggs

1 teaspoon grated lemon
 or orange zest

¾ cup desiccated coconut

1¾ cups plain flour

1 teaspoon baking powder

icing sugar, for dusting

Combine dates, bicarbonate of soda and boiling water.
Leave for 20 minutes then beat to a pulp.

Preheat oven to 180°C. Lightly grease and flour a
20-cm cake tin.

Cream butter, sugar, salt and vanilla extract. Add eggs
one at a time, beating well after each addition.

Fold in date pulp, zest and coconut, then add sifted flour
and baking powder.

Pour into prepared tin and bake for 40–45 minutes.

Dust with icing sugar or ice as required.

Meringues

2 egg whites

⅓ cup castor sugar

Preheat oven to 120°C. Grease and line baking trays.

Beat egg whites until stiff peaks form. Gradually add sugar until stiff glossy peaks form.

Drop dessertspoonfuls of mixture onto prepared trays.

Bake for 60–90 minutes or until crisp and firm, but not browned.

Serve plain or sandwiched together with whipped cream.

VARIATIONS

Add 2 teaspoons instant coffee granules, or a few drops food colouring or flavoured essence with the sugar.

MAKES 16 | GLUTEN FREE

Mexican muffins

1 cup plain flour

1 teaspoon salt

1 tablespoon baking powder

2 eggs, beaten

¾ cup water

1 cup refried beans

1 cup grated tasty cheese,
plus extra for sprinkling

2 spring onions, chopped

3 tomatoes, chopped

Preheat oven to 200°C. Grease muffin tins.

Sift flour into a bowl with salt and baking powder.
Add remaining ingredients and mix together until
just combined.

Spoon into prepared muffin tins and sprinkle with extra
grated cheese.

Bake for 15–20 minutes.

MAKES 12

Mince slice

2 cups self-raising flour

pinch of salt

125 g cold butter, cut into
   small pieces

1 teaspoon white sugar

FILLING

1 cup sultanas

1 cup currants

½ cup nuts

castor sugar, for sprinkling

icing sugar, for dusting

Preheat oven to 180°C. Lightly grease and line a
19-cm × 29-cm slice tin.

For the base, sift flour and salt, then rub in butter
with your fingertips until crumbly. Add sugar, then mix
in enough cold water to make a stiff dough.

Knead gently on a lightly floured surface.

For the filling, finely mince the fruit and nuts in a food
processor. Sprinkle with a little castor sugar, to taste.

Divide dough into two pieces and roll each out thinly.
Use the first sheet to line the base and sides of the tin.
Spread over the minced fruit mixture, then cover with
the second sheet of dough. Press dough together to
seal, then score squares in the top with a sharp knife.

Bake for 10–15 minutes. Dust with icing sugar just
before serving.

MAKES 36

Mint slice

BASE

1½ cups self-raising flour

½ cup soft brown sugar

1 cup desiccated coconut

180 g butter, melted

FILLING

1¼ cups icing sugar

1½ tablespoons milk

1 tablespoon white vegetable
    shortening, melted

1 teaspoon peppermint
    essence

TOPPING

½ cup drinking chocolate
    powder

3 tablespoons white
    vegetable shortening,
    melted

Preheat oven to 180°C. Lightly grease and line a
19-cm × 29-cm slice tin.

For the base, mix together sifted flour, sugar and
coconut. Stir in melted butter.

Press into the tin and bake for 15–20 minutes,
or until golden.

For the filling, mix together sifted icing sugar, milk,
shortening and peppermint essence. Pour over the
warm base. Leave to set.

For the topping, mix drinking chocolate and shortening
to a smooth paste. When filling has set, spread with
topping. Let topping set before cutting into small
squares.

MAKES 36

Mocha creams

200 g softened unsalted
butter

½ cup icing sugar

½ cup cornflour

1 cup plain flour

¼ cup cocoa, plus extra
for dusting

400 g milk chocolate,
chopped

CREAM

100 g softened unsalted
butter

1 cup icing sugar

2 teaspoons instant coffee
granules

2 teaspoons hot water

Preheat oven to 180°C. Line baking trays with
baking paper.

Cream butter and sifted icing sugar until light and fluffy.
Sift together flours and cocoa and fold into creamed
mixture until combined.

Roll dessertspoonfuls of mixture into balls. Place balls
2 cm apart on prepared trays and flatten slightly with
the back of a spoon.

Bake for 8 minutes, or until lightly browned. Cool on
trays for 5 minutes, then transfer to a wire rack.

Melt chocolate in a double boiler over simmering water,
or on MEDIUM in the microwave.

Once biscuits are cool, use a fork to dip them into the
melted chocolate. Place biscuits on a tray lined with
baking paper and refrigerate until the chocolate is set.

To make the mocha cream, cream butter until light and
fluffy. Gradually beat in sifted icing sugar until combined.
Dissolve coffee in hot water and add to mixture, beating
until just combined.

Spoon mocha cream into a piping bag fitted with a
1.5-cm fluted nozzle and pipe small rosettes onto each
biscuit. (If you don't have a piping bag, you can just
spread it on.) Refrigerate biscuits until ready to eat.

Dust with a little cocoa just before serving.

MAKES 40

Moll's fruit cake

1 × 225-g tin crushed
   pineapple, undrained

225 g butter

¾ cup soft brown sugar

725 g mixed dried fruit

1 cup self-raising flour

1 cup plain flour

½ teaspoon bicarbonate
   of soda

1 teaspoon baking powder

3 eggs, beaten

1 teaspoon almond essence

1 teaspoon lemon essence

1 teaspoon ground cloves

2 teaspoons mixed spice

Preheat oven to 140°C. Lightly grease a 23-cm cake tin and line with two layers of non-stick baking paper.

Combine pineapple, butter, sugar and mixed fruit in a saucepan and bring to the boil. Take off heat.

When cool, add sifted flours and remaining ingredients and mix.

Pour into prepared tin and bake for 90 minutes, or until a skewer inserted into the centre of the cake comes out clean. Leave to cool in tin before turning out.

Moroccan date & walnut cake

150 g softened butter

½ cup castor sugar

4 eggs

1 cup self-raising flour

1 teaspoon ground
   cinnamon

1 teaspoon ground nutmeg

½ teaspoon ground cloves

½ cup milk

½ teaspoon vanilla extract

1 cup chopped pitted dates

½ cup chopped walnuts

2 tablespoons plain flour

Preheat oven to 160°C. Lightly grease a 20-cm square cake tin and line the base with non-stick baking paper.

Cream the butter and sugar until light and fluffy. Add the eggs one at a time.

Sift the self-raising flour and spices together and stir into the egg mixture, combining well. Stir in the milk and vanilla extract.

Mix the dates and walnuts with the plain flour and fold through the cake batter.

Spoon into the prepared tin and bake for 30–60 minutes or until a skewer inserted into the centre of the cake comes out clean.

Cool in the tin for 5 minutes before turning out onto a wire rack.

Serve with fresh cream and orange segments.

Mrs Baillie's sunflower & honey squares

125 g butter

¾ cup honey

4½ cups Corn Flakes, crushed

⅔ cup sunflower seeds (kernels)

⅓ cup desiccated coconut

⅓ cup glacé cherries

Lightly grease a 19-cm × 29-cm slice tin.

Melt butter and honey in a saucepan and simmer for 5 minutes.

Combine Corn Flakes, sunflower seeds, coconut and cherries in a large bowl. Pour the liquid over and mix well to combine.

Press into tin and refrigerate until set. Cut into squares when cold.

MAKES 16 | NO BAKE

Muesli muffins

1½ cups self-raising flour

100 g cold butter, cut into small pieces

1½ cups muesli

1 apple, peeled, cored and grated

½ cup soft brown sugar

¼ cup chopped nuts (optional)

½ cup milk

½ cup water

Preheat oven to 190°C. Grease muffin tins.

Sift flour and rub in butter until mixture resembles breadcrumbs.

Add remaining ingredients and mix until just combined.

Three-quarters fill prepared muffin tins and bake for 20–25 minutes.

MAKES 12

Mum's chocolate walnut slice

125 g butter

½ cup white sugar

2 tablespoons cocoa

1 egg, beaten

250 g plain sweet biscuits, crushed

¾ cup walnuts, chopped

Lightly grease a 19-cm × 29-cm slice tin.

Stir butter and sugar in a saucepan over medium heat until butter has melted and sugar dissolved. Add sifted cocoa and egg and bring to the boil, stirring continuously.

Add crushed biscuits and nuts, and mix until well combined.

Press into tin and refrigerate until set. Top with icing when cold if desired (see pages 677–82).

MAKES 36 | NO BAKE

Nanna Molly's melting moments

250 g softened unsalted
  butter

¼ cup icing sugar

1½ cups plain flour

⅓ cup cornflour

FILLING

1½ cups icing sugar

40 g softened butter

2 teaspoons vanilla extract

2 teaspoons water

Preheat oven to 160°C. Line baking trays with
baking paper.

Cream butter and sugar until light and fluffy.
Gradually beat in sifted flour and cornflour.

Roll heaped teaspoonfuls of mixture into balls and place
on baking tray, flattening each slightly with a fork.

Bake for 15–20 minutes until firm and golden.
(Be careful not to burn them.)

For the filling, beat sifted icing sugar and butter together
until creamy. Mix in vanilla extract and water.

Once biscuits are cold, sandwich together with filling.

VARIATION
For the filling, you can substitute 1 tablespoon lemon
juice or passionfruit pulp for the vanilla and water.

MAKES 32

Nutmeg cannonballs

250 g softened butter

½ cup white sugar

2 teaspoons vanilla extract

2 cups plain flour

1½ cups ground almonds

½ cup icing sugar mixed with 3 teaspoons ground nutmeg

Cream the butter, sugar and vanilla until light and fluffy. Add the sifted flour and ground almonds and combine well.

Roll dough into balls 3 cm in diameter. Place on lightly greased baking trays and chill for at least 30 minutes.

Preheat oven to 150°C.

Bake for 15–20 minutes. Remove from oven and, while still warm, roll each ball in the icing sugar mixed with nutmeg.

MAKES 60

Nutty orange & lemon cake

3 eggs, separated

¾ cup castor sugar

grated zest of 1 lemon

grated zest of 1 small orange

1 teaspoon vanilla extract

½ cup finely ground
   hazelnuts

½ cup finely ground
   almonds

½ cup self-raising flour

pinch of salt

Preheat oven to 170°C. Lightly grease a 23-cm round cake tin and line the base with non-stick baking paper.

Whisk the egg yolks and sugar until thick and creamy (about 3 minutes). Stir in the lemon and orange zest and vanilla extract.

Mix the ground nuts together with the sifted flour and fold into the egg mixture.

In another bowl, whip the egg whites with a pinch of salt until stiff peaks form. Carefully fold two large spoonfuls of egg whites through the nutty cake batter. Tip the cake batter into the egg whites and carefully fold through.

Spoon into the prepared tin and bake for 25–30 minutes or until lightly browned and cooked through. Cool in the tin for 10 minutes before turning out onto a wire rack.

Serve warm or cold with fresh berries and whipped cream.

Oatcake crackers

1 cup plain flour

1 teaspoon bicarbonate
  of soda

1 teaspoon cream of tartar

1 tablespoon white sugar

125 g cold butter, cut into
  small pieces

1 cup rolled oats

Preheat oven to 180°C. Lightly grease baking trays.

Sift together the flour, bicarbonate of soda and cream of tartar. Mix in sugar, then rub in the butter with your fingertips until the mixture is crumbly. Stir in the rolled oats and enough hot water to make a stiff dough.

Roll the dough out thinly, cut into squares and place on baking trays.

Bake for 10–12 minutes or until lightly golden.

MAKES 30

Oat & orange muffins

1 orange, peeled and
   quartered

2 cups oat bran

¼ cup raw sugar

1 teaspoon mixed spice

2 teaspoons baking powder

¾ cup sultanas

¼ cup wheatgerm

2 tablespoons vegetable oil

¾ cup milk

1 teaspoon bicarbonate
   of soda

¼ cup chopped walnuts

Preheat oven to 190°C. Grease muffin tins.

Place orange in food processor, making sure to remove all pips first. Process until finely chopped.

In a mixing bowl, combine oat bran, sugar, mixed spice, baking powder, sultanas and wheatgerm.

Heat oil and milk slightly and dissolve bicarbonate of soda in milk mixture.

Add oat bran mixture and milk to orange in the food processor. Pulse to just combine.

Three-quarters fill prepared muffin tins and sprinkle with walnuts. Bake for 15 minutes or until firm.

MAKES 12

Oaty apple walnut muffins

100 g softened butter

2 teaspoons grated lemon
zest

¾ cup soft brown sugar

1 egg

1 cup self-raising flour

½ teaspoon ground
cinnamon

¼ teaspoon bicarbonate
of soda

¼ teaspoon salt

¾ cup unsweetened
stewed apple

1 cup quick-cooking
rolled oats

½ cup sultanas

½ cup chopped walnuts

Preheat oven to 180°C. Grease muffin tins.

Cream butter, lemon zest and sugar until light and fluffy.
Add egg and beat well.

Sift flour, cinnamon, bicarbonate of soda and salt into
a bowl. Add to creamed mixture alternately with
stewed apple.

Fold in oats, sultanas and walnuts.

Three-quarters fill prepared muffin tins and bake for
20–25 minutes.

MAKES 12

Old English matrimonials

1½ cups plain flour

pinch of salt

1 teaspoon baking powder

120 g cold butter, cut into
   small pieces

1¾ cups rolled oats

1 cup soft brown sugar

1½ cups blackberry,
   raspberry or strawberry
   jam

Preheat oven to 180°C. Lightly grease and line a
deep 19-cm × 29-cm slice tin.

Sift flour, salt and baking powder into a bowl, add
the butter and rub in with your fingertips until crumbly.
Stir in the oats and sugar.

Press half the mixture into the tin. Spread jam evenly
over the base.

Top with remaining mixture so that it completely covers
the jam. Press down lightly.

Bake for 30 minutes or until browned and beginning to
bubble around the edges. Cool in the tin before cutting
into squares.

MAKES 24

Old-fashioned gingerbread

225 g softened butter

1 cup castor sugar

3 eggs, lightly beaten

1 cup treacle

1 cup milk

3 cups plain flour

1 teaspoon ground
cinnamon

1 teaspoon grated nutmeg

2 teaspoons ground ginger

2 teaspoons bicarbonate
of soda

Preheat oven to 160°C. Lightly grease and line a 23-cm square cake tin.

Cream the butter and sugar until light and fluffy. Slowly add the eggs until well combined.

Heat the treacle and milk in a saucepan. Remove and cool a little before stirring into the egg-and-butter mixture.

Sift the flour, spices and bicarbonate of soda together. Fold into the wet ingredients.

Spoon the cake batter into the prepared tin and bake for 60 minutes or until a skewer inserted into the centre of the cake comes out clean.

Cool in the tin before turning the cake out onto a wire rack to cool completely.

Old French fig cake

225 g fresh ripe figs,
   chopped finely

125 g butter

2 cups castor sugar

1 egg, lightly beaten

3⅔ cups plain flour

2 teaspoons baking powder

¼ teaspoon salt

½ tablespoon grated lemon
   or orange zest

½ teaspoon vanilla extract

icing sugar, for dusting

Preheat oven to 150°C. Lightly grease a 20-cm cake tin and line the base with non-stick baking paper.

Place figs in a saucepan and simmer for 8 minutes. Add butter and sugar and keep stirring over gentle heat until melted. Allow to cool.

Stir egg into mixture. Add sifted flour, baking powder, salt, zest and vanilla extract. Mix well.

Pour into prepared tin and bake for 60–90 minutes.

Dust with icing sugar.

Olive & chilli muffins

2 cups plain flour

½ teaspoon salt

1 tablespoon baking powder

1 egg

¾ cup water

1½ cups grated cheddar
cheese

½ cup pitted black olives,
sliced

1 teaspoon very finely sliced
dried chilli

2 tablespoons polenta,
for sprinkling

Preheat oven to 200°C. Grease muffin tins.

Sift together flour, salt and baking powder. Add egg, water, cheese, olives and chilli and mix until just combined.

Spoon into prepared muffin tins and sprinkle with polenta.

Bake for 12–15 minutes.

MAKES 16

Olive & mint muffins

1 cup chopped pitted black
    olives

2 cups plain flour

½ cup grated onion

¾ cup olive oil

1½ tablespoons chopped
    fresh mint, or 1 teaspoon
    crushed dried mint

1 tablespoon castor sugar

1 heaped teaspoon baking
    powder

Preheat oven to 190°C. Brush muffin tins with olive oil and dust with flour.

Rinse olives and drain. Dry on paper towel.

Sift flour and combine with remaining ingredients, adding baking powder last.

Bake for 20–25 minutes, or until golden.

MAKES 16

Olive & salami muffins

1 cup plain flour

¼ teaspoon salt

1 tablespoon baking powder

1 egg, beaten

½ cup grated tasty cheese

⅔ cup pitted black olives, sliced

⅔ cup diced spicy salami

Preheat oven to 200°C. Grease muffin tins.

Sift together flour, salt and baking powder.

Make egg up to one cup with water and add to flour along with remaining ingredients. Mix until just combined.

Three-quarters fill prepared muffin tins and bake for 12–15 minutes.

MAKES 12

One-pot brownies

120 g butter

60 g dark cooking chocolate, chopped

½ teaspoon vanilla extract

1 cup castor sugar

2 eggs

¾ cup plain flour

¾ cup chopped walnuts

Preheat oven to 180°C. Lightly grease and line a 19-cm square cake tin.

Melt the butter and chocolate in a large saucepan over low heat. Remove from heat and cool for a few minutes so the eggs don't scramble when added.

Add vanilla and sugar and mix well. Add eggs one at a time, beating well after each addition. Fold in the sifted flour and walnuts.

Pour into prepared tin and bake for about 20 minutes. Cut into squares when cool.

MAKES 18

Open sesame slice

2 cups wholemeal
   self-raising flour

2 cups desiccated coconut

2 cups white sugar

2 cups rolled oats

2 eggs, beaten

240 g butter, melted

2 tablespoons honey

⅓ cup sesame seeds

Preheat oven to 180°C. Lightly grease and line a 19-cm × 29-cm slice tin.

Combine sifted flour with coconut, sugar and oats. Mix in eggs, then add butter and honey and combine well.

Press into the tin.

Sprinkle sesame seeds evenly over the top of the slice and press in firmly. Bake for 25 minutes or until golden brown.

Cut into squares while warm, but cool in the tray before turning out.

MAKES 24

Orange & almond cake

2 thin-skinned oranges

6 eggs

250 g castor sugar

2 cups ground almonds

1 teaspoon baking powder

Preheat oven to 180°C. Lightly grease a 24-cm round cake tin and line the base with non-stick baking paper.

Place the oranges in a saucepan of cold water and cover. Bring to the boil and cook at a simmer for 2 hours (or until soft). Cool, remove pips, then blend to a pulp in a food processor.

Beat the eggs until fluffy, adding the sugar slowly until a thick, pale mousse-like mixture forms. Carefully fold in the ground almonds and baking powder. Stir in the pulped oranges.

Pour batter into prepared tin and bake for 35–40 minutes or until cooked through. Cool in the tin before turning out.

Serve with fresh orange slices, chopped dates and plain creamy yoghurt.

Orange cake

1 cup plain flour

¾ cup white sugar

¼ cup milk

3 eggs, beaten

75 g butter, melted

grated zest of ½ orange

1½ teaspoons baking powder

orange butter icing
  (page 678)

Preheat oven to 180°C. Lightly grease and flour an 18-cm cake tin.

Sift flour and mix with remaining ingredients except baking powder. Leave for a few minutes. Beat for 3 minutes then add baking powder.

Pour into prepared tin and bake for 30 minutes.

Ice with orange icing.

Orange carrot muffins

1½ cups wholemeal plain
    flour

½ cup oat bran

2 teaspoons baking powder

½ teaspoon bicarbonate
    of soda

1 teaspoon ground
    cinnamon

1 egg

⅔ cup orange juice

½ cup buttermilk

2 tablespoons castor sugar

1 teaspoon grated orange
    zest

2 tablespoons vegetable oil

1 cup coarsely grated carrot

Preheat oven to 200°C. Grease muffin tins.

In a large bowl, mix together sifted flour, oat bran, baking powder, bicarbonate of soda and cinnamon.

In a separate bowl, beat together egg, juice, buttermilk, sugar, orange zest and oil. Mixture will look curdled, but don't worry.

Stir in grated carrot.

Add wet ingredients to dry ingredients, and stir until just moistened.

Spoon batter into prepared muffin tins and bake for approximately 20 minutes.

MAKES 12–16

Orange choc-chip muffins

2 cups plain flour

½ cup soft brown sugar, firmly packed

½ cup castor sugar

1½ teaspoons baking powder

½ teaspoon bicarbonate of soda

½ teaspoon salt

⅓ cup vegetable oil

¼ cup orange juice

¼ cup orange liqueur

1 egg

1 teaspoon grated orange zest

1 teaspoon vanilla extract

1 cup chocolate chips

icing sugar or cocoa, for dusting

Preheat oven to 200°C. Grease muffin tins.

In a large bowl sift together flour, sugars, baking powder, bicarbonate of soda and salt.

In a separate bowl mix together oil, orange juice, liqueur, egg, orange zest and vanilla.

Make a well in the centre of the dry ingredients and add orange mixture.

Stir to combine, then fold in chocolate chips.

Spoon batter into prepared muffin tins and bake for 15–20 minutes.

Serve dusted with icing sugar or cocoa.

VARIATION

Top with orange butter icing (page 678) and sprinkle with chocolate chips.

MAKES 16

Orange chocolate muffins

125 g softened butter

1 cup castor sugar

2 eggs

zest of 2 oranges

½ cup natural yoghurt

½ cup orange juice

1 teaspoon baking powder

½ teaspoon bicarbonate
  of soda

2 cups plain flour

90 g dark chocolate chips

Preheat oven to 190°C. Grease muffin tins.

In a large bowl cream butter and sugar until light and fluffy. Beat in eggs and add orange zest.

Add yoghurt, orange juice, baking powder and bicarbonate of soda and stir to combine.

Fold in sifted flour and chocolate chips.

Spoon batter into prepared muffin tins and bake for 15–20 minutes.

VARIATION

If desired, top with chocolate butter icing (page 678) and sprinkle with more chocolate chips.

MAKES 16

Orange honey creams

125 g softened butter

½ cup white sugar

1 egg, lightly beaten

4 tablespoons honey

2 cups plain flour

1 teaspoon baking powder

½ teaspoon salt

FILLING

60 g softened butter

2 teaspoons finely grated
orange zest

2 cups icing sugar

1 tablespoon honey

1 teaspoon orange juice

Preheat oven to 180°C. Lightly grease baking trays.

Cream butter and sugar until light and fluffy, then beat in egg and honey. Fold in the sifted dry ingredients.

Spoon mixture into a piping bag with a round tip attached, and pipe onto baking trays in 2-cm wide rounds, leaving space between for spreading.

Bake for 15 minutes.

For the filling, cream butter, add the zest, then gradually beat in sifted icing sugar. Add honey and juice and continue beating until smooth.

When biscuits are completely cold, sandwich together with filling.

MAKES 24

Orange-iced chocolate teacake

100 g softened butter

⅔ cup castor sugar

2 eggs, lightly beaten

2 tablespoons cocoa
   dissolved in 2 tablespoons
   hot water

grated zest of 1 orange

⅔ cup self-raising flour

2 tablespoons freshly
   squeezed orange juice

orange butter icing
   (page 678)

3 slices glacé orange, for
   decorating

Preheat oven to 180°C. Lightly grease a 20-cm round cake tin and line the base with non-stick baking paper.

Cream the butter and sugar until light and fluffy. Slowly add the eggs until combined. Beat in the cocoa mixture and orange zest. Fold in the sifted flour and mix in the orange juice.

Spoon the batter into the prepared tin and bake for 40–45 minutes or until a skewer inserted into the centre of the cake comes out clean. Cool in the tin for 10–15 minutes before turning out onto a wire rack.

When cold, use a palette knife to spread orange icing over the sides and top of the cake. Decorate with chopped glacé orange slices.

Orange muffins

zest and flesh of 2 oranges
  (pith and seeds discarded)

75 g softened butter

1 egg

1½ cups self-raising flour

¾ cup castor sugar

½ cup currants

Preheat oven to 190°C. Grease muffin tins.

Process orange zest and flesh in a food processor with butter and egg.

Mix in sifted flour and remaining ingredients until just combined.

Spoon into prepared muffin tins and bake for 15–20 minutes.

MAKES 12

Orange thins

250 g softened butter

1¼ cups white sugar

1 egg

grated zest of 1 orange

4 cups plain flour

pinch of salt

1 teaspoon ground
  cinnamon

½ teaspoon crushed
  cardamom seeds

½ cup almond meal

¼ cup orange juice

Preheat oven to 220°C. Lightly grease baking trays.

Cream butter, sugar, egg and zest until light and fluffy.

Sift together flour, salt and spices and add to creamed mixture with almond meal and juice. Mix well.

Roll dough out to a thickness of 3 mm and cut out shapes with a floured biscuit cutter. Gather any leftover dough, roll out again, and use to make more biscuits.

Place on prepared trays and bake for 5–7 minutes, or until crisp.

MAKES 120

Orange & toasted almond muffins

2½ cups plain flour

1 cup white sugar

3½ teaspoons baking
   powder

½ teaspoon salt

¼ teaspoon almond essence

1 tablespoon grated orange
   zest

⅓ cup vegetable oil

¾ cup evaporated milk

½ cup water

1 egg

1 cup toasted finely chopped
   almonds

ICING

1 cup icing sugar

1–2 tablespoons orange juice

2 teaspoons orange zest

Preheat oven to 190°C. Grease muffin tins.

In a large bowl combine sifted flour, sugar, baking powder, salt, almond essence, orange zest, oil, evaporated milk, water and egg. Beat with electric mixer at high speed for 30 seconds until blended.

Fold in ¾ cup of the chopped almonds.

Spoon batter into prepared muffin tins, filling to two-thirds full.

Bake for 15–18 minutes.

In a small bowl combine sifted icing sugar, orange juice and zest. Spread icing over muffins. Sprinkle with remaining chopped almonds.

MAKES 20–24

Overnight bran muffins

1½ cups plain flour

1 teaspoon bicarbonate
of soda

1 teaspoon ground
cinnamon

1 egg

1½ cups natural yoghurt

½ cup vegetable oil

1½ cups bran

½ cup soft brown sugar

125 g dates, chopped

Sift together flour, bicarbonate of soda and cinnamon. Mix with remaining ingredients until just combined.

Cover mixture and chill for up to 24 hours.

Preheat oven to 180°C. Grease muffin tins.

Spoon into prepared muffin tins and bake for 15–20 minutes.

MAKES 12

Paprika puffs

4 tablespoons self-raising
  flour

pinch of salt

pinch of smoked paprika,
  plus extra for sprinkling

80 g butter, melted

4 tablespoons grated tasty
  or parmesan cheese

sesame seeds or desiccated
  coconut, for coating

Preheat oven to 180°C. Lightly grease baking trays.

Sift together flour, salt and paprika. Add butter and cheese and mix until well combined.

Roll dough into small balls, then roll in sesame seeds or coconut to coat.

Place balls on baking trays and bake for 15 minutes, or until golden brown.

MAKES 36

Parkin

1¾ cups plain flour

1 cup rolled oats

85 g cold butter, cut into
small pieces

⅓ cup soft brown sugar,
firmly packed

1 tablespoon baking powder

½ teaspoon mixed spice

1 tablespoon boiling water

2 tablespoons golden syrup

blanched almonds, split in
half, or mixed peel, for
decorating

Preheat oven to 180°C. Lightly grease baking trays.

Combine sifted flour and oats. Rub in butter with your
fingertips until crumbly. Add sugar, baking powder and
mixed spice and mix well.

Add boiling water to the golden syrup and mix this into
the dry ingredients.

Roll mixture into balls the size of a walnut. Place on
baking trays and press a blanched almond half or a
piece of peel into the centre of each.

Bake for 15 minutes.

MAKES 30

Parmesan croissants

180 g softened butter

2 cups cottage cheese

2 cups plain flour

pinch of onion or garlic salt

1 cup finely grated parmesan cheese, plus extra for sprinkling

Cream the butter and cottage cheese until smooth. Add the sifted flour and salt and mix well.

Chill for 1 hour, or until easy to handle.

Preheat oven to 200°C. Lightly grease baking trays.

Divide dough into three or four portions. Roll each out to a round 23 cm in diameter.

Sprinkle each round with parmesan cheese and cut into 8 wedges.

To make the croissants, start with the rounded side of each wedge and roll towards the point. Place point-side down on baking trays and shape into crescents. Sprinkle tops lightly with extra cheese.

Bake for 20–25 minutes or until golden. Immediately remove from baking trays and cool on a wire rack.

MAKES 32

Passionfruit biscuits

60 g softened butter

¾ cup icing sugar

pulp of 4 passionfruit
  (about ⅓ cup pulp)

1¼ cups self-raising flour

1 cup cornflour

FILLING

60 g softened butter

¾ cup icing sugar

pulp of 1 passionfruit (about
  1 tablespoon pulp)

For biscuits, cream butter and icing sugar until light and fluffy. Add passionfruit pulp and sifted flours. Mix well, then chill mixture until firm.

Preheat oven to 180°C. Lightly grease baking trays.

Roll biscuit dough into small balls. Place on baking trays and flatten slightly with a fork.

Bake for 12–15 minutes.

For the filling, cream butter and icing sugar, then add just enough passionfruit pulp to produce a spreading consistency.

Once biscuits are cold, sandwich together with filling.

MAKES 70

Passionfruit cake

50 g softened butter

125 g castor sugar

2 eggs

1 tablespoon passionfruit
  juice

1 tablespoon water

½ cup plain flour

1 teaspoon baking powder

1½ tablespoons cornflour

FILLING

1 tablespoon gelatine

2 tablespoons water

1 cup cream

pulp of 5–6 passionfruit
  (about ½ cup pulp)

icing sugar, to taste

Preheat oven to 180°C. Lightly grease and flour two 15-cm round deep cake tins.

Cream butter and sugar until light and fluffy. In a separate bowl, beat eggs well, then add passionfruit juice and water. Sift dry ingredients and add alternately with egg mixture to creamed mixture.

Pour into prepared tins and bake for about 15 minutes. Turn onto a wire rack to cool.

To make passionfruit cream filling, dissolve gelatine in water over gentle heat. Whip cream stiffly, then add passionfruit and sugar to taste. Stir in dissolved gelatine.

Join cake with passionfruit cream and serve dusted with icing sugar.

Passionfruit cream-cheese slice

BASE

1 cup plain flour

2 tablespoons icing sugar

125 g cold butter, cut into
    small pieces

FILLING

3 teaspoons gelatine

¼ cup water

500 g softened cream cheese,
    chopped

280 g lemon butter

TOPPING

⅓ cup custard powder

1 cup castor sugar

2 tablespoons milk

1½ cups water

1 tablespoon butter

2 tablespoons lemon juice

pulp of 4 passionfruit
    (about ⅓ cup pulp)

Preheat oven to 180°C. Lightly grease and line a
20-cm × 30-cm lamington tin.

For the base, blend the sifted flour and icing sugar
with the butter in a food processor until combined.

Press dough into tin and bake for 20 minutes. Cool.

For the filling, sprinkle the gelatine over the water in
a cup. Stand cup in a small saucepan of simmering
water and stir until the gelatine dissolves. Beat cream
cheese until smooth, then add the gelatine and lemon
butter. Beat again until well combined. Spread over the
cooked base.

For the topping, combine custard powder, sugar, milk
and water in a small saucepan and heat until mixture
boils and thickens. Take off the heat and stir in the
butter, then let cool for 10 minutes. Stir in the lemon
juice and passionfruit pulp. Pour over the slice.

Chill in the refrigerator until set, then cut into large
squares.

MAKES 12

Passionfruit crunch muffins

2 cups plain flour

1 egg

½ cup milk

⅓ cup honey

⅓ cup vegetable oil

1 teaspoon baking powder

pulp of 5–6 passionfruit
(about ½ cup pulp)

TOPPING

50 g cold butter, cut into
small pieces

½ cup soft brown sugar

½ cup rolled oats

Preheat oven to 180°C. Grease muffin tins.

Sift flour and add to remaining muffin ingredients.
Mix together until just combined.

Three-quarters fill prepared muffin tins.

To make topping, rub butter into sugar with your
fingertips until crumbly. Mix in rolled oats.

Sprinkle topping over muffins.

Bake for 15–20 minutes.

MAKES 16

Passionfruit fingers

BASE

180 g softened butter

1 cup icing sugar

pulp of 4 passionfruit
   (about ⅓ cup pulp)

1½ cups self-raising flour

1 cup cornflour

pinch of salt

ICING

90 g butter, melted

2 cups icing sugar

pulp of 2 passionfruit (about
   2 tablespoons pulp)

Preheat oven to 180°C. Lightly grease and line a 19-cm × 29-cm slice tin.

For the base, cream the butter and sifted icing sugar until light and fluffy, then beat in the passionfruit pulp. Add the sifted flour, cornflour and salt and mix well to combine.

Press into prepared tin and bake for 30 minutes.

To make passionfruit icing, beat together the butter, sifted icing sugar and passionfruit pulp until smooth.

Once slice is cool, top with icing and cut into fingers.

MAKES 24

457

Passover ginger muffins

¾ cup potato flour or
    rice flour

½ teaspoon ground
    cinnamon

½ teaspoon ground ginger

pinch of ground cloves

1 egg, plus 4 egg whites

2 tablespoons honey

2 teaspoons grated orange
    zest

2 tablespoons orange juice

2 tablespoons castor sugar

Preheat oven to 200°C. Grease muffin tins.

In a large bowl, sift together potato flour and spices.

In a small bowl, whisk together 1 whole egg, honey, orange zest and juice. Add to dry ingredients, and stir together until just blended. Batter will be stiff.

In a deep, medium-sized bowl, beat egg whites until soft peaks form. Add sugar, and beat until whites are thick and glossy.

Stir about a quarter of egg white mixture into potato flour batter, then fold in remaining egg whites.

Spoon batter into muffin tins and bake for about 15 minutes.

Let cool for about 10 minutes before removing from tins. Best served warm.

MAKES 12 | GLUTEN FREE

Peach muffins

2 cups tinned or fresh
  peaches, drained

4 cups plain flour

2 cups castor sugar

2 teaspoons baking powder

½ teaspoon salt

3 eggs

¾ cup vegetable oil

2 cups milk

TOPPING

½ cup castor sugar mixed
  with 1 teaspoon ground
  cinnamon

Preheat oven to 200°C. Grease muffin tins.

Dice drained peaches to the size of peas.

Sift together flour, sugar, baking powder and salt.

In a separate bowl combine eggs, oil and milk.

Add flour mixture and combine gently. Fold in peaches.

Spoon into prepared muffin tins and sprinkle with
cinnamon sugar topping.

Bake for 20–25 minutes.

MAKES 30

Peanut biscuits

75 g softened butter

1 cup soft brown sugar,
    firmly packed

4 tablespoons crunchy
    peanut butter

1 egg

⅓ cup rice flour

3 tablespoons cornflour

½ teaspoon bicarbonate
    of soda

¼ teaspoon cream of tartar

½ teaspoon ground
    cinnamon

½ cup chopped peanuts

¼ cup ground almonds

¼ cup fine polenta

Preheat oven to 180°C. Lightly grease baking trays.

Cream butter, sugar and peanut butter until smooth, then beat in the egg.

In a separate bowl, sift together flours, bicarbonate of soda, cream of tartar and cinnamon. Stir in peanuts, almonds and polenta, then fold into the creamed mixture.

Roll dough into walnut-sized balls and place on trays. Flatten with a fork.

Bake for 12–15 minutes, or until the biscuit edges are light brown.

MAKES 30 | GLUTEN FREE

Peanut butter muffins

1½ cups plain flour

2 teaspoons baking powder

½ cup castor sugar

½ teaspoon salt

60 g butter

½ cup crunchy peanut
   butter

2 eggs, beaten

1 cup milk

Preheat oven to 190°C. Grease muffin tins.

In a large bowl sift together flour, baking powder,
sugar and salt.

Cut in butter and peanut butter and mix until crumbly.

Add eggs and milk and stir until just combined.

Spoon batter into prepared muffin tins and bake
for 15–20 minutes.

VARIATION

Brush tops of hot muffins with melted jam, then
sprinkle with chopped peanuts.

MAKES 12

Peanut butterscotch cake

TOPPING

125 g butter

2 tablespoons soft brown
   sugar

2 tablespoons white sugar

2 tablespoons honey

1½ cups finely chopped
   peanuts

CAKE

1⅔ cups plain flour

½ teaspoon salt

3 teaspoons baking powder

125 g cold butter, cut into
   small pieces

½ cup white sugar

2 eggs, beaten

¼ cup milk

½ teaspoon vanilla extract

Preheat oven to 190°C.

Lightly grease a 23-cm square tin and line base with non-stick baking paper.

To make nut topping, melt butter with sugars and honey in a saucepan. Stir in peanuts. Pour nut mixture into prepared tin.

To make cake mixture, sift together flour, salt and baking powder. Rub in butter until crumbly, add sugar and mix. Pour eggs into centre, add milk and vanilla extract, and mix well.

Pour cake mixture on top of nut mixture. Bake for 40 minutes, then reduce oven temperature to 180°C and bake for a further 20 minutes.

Turn out immediately onto a wire rack and carefully remove baking paper. Replace any nut topping that comes away – it will set in position as it cools.

Peanut slice

125 g butter

4 tablespoons golden syrup

4 tablespoons crunchy
  peanut butter

180 g wholemeal biscuits,
  crushed

Lightly grease a 19-cm square tin.

Stir the butter and golden syrup in a saucepan over medium heat until the butter melts.

Remove from the heat and immediately add the peanut butter, beating well to combine.

Add crushed biscuits and mix until a soft dough forms.

Press into tin and smooth the top. Chill for at least 2 hours before cutting into squares and turning out of the tin.

MAKES 16 | NO BAKE

Pear, chocolate & almond traybake

125 g butter

200 g dark cooking
   chocolate, chopped

3 eggs

1 cup castor sugar

1 cup self-raising flour

1 cup ground almonds

2 large Beurre Bosc pears,
   peeled, cored and thinly
   sliced

pouring custard (page 683)
   or cream, to serve

Preheat oven to 180°C. Lightly grease and line
a 28-cm × 18-cm lamington tin.

Melt the butter in a saucepan over a medium heat.
Remove and stir in the chocolate until melted.

Beat the eggs and sugar until pale and thick.
Slowly pour in the chocolate mixture and stir gently
to combine.

Carefully fold in the sifted flour and ground almonds.

Pour the batter into the prepared tin. Arrange the pear
slices over the top of the batter.

Bake for 40–45 minutes or until firm and cooked
through.

Cool on a wire rack. Cut into slices and serve with
pouring custard or cream.

Pear & honey muffins

2 cups wholemeal plain
  flour

1 teaspoon baking powder

1 teaspoon bicarbonate
  of soda

1 egg

1 cup natural yoghurt

¼ cup lemon juice

50 g butter, melted

½ cup honey, plus extra
  for pouring

½ cup soft brown sugar

2 large pears, peeled, cored
  and diced

Preheat oven to 190°C. Grease muffin tins.

Sift together flour, baking powder and bicarbonate of
soda. Mix with remaining ingredients until just combined.

Three-quarters fill prepared muffin tins and bake for
15–20 minutes.

Drizzle a little extra honey on top of each muffin while
still warm.

MAKES 16

Pear & prune cake

1¼ cups castor sugar

100 g softened butter

3 large eggs

1½ cups plain flour

1 teaspoon ground
   cinnamon

1 teaspoon baking powder

⅓ cup milk

1 tablespoon brandy

2 firm ripe pears, peeled,
   cored and diced

100 g pitted prunes,
   roughly chopped

Preheat oven to 180°C. Lightly grease a 20-cm round springform cake tin and line the base with non-stick baking paper.

Reserve 2 tablespoons of the sugar. Cream the butter and remaining sugar until light and fluffy. Add the eggs one at a time until well combined.

Sift the flour, cinnamon and baking powder into another bowl. Spoon the flour mixture into the butter mixture, alternately with the milk, to form a smooth batter.

Stir in the brandy. Fold the pears and prunes into the batter.

Pour into the prepared tin and sprinkle reserved castor sugar over the top. Bake for 45–55 minutes or until a skewer inserted into the centre of the cake comes out clean. Cool in the tin on a wire rack.

Turn out and serve with ice-cream or whipped cream.

Pear & raisin crumble

2 tablespoons plain flour

1.2 kg ripe pears, peeled, cored and cut into small chunks

½ cup soft brown sugar

½ cup raisins

2 tablespoons sherry

1 tablespoon finely chopped crystallised ginger

TOPPING

1 cup plain flour

1 cup walnuts, finely chopped

⅔ cup soft brown sugar

120 g butter, cut into tiny pieces

pouring custard (page 683) or natural yoghurt, to serve

Preheat oven to 190°C. Grease six 150-ml ramekin dishes.

For the fruit mixture, sift flour and combine with remaining ingredients. Spoon into the prepared dishes.

To make the topping, combine sifted flour, chopped walnuts, sugar and butter until the mixture starts to clump together.

Spoon the topping over the fruit mixture and bake for 30 minutes or until the topping is golden and crisp.

Cool a little before serving with yoghurt or pouring custard.

SERVES 8

Pecan cinnamon muffins

1½ cups plain flour

¼ cup castor sugar

¼ cup soft brown sugar,
  firmly packed

2 teaspoons baking powder

½ teaspoon salt

½ teaspoon ground
  cinnamon

1 egg, lightly beaten

½ cup vegetable oil

½ cup milk

½ cup chopped pecans

Preheat oven to 200°C. Grease muffin tins.

Sift flour, castor sugar, brown sugar, baking powder, salt and cinnamon into a mixing bowl.

Combine egg, oil and milk in a small bowl and blend well.

Add egg mixture to dry ingredients, stirring just enough to moisten. Fold in pecans.

Spoon batter into prepared muffin tins, filling each cup two-thirds full.

Bake for 20 minutes or until golden brown.

MAKES 12

Persimmon muffins

1 cup wholemeal plain flour

1 cup plain flour

1 teaspoon baking powder

½ teaspoon salt

½ teaspoon ground
cinnamon

½ teaspoon ground nutmeg

¼ teaspoon ground cloves

½ cup mashed persimmon
pulp

½ cup raisins

1 egg

½ cup milk

⅓ cup vegetable oil

½ cup honey

ICING

1½ cups icing sugar

½ teaspoon vanilla extract

2 tablespoons brandy

Preheat oven to 200°C. Grease muffin tins.

Sift together flours, baking powder, salt and spices.

In a separate bowl mix together remaining muffin ingredients.

Add wet mixture to dry ingredients and combine until just moistened.

Spoon batter into prepared muffin tins and bake for 18 minutes.

Allow to cool before icing.

To make icing, mix ingredients together thoroughly.

MAKES 16

Pineapple & carrot cake

3 eggs, beaten

½ cup vegetable oil

1 cup soft brown sugar

1 cup white sugar

2 teaspoons vanilla extract

2 cups wholemeal plain
flour

2 teaspoons ground
cinnamon

1 teaspoon ground nutmeg

½ teaspoon salt

2 teaspoons bicarbonate
of soda

¼ cup sour cream

3 cups grated carrot

1 cup desiccated coconut

1 × 225-g tin crushed
pineapple, drained

cream cheese icing
(page 682)

Preheat oven to 180°C. Lightly grease and flour a 22-cm ring tin.

Combine eggs, oil, sugars and vanilla extract in a large bowl and mix well.

Stir in sifted flour, spices, salt and bicarbonate of soda.

Fold in sour cream, grated carrot, coconut and crushed pineapple.

Pour into prepared tin and bake for 90 minutes, or until a skewer inserted into the centre of the cake comes out clean. Top with cream cheese icing.

Pineapple muffins

2 cups plain flour

1 teaspoon baking powder

1 cup castor sugar

1 teaspoon salt

1 egg

1 cup milk

1 tablespoon butter, melted

½ cup drained crushed
   pineapple

Preheat oven to 200°C. Grease muffin tins.

Sift dry ingredients into a large bowl.

In a separate bowl, beat egg with milk, and add butter and pineapple.

Make a well in the centre of the dry ingredients, add liquid and stir until just moist and lumpy.

Three-quarters fill greased muffin tins and bake for 15–20 minutes.

MAKES 16

Pine nut & yoghurt muffins

2 cups plain flour

¼ cup castor sugar

1 teaspoon bicarbonate
  of soda

¼ teaspoon salt

1 cup natural yoghurt

¼ cup milk

60 g butter, melted and
  cooled slightly

1 egg

2 tablespoons honey

1 teaspoon vanilla extract

¾ cup chopped dried
  apricots

½ cup chopped pine nuts

Preheat oven to 200°C. Grease muffin tins.

In a large bowl sift together flour, sugar, bicarbonate of soda and salt.

In a separate bowl mix together yoghurt, milk, butter, egg, honey and vanilla until well combined.

Make a well in the centre of the dry ingredients and add yoghurt mixture. Stir to just combine.

Mix in dried apricots and all but 2 tablespoons of the pine nuts.

Spoon batter into prepared muffin tins and sprinkle with reserved pine nuts.

Bake for 15–20 minutes.

MAKES 16

Pistachio chocolate muffins

80 g cold butter, cut into
    small pieces

2 cups plain flour

3 teaspoons baking powder

1 teaspoon salt

⅓ cup castor sugar

2 eggs

1 cup milk

2 teaspoons rum

1 cup chopped pistachio
    nuts

½ cup chocolate chips

Preheat oven to 200°C. Grease muffin tins.

Rub butter into sifted flour, baking powder and salt until crumbly. Add sugar.

In a separate bowl, beat together eggs, milk and rum.

Make a well in the centre of the dry ingredients and add milk mixture, half of the chopped nuts and the chocolate chips. Mix very lightly until just combined.

Three-quarters fill prepared muffin tins. Chop remaining nuts finely and sprinkle over muffins.

Bake for 20–25 minutes.

MAKES 16

Pistachio muffins

2 cups plain flour

¼ teaspoon salt

2 teaspoons baking powder

1 egg

½ cup water

50 g butter, melted

1 cup natural yoghurt

¼ cup castor sugar

1 cup chopped pistachio
  nuts

Preheat oven to 190°C. Grease muffin tins.

Sift flour, salt and baking powder into a large bowl.
Add remaining ingredients and mix together until
just combined.

Spoon into prepared muffin tins and bake for
15–20 minutes.

MAKES 16

Pizza muffins

2 cups plain flour

½ teaspoon salt

1 tablespoon baking powder

1 onion, chopped

1 cup grated tasty cheese

1 rasher bacon, cooked and
chopped

1 tomato, chopped

1 egg, lightly beaten

Preheat oven to 200°C. Grease muffin tins.

Sift flour, salt and baking powder into a large bowl. Mix in onion, cheese, bacon and tomato.

Make egg up to 1 cup with water, then mix with dry ingredients until just combined.

Spoon into prepared muffin tins and bake for 20 minutes.

MAKES 16

Plum & lemon muffins

10–12 ripe dark plums

3 cups plain flour

1 tablespoon baking powder

¾ cup white sugar

1 tablespoon grated
   lemon zest

50 g butter, melted

2 eggs, lightly beaten

1¼ cups milk

2 tablespoons castor sugar

Preheat oven to 200°C. Grease muffin tins.

Peel and stone plums, and roughly chop flesh. Set aside.

Sift flour and baking powder into a large bowl and stir in white sugar and lemon zest.

In a separate bowl, combine melted butter, eggs and milk.

Pour milk mixture into flour mixture. Gently stir to just mix. Fold in chopped plums.

Three-quarters fill prepared muffin tins. Sprinkle with castor sugar.

Bake for 15–20 minutes.

MAKES 20–24

Plum kuchen

1½ cups plain flour

1½ teaspoons baking powder

1 teaspoon ground cinnamon

pinch of salt

100 g softened butter

⅔ cup white sugar

2 large eggs

2 teaspoons vanilla extract

½ teaspoon almond essence

½ cup sour cream

5 large plums, each cut into 8 slices

¼ cup castor sugar mixed with ½ teaspoon ground cinnamon

40 g butter, melted

Preheat oven to 175°C. Lightly grease a 2-litre ovenproof dish.

Sift the dry ingredients into a bowl. In another bowl, cream the softened butter and white sugar until light and fluffy. Beat in the eggs one at a time, then stir in the vanilla and almond essence.

Stir in the dry ingredients, alternately with the sour cream, to make a smooth batter. Spread into the prepared tin and arrange the plum slices in four rows on top.

Sprinkle cinnamon sugar over the plums. Drizzle with the melted butter.

Bake for 40 minutes or until firm and springy to the touch.

Cool for at least 30 minutes before cutting and serving.

Polenta fruit biscuits

250 g softened butter

1 cup icing sugar

½ cup polenta

1 egg, separated

2 cups plain flour

mixed crystallised fruit
   (pineapple, cherries,
   pawpaw, ginger, etc.),
   for decorating

Preheat oven to 180°C. Lightly grease baking trays.

Cream the butter and sugar until light and fluffy.
Add polenta and mix well to combine, then stir in
the egg yolk.

Beat egg white until stiff peaks form, then fold into the
mixture. Fold in the sifted flour.

Roll teaspoonfuls of mixture into balls and place onto
prepared trays. Press a piece of crystallised fruit into
the centre of each biscuit.

Bake for 10 minutes or until golden.

MAKES 48

Pooh's peanut crisps

2 tablespoons honey

¾ cup crunchy peanut
butter

1 cup water

3 cups wholemeal plain
flour

pinch of salt

Preheat oven to 200°C. Lightly grease baking trays.

Mix together honey, peanut butter and water. Add sifted flour and salt and mix to form a stiff dough.

On a very lightly floured surface, roll dough out very thinly. Cut into 6-cm × 3-cm rectangles and prick all over with a fork.

Bake for 10–12 minutes or until crisp.

MAKES 30

Poppy seed, cheese & onion muffins

½ cup chopped onion

3 tablespoons butter

1 egg, lightly beaten

½ cup milk

1½ cups self-raising flour

pinch of salt

1 cup grated tasty cheese

1 tablespoon poppy seeds

Preheat oven to 220°C. Grease muffin tins.

Fry onion in 1 tablespoon of the butter until lightly brown.

Mix beaten egg and milk together.

Sift flour and salt into a separate bowl. Rub in 1 tablespoon of butter.

Mix dry ingredients with egg and milk to make a light scone batter.

Add onion and half the cheese.

Place small rounds into muffin tins and sprinkle with remaining grated cheese and poppy seeds. Melt remaining tablespoon of butter and drizzle over top of muffins.

Bake for 15 minutes.

MAKES 12–14

Portuguese pine nut biscuits

1 cup cornflour

¾ cup plain flour

½ teaspoon ground
  cinnamon

1¼ cups pine nuts

90 g butter, melted

⅔ cup castor sugar

4 eggs

pinch of salt

Preheat oven to 190°C. Lightly grease baking trays and dust with flour.

Combine sifted flours and cinnamon with all other ingredients in a bowl – reserving a handful of the pine nuts – and mix until well combined.

Roll dough into small balls, press a few of the reserved pine nuts onto the top of each biscuit and place on prepared trays.

Bake in the oven for 12–15 minutes, or until golden brown.

MAKES 36

Posh choc–shortbread squares

BASE

1 cup self-raising flour

¼ cup white sugar

½ cup desiccated coconut

115 g butter, melted

TOPPING

1 cup icing sugar

1 tablespoon cocoa

1 cup desiccated coconut

60 g butter, melted

¼ cup condensed milk

Preheat oven to 180°C. Lightly grease and line a 19-cm × 29-cm slice tin.

For the base, combine sifted flour, sugar and coconut, then pour over melted butter and mix well.

Press into the tin and bake for 15 minutes.

For the topping, sift together icing sugar and cocoa, then add remaining ingredients and combine well. Spread over the base while still hot.

Cool, then cut into squares.

MAKES 24

Potato caramel cake

150 g softened butter

2 cups castor sugar

4 eggs, separated

½ cup milk

½ cup hot mashed potato

½ teaspoon salt

¾ teaspoon ground cloves

¾ teaspoon ground
   cinnamon

¾ teaspoon ground nutmeg

1 cup grated dark cooking
   chocolate

2 teaspoons baking powder

2 cups plain flour

1 cup chopped walnuts

chocolate butter icing
   (page 678)

Preheat oven to 180°C. Lightly grease and flour a 20-cm square cake tin.

Cream butter, sugar and egg yolks. Add milk, mashed potato, salt, spices and chocolate.

Sift baking powder with flour and stir into mixture.

Beat egg whites until stiff peaks form, then fold into batter.

Add chopped walnuts just as cake is ready for the oven.

Pour into prepared tin and bake for 60–75 minutes, or until a skewer inserted into the centre of the cake comes out clean. When cool, ice with chocolate icing.

Potato fry muffins

2 potatoes, peeled and
  cubed

1 clove garlic, crushed

1 teaspoon mustard seeds

1 teaspoon turmeric

1 tablespoon vegetable oil

1 egg, lightly beaten

1 cup plain flour

1 tablespoon baking powder

1 teaspoon salt

1 cup grated tasty cheese

Preheat oven to 180°C. Grease muffin tins.

Fry potato with garlic, mustard seeds, turmeric and oil until potato is tender but not soft. Be careful as the mustard seeds may jump.

Transfer to a bowl.

Make egg up to 1 cup with water.

Add egg, sifted flour and remaining ingredients to potato mixture and stir until just combined.

Spoon into prepared muffin tins and bake for 12–15 minutes.

MAKES 12–16

Potato & sun-dried tomato muffins

3 cups grated potato

½ cup plain flour

½ teaspoon salt

1 teaspoon baking powder

1 clove garlic, crushed

8 sun-dried tomatoes,
  finely chopped

¼ cup olive oil

2 eggs, separated

Preheat oven to 200°C. Grease muffin tins.

Rinse and drain potato.

Sift flour, salt and baking powder into a large bowl.
Mix in all remaining ingredients except egg whites.

Beat egg whites until soft peaks form. Fold into mixture.

Spoon into muffin tins. Bake for 20–25 minutes.

MAKES 12–16

Pumpkin cake

250 g softened butter

2½ cups castor sugar

3 eggs

3 cups wholemeal plain
    flour

1 teaspoon bicarbonate
    of soda

1 teaspoon baking powder

1 teaspoon ground
    cinnamon, plus extra
    for sprinkling

1 teaspoon allspice

½ teaspoon ground nutmeg

2 cups mashed pumpkin

1 cup chopped walnuts, plus
    extra for decorating

lemon butter icing
    (page 677)

Preheat oven to 125°C. Lightly grease and flour a 23-cm cake tin.

Cream butter and sugar until light and fluffy. Add eggs one at a time, beating well after each addition.

Sift dry ingredients, and add alternately with pumpkin to creamed mixture. Add chopped walnuts and beat well.

Pour into prepared tin and bake for 90 minutes, or until a skewer inserted into the centre of the cake comes out clean.

Ice with lemon icing. Sprinkle with walnuts and extra cinnamon.

Pumpkin & chocolate chip muffins

1 cup sliced almonds

1¾ cups plain flour

1 teaspoon allspice

1 teaspoon garam masala

¼ teaspoon baking powder

1 teaspoon bicarbonate
   of soda

¼ teaspoon salt

1 cup castor sugar

2 eggs

1 cup mashed pumpkin

150 g butter, melted

1 cup chocolate chips

Preheat oven to 180°C. Grease muffin tins.

Place almonds on an oven tray and bake for about 5 minutes or until lightly browned.

Sift flour, allspice, garam masala, baking powder, bicarbonate of soda and salt into a large bowl. Add sugar.

In a separate bowl, beat eggs and add pumpkin and melted butter. Beat to combine.

Fold almonds and chocolate chips into this mixture.

Quickly fold in dry ingredients.

Three-quarters fill prepared muffin tins and bake for 20 minutes or until well risen.

MAKES 16

Pumpkin date puffs

185 g softened butter

1 cup white sugar

2 eggs

½ teaspoon vanilla extract

1 cup cold mashed pumpkin

1 cup self-raising flour

1½ cups plain flour

pinch of salt

½ teaspoon bicarbonate
  of soda

¼ teaspoon ground nutmeg

¼ teaspoon mixed spice

1 cup dates, chopped

½ cup walnuts, chopped

Preheat oven to 190°C. Lightly grease baking trays.

Cream butter and sugar until light and fluffy.
Gradually beat in the eggs and vanilla, then the
mashed pumpkin.

Sift together the flours, salt, bicarbonate of soda
and spices. Add to the pumpkin mixture and mix well.
Stir in the dates and walnuts.

Drop dessertspoonfuls of mixture onto baking trays
and bake for 10–12 minutes.

MAKES 40

Pumpkin fruit cake

125 g sultanas

125 g raisins

125 g mixed peel

125 g dried apricots,
    finely chopped

1 cup orange or apple juice

1 tablespoon honey

1 teaspoon bicarbonate
    of soda

4 egg whites

1 cup cold mashed pumpkin

1¾ cups wholemeal
    self-raising flour

1 teaspoon mixed spice

Preheat oven to 165°C. Lightly grease and line a 20-cm round cake tin.

In a small saucepan combine fruit, juice and honey. Bring to the boil, stirring gently. Remove from heat and add bicarbonate of soda. Allow to cool.

In a large bowl beat egg whites lightly, add fruit mixture and mashed pumpkin and beat until smooth. Stir in sifted flour and mixed spice, combining well.

Pour into prepared tin and bake for 90 minutes or until a skewer inserted into the centre of the cake comes out clean.

VARIATION
This cake is even more delicious if the dried fruit is soaked in the orange juice overnight. For a special occasion several teaspoons of brandy can be added.

Pumpkin muffins

40 g softened butter

½ cup white sugar

1 egg

¾ cup plain flour

1 teaspoon baking powder

1 teaspoon bicarbonate
  of soda

½ teaspoon ground
  cinnamon

¼ teaspoon ground nutmeg

¾ cup wholemeal plain
  flour

¼ cup sultanas

½ cup mashed pumpkin

milk, to mix

cream cheese icing
  (page 682) (optional)

Preheat oven to 180°C. Grease muffin tins.

Cream butter and sugar until light and fluffy, then add egg and beat.

Sift flour, baking powder, bicarbonate of soda and spices into the creamed mixture.

Stir in sifted wholemeal flour, sultanas, pumpkin and sufficient milk to make a moist mixture.

Spoon batter into prepared muffin tins and bake for 15–20 minutes.

If desired, ice with cream cheese icing.

MAKES 12

Raisin country cake

3⅓ cups plain flour

2 teaspoons baking powder

175 g soft brown sugar

2 teaspoons mixed spice

pinch of ground nutmeg

grated zest of ½ lemon

175 g cold butter, cut into
    small pieces

2 cups raisins

1½ cups currants

¾ cup mixed peel

2 eggs, beaten

½ cup milk

2 tablespoons golden syrup

½ cup stout

Preheat oven to 160°C. Lightly grease a 27-cm cake tin and line the base with non-stick baking paper.

Sift flour, baking powder, sugar, mixed spice and nutmeg into a bowl. Add lemon zest, then rub in butter.

Add fruit and peel, make a well in the centre and pour in eggs, milk and golden syrup. Mix well. Stir in enough stout to make a dropping consistency.

Spoon into the prepared tin and bake for 2 hours, or until a skewer inserted into the centre of the cake comes out clean.

Raisin muffins

1½ cups wholemeal plain
    flour

⅓ cup soft brown sugar

3 teaspoons baking powder

½ teaspoon salt

1 teaspoon ground
    cinnamon

½ cup wheatgerm

¾ cup raisins

⅔ cup milk

⅓ cup vegetable oil

2 eggs, lightly beaten

Preheat oven to 200°C. Grease muffin tins.

Sift flour into a large bowl, adding any husks in sifter to the bowl.

Mix in sugar, baking powder, salt, cinnamon, wheatgerm and raisins.

Add milk, oil and lightly beaten eggs. Mix until dry ingredients are just moistened.

Three-quarters fill prepared muffin tins and bake for 20 minutes.

MAKES 12

Raisin orange cake

125 g softened butter

1 cup white sugar

1 teaspoon vanilla extract

2 eggs, beaten

1 medium-sized orange

1 cup raisins

½ cup chopped walnuts

2 cups plain flour

pinch of salt

½ cup warm water

1 teaspoon bicarbonate
   of soda

orange butter icing
   (page 678)

Preheat oven to 180°C. Lightly grease and flour a
15-cm round deep cake tin.

Cream butter, sugar and vanilla extract until light and
fluffy. Add eggs and mix well.

Cut orange into quarters. Remove peel, pith and
seeds. Put flesh into a blender with raisins and walnuts.
Blend until finely minced. Add to creamed mixture.

Fold in sifted flour and salt alternately with warm water
in which bicarbonate of soda has been dissolved.

Pour into prepared tin and bake for 60–70 minutes.
Ice with orange icing when cool.

Raspberry drops

125 g softened butter

¾ cup white sugar

¼ teaspoon vanilla extract

2 eggs, beaten

1¼ cups plain flour

¼ cup cornflour

½ cup desiccated coconut

raspberry jam, for filling

Preheat oven to 180°C. Lightly grease baking trays.

Cream butter and sugar until light and fluffy. Stir in vanilla extract and eggs. Add sifted flours and coconut. Beat until well combined.

Roll mixture into small balls and place on baking trays. Press a hole into the centre of each biscuit using the end of a teaspoon and fill with raspberry jam.

Bake for 15 minutes. Cool on trays.

MAKES 30

Red devil cake

1 cup grated dark cooking
  chocolate

½ cup milk, mixed with
  ½ tablespoon lemon juice
  or vinegar

2 cups soft brown sugar

4 egg yolks

120 g softened butter

1 teaspoon bicarbonate
  of soda

½ cup milk

2 cups plain flour

2 egg whites

chocolate butter icing
  (page 678)

Preheat oven to 180°C. Lightly grease and flour a
20-cm round cake tin.

Gently heat chocolate, soured milk, half the brown sugar
and 1 egg yolk until chocolate has melted. Set aside
to cool.

Cream butter and remaining sugar until light and fluffy.
Add remaining egg yolks, bicarbonate of soda dissolved
in milk, and sifted flour.

Beat egg whites until stiff and fold into creamed mixture
with chocolate mixture.

Pour into prepared tin and bake for 50–60 minutes.

Ice with chocolate icing.

VARIATION
This mixture can also be baked in two sandwich tins
and filled with chocolate icing. Halve the cooking time
if using this method.

Refrigerator biscuits

185 g softened butter

1 cup soft brown sugar,
   firmly packed

1 egg

1 teaspoon vanilla extract

2¼ cups plain flour

½ teaspoon salt

½ teaspoon baking powder

egg white, for brushing

castor sugar, for sprinkling

Cream the butter and sugar until light and fluffy.
Add egg and vanilla and beat well.

In a separate bowl sift together flour, salt and baking
powder, then stir into creamed mixture.

Roll mixture into long logs about 5 cm in diameter.
Wrap tightly in foil and chill in the refrigerator until cold.

Preheat oven to 180°C. Lightly grease baking trays.

Cut dough into thin slices. Place on baking trays, brush
each slice with egg white and sprinkle with castor sugar.

Bake for 7–10 minutes.

(This biscuit dough can be stored in the refrigerator
for up to 2 weeks, or frozen for 2 months.)

VARIATION

Before refrigerating, divide dough into five portions.
Leave the first portion plain. To the second portion add
2 teaspoons instant coffee granules dissolved in a little
water. To the third portion add ⅓ cup desiccated coconut
and ½ teaspoon lemon essence. To the fourth portion
add 1 teaspoon ground ginger, then top each biscuit
round with a piece of crystallised ginger. To the final
portion add ½ tablespoon cocoa and ½ teaspoon
cinnamon, then top each biscuit round with a chocolate
button or almond.

MAKES 60

Rhubarb & lemon cake

1 cup castor sugar

finely grated zest of
    2 lemons

4 eggs, lightly beaten

¼ cup milk

1¾ cups self-raising flour

1 tablespoon freshly
    squeezed lemon juice

140 g butter, melted

⅔ cup light olive oil

300 g fresh rhubarb,
    trimmed and cut into
    small chunks

Preheat oven to 180°C. Lightly grease and flour a 26-cm round springform cake tin and line the base with non-stick baking paper.

Using an electric mixer, blend the sugar with the lemon zest for 1 minute. Add the eggs and beat until pale and thick (about 3 minutes).

Stir in the milk and sifted flour to make a smooth batter. Blend in the lemon juice, melted butter and oil.

Pour one-third of the batter into the prepared tin, making sure the base is covered. Arrange the rhubarb over the top and then pour the remaining batter over the rhubarb.

Bake for 50 minutes or until the cake pulls away from the sides of the tin. Cool for 10 minutes before turning out onto a wire rack.

Rhubarb muffins

2 cups plain flour

1 tablespoon baking powder

½ teaspoon salt

¾ cup castor sugar

1 cup milk

100 g butter, melted and
    cooled slightly

1 egg

1½ cups finely chopped
    rhubarb

3 tablespoons raw sugar
    mixed with 1 tablespoon
    ground cinnamon

Preheat oven to 220°C. Grease muffin tins.

Sift together flour, baking powder and salt. Add sugar
and combine.

In a separate bowl mix together milk, butter and egg.

Add milk mixture to dry ingredients and combine, then
stir in rhubarb.

Spoon batter into prepared muffin tins. Sprinkle over
cinnamon sugar.

Bake for 15 minutes.

Serve with whipped cream.

MAKES 16

Rhubarb & ricotta crumble

CRUMBLE

150 g cold butter, cut into
  small pieces

1 cup plain flour

1 cup soft brown sugar

100 g rolled oats

FILLING

2 cups ricotta

3 eggs

¼ cup castor sugar

2 tablespoons orange juice

400 g cooked rhubarb,
  puréed

Preheat oven to 180°C. Lightly grease and line a 23-cm springform tin.

To make crumble, combine the butter, sifted flour, brown sugar and rolled oats in a food processor and pulse until the mixture starts to clump together. Reserve ¾ cup of the mixture, and press the rest into the prepared tin.

Bake for 15–20 minutes or until lightly browned and firm.

To make the filling, combine the ricotta, eggs, castor sugar and orange juice. Mix well until smooth.

Spread the puréed rhubarb over the baked crumble base. Pour in the ricotta mixture. Sprinkle the reserved crumble over the top, and bake for 35–40 minutes. Cool to room temperature.

SERVES 6

Rich chocolate & date cake

250 g whole unblanched
  almonds

250 g dark cooking
  chocolate, chopped

250 g chopped pitted dates

6 egg whites

pinch of salt

½ cup castor sugar

Preheat oven to 180°C. Lightly grease a 23-cm round springform cake tin and line the base with non-stick baking paper.

Chop the nuts and chocolate together using a food processor. Transfer to a mixing bowl and stir in the chopped dates.

In another bowl, whisk the egg whites and salt until soft peaks form. Slowly whisk in the sugar until thick and glossy.

Fold the chocolate mixture through the meringue.

Pour into the prepared tin and bake for 45 minutes or until firm. Cool in the tin and then carefully turn out onto a serving plate.

Cut into thin wedges and serve with fresh fruit slices and cream.

Rich chocolate rum cake

1¼ cups plain flour

1½ teaspoons baking powder

¾ teaspoon bicarbonate
   of soda

pinch of salt

100 g dark cooking
   chocolate, chopped

1½ cups castor sugar

½ cup boiling water

3 eggs, lightly beaten

1 heaped tablespoon cocoa

225 g softened butter,
   cut into 8 pieces

¾ cup sour cream

1 tablespoon dark rum

Preheat oven to 170°C. Lightly grease a 23-cm round springform cake tin and line the base with non-stick baking paper.

Blend the sifted flour, baking powder, bicarbonate of soda and salt in a food processor for 3 seconds. Remove and reserve.

Process the chocolate and half of the sugar until the mixture resembles fine breadcrumbs. With the food processor still running, pour in the boiling water and process until the chocolate has melted. Pour in the eggs, cocoa and remaining sugar and process for 2 minutes. Add the butter and process for 1 minute. Add the sour cream and rum and blend.

Spoon the flour into the food processor. Pulse the mixture three or four times until the flour is incorporated. Be careful not to over-process.

Spoon the mixture into the prepared tin. Bake for 75 minutes or until a skewer inserted into the centre of the cake comes out clean. Cool in the tin for 10 minutes before turning out onto a wire rack.

Rich chocolate shortbread crescents

250 g softened butter

¼ cup icing sugar

1 cup cornflour

¾ cup plain flour

2 tablespoons cocoa

90 g dark cooking chocolate, chopped

Preheat oven to 180°C. Lightly grease baking trays.

Cream butter and sifted icing sugar until light and fluffy. Add sifted cornflour, flour and cocoa and combine well.

Put mixture into a piping bag fitted with 1-cm star tip. Pipe onto trays in small crescents (about 3 cm long) and bake for 12 minutes.

Cool on trays and do not decorate until completely cold.

To decorate, melt chocolate in a double boiler over simmering water, or on MEDIUM in the microwave. Drizzle over the top of the crescents, or dip the ends of each cresent into the chocolate.

Allow to set before storing in an airtight container.

MAKES 30

Rich old-fashioned fruit cake

1 kg mixed dried fruit

½ cup finely chopped glacé ginger

1 teaspoon grated orange zest

1 cup apple purée

2 tablespoons apricot jam

2 tablespoons orange juice

250 g softened butter

1¼ cups soft brown sugar

1 teaspoon vanilla extract

4 eggs, lightly beaten

3 cups plain flour

1 teaspoon baking powder

1 teaspoon mixed spice

1 teaspoon ground ginger

glacé cherries and whole almonds, for decorating

2–4 tablespoons whisky

In a large bowl mix fruit, glacé ginger, orange zest, apple purée, apricot jam and orange juice. Cover and allow to stand overnight.

Preheat oven to 150°C. Lightly grease a 20-cm round tin and line with two layers of non-stick baking paper.

Cream butter, sugar and vanilla extract until light and creamy. Add eggs one at a time. Add sifted dried ingredients alternately with fruit mixture.

Pour into prepared tin. Decorate with rows of cherries and almonds. Bake for 3–3½ hours. Cover with baking paper for the last hour to prevent burning.

Remove from oven and pour whisky on top. Leave in tin to cool completely before turning out.

Roasted pecan & ginger cake

130 g softened butter

1 cup soft brown sugar

2 eggs, lightly beaten

1 cup plain flour

½ tablespoon baking
  powder

2 teaspoons ground ginger

⅔ cup roasted pecans, finely
  chopped

⅔ cup milk

½ teaspoon freshly grated
  ginger

½ teaspoon vanilla extract

10 pecan halves, for
  decorating

Preheat oven to 180°C. Lightly grease a 22-cm round cake tin and line the base with non-stick baking paper.

Cream the butter and sugar until light and fluffy. Slowly add the eggs. Sift the flour, baking powder and ground ginger into another bowl and stir in the pecans.

Add the flour mixture to the butter mixture a little at a time, alternately with the milk, finishing with the flour mixture. Stir in the fresh ginger and vanilla extract.

Pour into the prepared tin and decorate the top with the pecan halves.

Bake for 35–40 minutes or until lightly browned and cooked through. Cool in the tin on a wire rack for 10 minutes before turning out of the tin to cool completely.

Rocky road

375 g milk chocolate, chopped

30 g white vegetable shortening, chopped

200 g pink and white marshmallows, chopped

⅓ cup desiccated coconut

⅓ cup glacé cherries, chopped

⅓ cup macadamia nuts, chopped

Grease and line a 20-cm square cake tin.

Melt chocolate and shortening in a double boiler over simmering water, or on MEDIUM in the microwave.

Combine melted chocolate with remaining ingredients and mix well. Pour into tin.

Freeze for 20 minutes or until set, and cut into pieces to serve.

MAKES 36 | NO BAKE

Rocky road muffins

¼ cup milk

1 egg

1 cup natural yoghurt

50 g butter, melted

2 cups plain flour

1 teaspoon baking powder

½ cup castor sugar

½ cup small marshmallows

90 g chocolate, chopped

½ cup peanuts

½ cup jubes, chopped

TOPPING

1 tablespoon cocoa

1 tablespoon butter

1 tablespoon milk

icing sugar, to mix

jubes or marshmallows,
   for decorating

Preheat oven to 180°C. Grease muffin tins.

Mix milk, egg, yoghurt and butter in a large bowl.

Add sifted flour and remaining ingredients and mix
until just combined.

Spoon into prepared muffin tins and bake for
12–15 minutes.

For topping, heat cocoa, butter and milk and stir until
smooth. Add enough sifted icing sugar to make a paste.
Spread over muffins and place marshmallows or jubes
in icing before it sets.

MAKES 16

Roly poly with hot jam sauce

1½ cups self-raising flour

½ cup plain flour

60 g softened butter

¾ cup buttermilk

½ cup strawberry jam

SAUCE

¼ cup blackberry jam

finely grated zest and juice
  of 1 large orange

Preheat oven to 175°C. Lightly grease a shallow baking dish.

Sift the flours into a mixing bowl. Add the butter and rub together until the mixture resembles fine breadcrumbs. Slowly pour in the buttermilk until the mixture comes together and forms a sticky dough.

On a floured board, roll out the dough to approximately 25 cm × 20 cm. Spread the jam over the dough, leaving a border around the edges. Roll up evenly, starting from the short side.

Wrap the roll in non-stick baking paper and place in the prepared dish. Bake for 40–45 minutes or until golden.

To make the hot jam sauce, heat the jam, orange zest and juice over a gentle heat until well combined. Spoon over the roly poly and serve immediately.

SERVES 6

Rum & lime glazed banana bread

120 g softened butter

¾ cup soft brown sugar

2 eggs, lightly beaten

1 cup mashed banana

¼ cup buttermilk

1 tablespoon fresh lime juice

½ teaspoon salt

½ teaspoon ground ginger

2 cups self-raising flour

½ teaspoon bicarbonate
  of soda

GLAZE

¼ cup soft brown sugar

1 tablespoon rum

1 tablespoon butter

¼ cup fresh lime juice

Preheat oven to 175°C. Lightly grease and line a 25-cm × 15-cm loaf tin.

Cream butter and sugar until light and fluffy. Stir in the eggs, mashed banana, buttermilk and lime juice and combine.

Sift the salt, ginger and flour into a mixing bowl with the bicarbonate of soda. Stir into the cake batter and combine until smooth.

Spoon into prepared tin and bake for 60 minutes. Allow cake to stand for 10 minutes before turning out onto a wire rack.

Meanwhile, heat all the glaze ingredients in a saucepan. Stir for about 5 minutes to form a smooth syrup.

Coat the top and sides of the cake with the glaze. Serve while warm or at room temperature.

Ruth's sponge cake

2 tablespoons chilled water

¾ cup castor sugar

4 eggs, separated

1½ cups cornflour

1 teaspoon baking powder

1 teaspoon vanilla extract

whipped cream and jam,
   for filling

icing sugar, for dusting

Preheat oven to 190°C. Lightly grease and flour two 20-cm round cake tins.

Warm water and sugar in a saucepan until sugar dissolves.

Beat egg whites until stiff peaks form. Add sugar mixture to egg whites and beat well. Add yolks one at a time, and beat until thick. Stir in sifted cornflour and baking powder. Lastly add vanilla extract.

Pour into prepared tins and bake for 20–25 minutes. If you are brave enough, take the sponge straight from the oven and, still in the tin, drop it on the floor to get rid of excess air.

Fill with whipped cream and jam and dust with icing sugar.

GLUTEN FREE

Salmon muffins

1 cup plain flour

1 teaspoon salt

1 tablespoon baking powder

1 × 185-g tin salmon,
    drained and mashed
    (reserve liquid)

1 egg

1 cup grated mild cheese

Preheat oven to 200°C. Grease muffin tins.

Sift flour, salt and baking powder into a large bowl.

Make liquid from salmon up to ¾ cup with water and mix into flour with remaining ingredients. Stir until just combined.

Three-quarters fill prepared muffin tins and bake for 12–15 minutes.

VARIATION
Make a small diagonal split in the top of each muffin before serving, spread with cream cheese and tuck in a small piece of smoked salmon.

MAKES 12

Sara's apricot slice

BASE

2 cups self-raising flour

¾ cup castor sugar

125 g cold butter, cut into
small pieces

1 egg, beaten

apricot jam, for spreading

TOPPING

1 egg, beaten

⅓ cup castor sugar

2 cups desiccated coconut

Preheat oven to 180°C. Lightly grease and line
a 19-cm × 29-cm slice tin.

For the base, mix together sifted flour and sugar.
Rub in the butter with your fingertips until crumbly.
Add the beaten egg and mix to a stiff dough.

Press into tin and spread with a layer of jam.

For the topping, mix all ingredients together.
Sprinkle over slice.

Bake for about 30 minutes. Cool in the tin and
then cut into squares.

MAKES 36

Savoury biscotti

3½ cups plain flour

1 teaspoon baking powder

1 teaspoon salt

½ teaspoon freshly ground
  black pepper

½ cup grated parmesan
  cheese

1 tablespoon dried rosemary

1 teaspoon dried oregano
  or marjoram

3 eggs

⅔ cup water

Preheat oven to 180°C. Lightly grease baking trays.

In a large bowl, combine the sifted flour, baking powder, salt and pepper with the cheese and herbs.

In a separate bowl, beat the eggs with the water. Add to the dry mixture and mix until combined.

On a lightly floured surface, knead dough until smooth. Divide dough into three portions. Roll each portion into a log about 3 cm in diameter.

Place logs on baking trays and flatten slightly. Bake for 30 minutes.

Turn off oven, remove logs and set aside to cool for 10 minutes. Slice logs diagonally into 1-cm thick slices, then return to the oven for another 20–30 minutes, or until crisp.

MAKES 24

Schoolboy squares

1 cup self-raising flour

1 dessertspoon cocoa

3 Weet-Bix biscuits, crushed

½ cup white sugar

1 cup desiccated coconut

½ cup currants

125 g butter, melted

chocolate glacé icing
 (page 680)

Preheat oven to 180°C. Lightly grease and line a 19-cm × 29-cm slice tin.

Sift together flour and cocoa, then mix in other dry ingredients. Pour over melted butter and combine well.

Press mixture into tin.

Bake for 10–15 minutes or until golden. While still warm, ice with chocolate icing and cut into bars.

MAKES 30

Scottish oatcakes

100 g rolled oats

½ teaspoon salt

pinch of bicarbonate of soda

1 tablespoon vegetable oil

2 tablespoons hot water

Preheat oven to 180°C. Lightly grease baking trays.

Place oats, salt and bicarbonate of soda in a large bowl. Stir in the oil and hot water and mix to a firm dough.

Roll out on a lightly floured surface and cut out rounds using a 7.5-cm biscuit cutter. Gather any leftover dough, roll out again and use to make more rounds. You should end up with 8 rounds. Cut each of these into quarters.

Place on trays and bake for 8–10 minutes or until golden and crisp.

MAKES 32

Scrummy six-layer slice

125 g butter, melted

1 cup sweet biscuit crumbs

1 cup desiccated coconut

375 g chocolate chips

1 × 395-g tin condensed
   milk

1 cup nuts (almonds,
   hazelnuts, etc.),
   roughly chopped

Preheat oven to 180°C. Lightly grease and line a
19-cm × 29-cm slice tin.

Each of the ingredients in this slice forms a layer.
First pour the melted butter into the tin, then sprinkle
over the biscuit crumbs, followed by the coconut.
Next scatter over the chocolate chips in an even layer,
then pour over the condensed milk. The final layer is
made of the nuts.

Bake for about 30 minutes. Cool, then cut into fingers.

MAKES 36

Self-saucing chocolate muffins

1 cup self-raising flour

2 tablespoons cocoa

½ cup white sugar

½ cup milk

1 tablespoon butter, melted

1 cup soft brown sugar

1½ cups boiling water

Preheat oven to 180°C. Grease muffin tin.

Sift flour and half the cocoa into a bowl. Stir in white sugar.

Add milk and melted butter, and stir until just combined.

Half-fill prepared muffin tins with mixture.

Mix remaining cocoa with soft brown sugar and boiling water, and add to each muffin cup to take level up to three-quarters full.

Bake for 15–20 minutes.

To turn muffins out, place serving dish over muffin tin and carefully flip over. Scoop out any remaining sauce.

MAKES 12

Sesame potato biscuits

2 cups plain flour

1½ teaspoons salt

240 g cold butter, cut into
    small pieces

1 cup cold mashed potato

3 egg yolks

2 tablespoons sour cream

1 egg, extra

¼ cup sesame seeds

Sift together flour and salt. Using your fingertips, rub in the butter until crumbly.

Stir in mashed potato, egg yolks and sour cream.

Knead dough for 1 minute until smooth, then wrap in foil and chill for 20 minutes. Repeat this kneading and chilling process three times.

Preheat oven to 200°C. Lightly grease baking trays.

Roll out dough to 5 mm in thickness and cut into rounds using a biscuit cutter.

Beat extra egg and brush it over biscuits. Sprinkle with sesame seeds.

Bake for 15–20 minutes until lightly brown.

MAKES 24

Sesame pound cake

⅓ cup sesame seeds

110 g softened butter

1 cup castor sugar

4 eggs

2 cups plain flour

½ teaspoon salt

1 teaspoon baking powder

½ cup milk

1 teaspoon vanilla extract

1 teaspoon sesame oil

1 teaspoon grated lemon zest

Preheat oven to 160°C. Lightly grease and line a 23-cm springform tin.

Toast sesame seeds in a frying pan for 2 minutes until golden.

Cream butter and sugar until light and fluffy. Add eggs one at a time, beating well after each addition.

In another bowl, sift together flour, salt and baking powder, and stir in all but 1 tablespoon of sesame seeds.

In a large cup combine milk, vanilla extract, oil and lemon zest. To butter mixture add sifted dry ingredients alternately with milk mixture, stirring well. Do not beat or over-stir.

Pour into prepared tin, sprinkle with remaining sesame seeds and bake for 50–60 minutes, or until a skewer inserted into the centre of the cake comes out clean.

Sesame snack bars

1½ cups white sugar

¾ cup water

75 g sesame seeds, toasted

1 teaspoon ground
   cinnamon

pinch of ground cloves

½ teaspoon lemon juice

Gently heat sugar and water in a saucepan until sugar has dissolved, then bring to the boil. Continue boiling, without stirring, until the syrup begins to turn golden brown.

Add the remaining ingredients and continue boiling for 3 minutes, stirring continuously.

Remove from the heat, pour onto a wet marble slab (or chopping board) and using a wet rolling pin, roll out to a thickness of about 1 cm. Using a palette knife, quickly lever off the slab and cut into bars. (Don't worry if it sets too quickly – you can simply leave it to harden completely, then snap into chunks.)

MAKES 24 | GLUTEN FREE
NO BAKE | DAIRY FREE

Sherry banana cake

125 g softened butter

¾ cup castor sugar

2 eggs

1 teaspoon vanilla extract

3 bananas, mashed

1½ cups plain flour

1½ teaspoons baking powder

½ teaspoon salt

½ teaspoon bicarbonate
   of soda

1 tablespoon milk

TOPPING

½ teaspoon gelatine

2 teaspoons water

⅔ cup cream

2 teaspoons icing sugar

1 teaspoon sherry

chopped walnuts or grated
   dark chocolate for
   decorating

Preheat oven to 180°C. Lightly grease and flour a 23-cm cake tin.

Cream butter and sugar, then beat in eggs and add vanilla. Fold in mashed banana. Add sifted flour, baking powder and salt. Dissolve bicarbonate of soda in milk and stir into mixture.

Pour into prepared tin and bake for 30–35 minutes. Turn onto a wire rack to cool.

To make sherry cream topping, stir gelatine in water over gentle heat until dissolved. Whisk cream until thick, then beat in icing sugar and cooled gelatine. Fold in sherry. Spread over cooled cake and sprinkle with nuts or chocolate.

Sherry trifle

1 small plain sponge cake

2–3 tablespoons strawberry or raspberry jam

1½ cups medium dry sherry

8 amaretti biscuits (almond macaroons), crushed

1 cup cream

2 cups vanilla custard

2 tablespoons toasted flaked almonds

Cut the cake in half and spread the jam between the layers. Cut cake into small chunks and use to line the bottom of an attractive glass bowl or dish.

Pour the sherry over the top and set aside for about 30 minutes.

Sprinkle over the crushed amaretti biscuits.

Whip the cream until stiff peaks form, then mix half of it carefully through the custard. Pour the custard mixture over the sponge and biscuits.

Using a piping bag, pipe the rest of the cream to decorate the top. Sprinkle over toasted flaked almonds.

Refrigerate for an hour before serving.

SERVES 6–8 | NO BAKE

Sheryl's shortbread

1¼ cups gluten-free flour mix (page 6)

¼ cup white sugar

100 g cold butter, cut into small pieces

Preheat oven to 150°C. Lightly grease a 20-cm fluted flan tin.

Combine sifted flour and sugar. Using your fingertips, rub in the butter until a fine crumbly mixture forms. Roll dough into a ball.

Press into tray and score diamond shapes. Bake for 30–40 minutes until light brown. Cool in the tin, then cut along the scored lines.

VARIATIONS
For ginger shortbread, add 1 dessertspoon ground ginger with the flour. For cinnamon shortbread, add 1 dessertspoon ground cinnamon with the flour.

MAKES 8 | GLUTEN FREE

Shona's midnight munchies

100 g butter

¼ cup castor sugar

¼ cup dark treacle

1 cup plain flour

2 teaspoons baking powder

½ teaspoon salt

100 g rolled oats

¾ cup sultanas

Preheat oven to 180°C. Lightly grease and line a 19-cm × 29-cm slice tin.

Place the butter, sugar and treacle into a saucepan and heat gently until butter has melted and sugar dissolved.

In a bowl, sift together flour, baking powder and salt. Stir in oats and sultanas, then pour over butter mixture. Mix thoroughly.

Press mixture into prepared tin and bake for 20 minutes.

MAKES 24

Simple tarte tatin

⅔ cup soft brown sugar

½ teaspoon ground
  cardamom

100 g butter

6–8 Golden Delicious
  apples, peeled, cored and
  quartered

1 sheet frozen puff pastry,
  thawed

pouring custard (page 683)
  or cream, to serve

Preheat oven to 220°C.

Sprinkle the sugar and cardamom over the bottom of a 24-cm ovenproof frying pan or skillet and dot with the butter.

Tightly pack the apple quarters into the pan, with the rounded sides pressed down into the sugar.

Cook over a high heat until the sugar and butter caramelise the apples. Remove from the heat and place the puff pastry on top, trimming the edges a little.

Place the frying pan in the oven on a preheated oven tray and bake for 10–15 minutes or until the pastry is cooked. Remove from the oven and cool a little.

Carefully invert the tart onto a plate and serve with pouring custard or cream.

SERVES 6

Sliced banana muffins

1½ cups plain flour

⅓ cup castor sugar

50 g cold butter, cut into
  small pieces

1 teaspoon baking powder

2 bananas, thinly sliced

1 egg

½ cup milk

100 g dark cooking
  chocolate, chopped

Preheat oven to 190°C. Grease muffin tins.

Rub butter into sifted flour and sugar until mixture
resembles breadcrumbs.

Add remaining ingredients and mix until just combined.

Spoon into prepared muffin tins and bake for about
20 minutes.

MAKES 12

Snickerdoodles

60 g softened butter

¾ cup castor sugar

1 egg

¾ cup plain flour

½ cup self-raising flour

pinch of salt

¼ cup wheatgerm

½ teaspoon vanilla extract

2 tablespoons castor sugar
    mixed with 2 teaspoons
    ground cinnamon

Preheat oven to 190°C. Lightly grease baking trays.

Cream butter and sugar until light and fluffy. Add egg and mix well. Stir in sifted flours, salt, wheatgerm and vanilla until well combined.

Roll mixture into 2-cm balls, then roll the balls in the cinnamon sugar to coat.

Place balls on trays, leaving space between each for spreading. Bake for 10–12 minutes.

MAKES 24

Snow on the trees

25 g butter

½ cup castor sugar

2 tablespoons cocoa

1 egg, beaten

2 tablespoons desiccated
coconut, plus extra for
sprinkling

2 cups sweet biscuit crumbs

¼ cup dates, chopped

¼ cup glacé cherries,
chopped

glacé icing (page 679)

few drops green food
colouring

Preheat oven to 180°C. Grease a 23-cm square cake tin and line the base.

Place butter, sugar and cocoa in a small saucepan and heat for 2 minutes. Remove from heat and cool for a few minutes so egg doesn't scramble when added.

Mix in egg, coconut, biscuit crumbs, dates and cherries.

Press mixture firmly into tin and bake for 15 minutes.

Make icing and stir in a few drops of green food colouring.

When slice is cold, top with a thin layer of icing, then sprinkle with extra coconut. Cut into squares to serve.

MAKES 24

Sophie's plum duff

225 g raisins

225 g sultanas

225 g currants

175 g mixed peel

2¾ cups suet

200 g white sugar

2⅓ cups plain flour

2 teaspoons mixed spice

2 teaspoons ground
  cinnamon

¼ teaspoon ground nutmeg

2 teaspoons baking powder

pinch of salt

3 eggs, beaten

1 cup milk

In a large bowl combine fruit, suet, sugar and sifted dry ingredients. Add beaten eggs and milk and stir well.

Spoon into two or three greased pudding basins and steam for 2½–3 hours.

Alternatively, this pudding may be cooked in a pudding cloth. Scald a square of calico in boiling water, wring out and dust with flour while still warm. Place mixture in centre and gather up ends, shaping mixture into a ball, then tie tightly with string. Put into boiling water with a plate on the bottom of the pan. If making as one pudding, boil 4½ hours, topping up water as needed. Hang to dry before storing.

To serve, boil 60 minutes.

This pudding will keep for many months. Serve with brandy sauce.

Sour cream apple slice

BASE

125 g butter, melted

1 × 600-g packet vanilla
cake mix

1 cup desiccated coconut

FILLING

500 g stewed apple (or pie
apple), well drained

TOPPING

1 egg, beaten

1 × 300-ml carton sour
cream

ground cinnamon, for
sprinkling

castor sugar, for sprinkling

Preheat oven to 180°C. Lightly grease and line a
25-cm × 30-cm Swiss roll tin.

For the base, mix melted butter with cake mix and
coconut until well combined.

Press into tin and bake in oven for 10–15 minutes,
until golden brown. Set aside to cool. (Leave oven on.)

Spread apple filling evenly over base.

For the topping, fold egg into sour cream. Pour sour
cream mixture evenly over apple and sprinkle with
cinnamon and castor sugar.

Bake for a further 20 minutes. Cool in the tin before
cutting into squares or fingers.

MAKES 36

Sour cream jalapeno corn muffins

1½ cups polenta

½ cup plain flour

1 tablespoon white sugar

1 tablespoon baking powder

1 teaspoon salt

2 eggs

1 cup sour cream

1–1½ teaspoons seeded, finely chopped jalapeno pepper

Preheat oven to 180°C. Grease muffin tin.

Thoroughly mix polenta, sifted flour, sugar, baking powder and salt in large bowl.

Whisk eggs and sour cream in a small bowl. When smooth, stir in jalapeno pepper.

Pour over flour mixture. Fold in with a rubber spatula until well mixed. Batter will be very stiff.

Scoop batter into prepared muffin tin.

Bake for 20–25 minutes, or until firm to the touch in the centre.

Let cool 5 minutes in tin before turning out onto a wire cooling rack.

MAKES 12

Sour cream poppy seed cake

80 g butter

½ cup poppy seeds

1 cup honey

1 teaspoon vanilla extract

4 eggs

1½ cups plain flour

1 teaspoon bicarbonate
of soda

¼ teaspoon salt

½ cup wholemeal plain
flour

1 cup sour cream

TOPPING

250 g softened cream cheese

¼ cup maple syrup or honey

Preheat oven to 180°C. Grease and flour a bundt tin.

Cream butter with poppy seeds until light and fluffy.
Add honey and vanilla extract and beat well. Add eggs
one at a time, beating well after each addition.

Sift plain flour, bicarbonate of soda and salt into a bowl.
Stir in sifted wholemeal flour.

Fold dry ingredients into creamed mixture alternately
with sour cream. Mix well.

Pour into prepared tin and bake for 50–60 minutes.
Allow to cool.

To make topping, beat cream cheese with maple syrup
until smooth and creamy. Spread over cake.

Spiced apple muffins

2 cups wholemeal plain flour

¼ teaspoon salt

1 tablespoon baking powder

1 teaspoon ground cinnamon

1 teaspoon mixed spice

2 eggs

1 cup water

½ cup soft brown sugar

2 cups cooked diced apple (or tinned pie apple)

coffee sugar, for sprinkling

Preheat oven to 190°C. Grease muffin tins.

Sift flour, salt, baking powder and spices into a large bowl. Add remaining ingredients and mix until just combined.

Three-quarters fill prepared muffin tins and sprinkle with coffee sugar.

Bake for 20–25 minutes.

MAKES 16

Spiced apricot turnover biscuits

100 g softened unsalted
  butter

¾ cup castor sugar

2 eggs, lightly beaten

2⅔ cups self-raising flour

1 teaspoon ground cloves

1 × 400-g tin apricots
  (or peaches or pie apples)

1½ tablespoons soft brown
  sugar, for sprinkling

2 tablespoons castor sugar
  mixed with 1 teaspoon
  ground cinnamon,
  for sprinkling

ICING

3 cups icing sugar

⅓ cup boiling water

Cream butter and sugar until light and fluffy. Add eggs one at a time, beating well after each addition.

Add sifted flour and cloves and mix to form a soft dough. Turn onto a floured surface and knead gently. Cover with cling wrap and chill for at least 20 minutes.

Preheat oven to 180°C. Line baking trays with baking paper.

Divide dough into 2 pieces. Roll out each piece to about 5 mm thick. Using a 9-cm biscuit cutter, cut 11 rounds from the first piece of dough. Using an 8-cm biscuit cutter, cut another 11 rounds from the second piece of dough.

Drain and purée the tinned apricots, then place a tablespoon of the purée on each of the smaller rounds, leaving a border around the edge. Sprinkle over some of the brown sugar. Top with the larger rounds, pressing edges together to seal.

Bake for 15 minutes, or until lightly browned. Let biscuits cool on trays for 5 minutes before transferring to a wire rack to cool completely.

For the icing, sift icing sugar into a bowl. Stir in boiling water until smooth. Spoon icing over biscuit tops and sprinkle with cinnamon sugar.

MAKES 10

Spiced fruit muffins

50 g softened butter

½ cup castor sugar

1 egg

1 apple, peeled and grated

½ teaspoon bicarbonate
   of soda

1 dessertspoon boiling water

¾ cup plain flour

½ teaspoon ground
   cinnamon

½ teaspoon mixed spice

¼ cup sultanas

Preheat oven to 200°C. Grease muffin tins.

Cream butter and sugar until light and fluffy.

Add egg and beat well.

Stir in grated apple, bicarbonate of soda dissolved in water, sifted flour and spices. Mix lightly, then fold in sultanas.

Three-quarters fill prepared muffin tins and bake for 15 minutes or until firm.

MAKES 10

Spiced honey cake

1 cup honey

2 cups warm water

2 cups white sugar

4 cups plain flour

1 teaspoon baking powder

2 teaspoons ground
cinnamon

1 teaspoon ground nutmeg

1 teaspoon ground ginger

1 teaspoon ground mace

½ teaspoon ground cloves

icing sugar, for dusting

Preheat oven to 180°C. Lightly grease and flour a 20-cm cake tin.

Mix honey and warm water, then add to sugar and sifted dry ingredients, blending well.

Pour into prepared tin and bake for 50–60 minutes.

Dust with icing sugar.

Spiced jumbles

240 g softened butter

1 cup white sugar

1 teaspoon ground nutmeg

1 teaspoon ground cinnamon

1 teaspoon ground ginger

1 egg, beaten

3 cups plain flour

Preheat oven to 180°C.

Cream butter and sugar until very light. Add spices, then beat in egg.

Add sifted flour a cup at a time to form a soft dough that is not sticky, adding more flour if necessary.

Roll out on a lightly floured surface to 5 mm in thickness, and then cut into shapes with biscuit cutters.

(Alternatively, you can roll small pieces of dough into long ropes about 2 cm in diameter and then twist them into figures-of-eight.)

Bake on ungreased baking trays for 12–15 minutes.

MAKES 36

Spiced lemon muffins

2 cups plain flour

1½ teaspoons ground
   cinnamon

1 tablespoon baking powder

1 tablespoon grated lemon
   zest

½ cup castor sugar

2 eggs

½ cup vegetable oil

1 cup natural yoghurt

¼ cup milk

¼ cup raw sugar mixed with
   1 teaspoon ground
   cinnamon

TOPPING

2 eggs

½ cup castor sugar

grated zest and juice
   of 2 lemons

40 g butter

Preheat oven to 200°C. Grease muffin tins.

In a large bowl sift together flour, cinnamon and baking powder. Add lemon zest and sugar.

In a separate bowl beat eggs, oil, yoghurt and milk.

Add yoghurt mixture to dry ingredients and stir to combine.

Spoon into prepared muffin tins and sprinkle with cinnamon sugar.

Bake for 15–20 minutes.

To make topping, combine eggs and sugar in a heatproof bowl. Stir in lemon zest, lemon juice and butter. Cook in the bowl over a saucepan of boiling water for 15 minutes, stirring occasionally, until mixture thickens. Spread onto cooled muffins.

MAKES 16

Spicy All-Bran muffins

1¼ cups All-Bran, plus
   extra for sprinkling

1½ cups skim milk

1 egg yolk

60 g butter, melted

½ cup chopped raisins
   or dates

1½ cups self-raising flour

1 teaspoon ground
   cinnamon

½ teaspoon ground nutmeg

¼ cup castor sugar

2 egg whites

Preheat oven to 200°C. Grease muffin tins.

Place All-Bran and milk in a large bowl and let stand for 5 minutes until softened.

Beat in egg yolk, melted butter and raisins.

Sift together flour and spices. Stir in sugar, then add to All-Bran mixture.

Beat egg whites until stiff peaks form. Fold into batter.

Three-quarters fill prepared muffin tins and sprinkle with extra All-Bran.

Bake for 25–30 minutes.

MAKES 12–16

Spicy apple slice

125 g butter

½ cup castor sugar, plus extra for sprinkling

1 egg

1 cup plain flour

1 teaspoon ground cinnamon

1 teaspoon ground ginger

1½ cups stewed apple (or pie apple), well drained

Preheat oven to 180°C. Lightly grease and line a 19-cm × 29-cm slice tin.

Cream butter and sugar until light and fluffy. Add egg and beat well.

In a separate bowl sift together flour, cinnamon and ginger. Fold into creamed mixture.

Spread half the mixture into the tin. Cover with the apple and then spread remaining mixture on top. Brush with water and sprinkle generously with castor sugar.

Bake for about 45 minutes, or until golden brown. Serve warm or cold.

MAKES 16

Spicy nut muffins

1 tablespoon olive oil

1 cup nuts (almonds, peanuts, cashews, walnuts)

1 clove garlic, crushed

1 teaspoon salt

¼ teaspoon each ground cumin, coriander, chilli powder, ginger and cinnamon

2 cups self-raising flour

1 egg, beaten

¼ cup water

1 cup natural yoghurt

50 g butter, melted

2 tablespoons honey

Preheat oven to 200°C. Grease muffin tins.

Heat oil in a frying pan and gently fry nuts, garlic, salt and spices for 15 minutes. Leave to cool.

Sift flour into a large bowl and add remaining ingredients. Mix until just combined.

Add spiced nuts, reserving ¼ cup for decoration.

Three-quarters fill prepared muffin tins and sprinkle with reserved nuts.

Bake for 15–20 minutes.

MAKES 16

Spicy pear & grain muffins

1 egg, beaten

1 cup buttermilk

2 tablespoons vegetable oil

2 pears, grated

1¼ cups wholemeal plain
   flour

¾ cup polenta

½ cup rolled oats

¼ cup chopped raisins
   or currants

1½ teaspoons baking powder

½ teaspoon bicarbonate
   of soda

1 teaspoon ground
   cinnamon

½ teaspoon ground nutmeg

½ teaspoon allspice

Preheat oven to 180°C. Grease muffin tins.

Beat together egg, buttermilk and oil. Add pears.

In a separate bowl, combine sifted flour with remaining
ingredients.

Add wet ingredients to dry ingredients, and stir until just
blended.

Spoon into prepared muffin tins and bake for about
20–25 minutes.

MAKES 16

Spicy prune cake

125 g softened butter

1 cup castor sugar

2 eggs

⅔ cup drained stewed
  pitted prunes, chopped
  (reserve juice)

⅔ cup sour cream

1½ cups plain flour

½ teaspoon bicarbonate
  of soda

½ teaspoon salt

½ teaspoon ground nutmeg

½ teaspoon ground
  cinnamon

½ teaspoon allspice

ICING

1 tablespoon softened butter

2 cups icing sugar

½ teaspoon ground
  cinnamon

2 tablespoons reserved
  prune juice

Preheat oven to 180°C. Lightly grease and flour two sandwich tins.

Cream butter and sugar until light and fluffy. Add eggs one at a time, beating well, then add prunes and sour cream. Fold in sifted dry ingredients.

Pour into prepared tins and bake for 30–40 minutes. Turn out onto a wire rack to cool.

To make icing, beat ingredients together, adding enough prune juice to make a smooth, spreadable icing.

Fill and ice cake when cold.

Spicy prune muffins

1 teaspoon bicarbonate
of soda

¾ cup warm milk

2 cups self-raising flour

1 egg

⅓ cup vegetable oil

1 teaspoon mixed spice

½ cup soft brown sugar

¾ cup pitted prunes soaked
in ¼ cup liqueur

Preheat oven to 190°C. Grease muffin tins.

Stir bicarbonate of soda into milk.

Sift flour into a bowl and mix in remaining ingredients
until just combined. Add milk mixture and stir gently
to combine.

Spoon into prepared muffin tins and bake for
20–25 minutes.

MAKES 16

Spicy pumpkin muffins

1 cup plain flour

1 cup wholemeal plain flour

¼ cup castor sugar

1 tablespoon baking powder

2 teaspoons ground
   cinnamon

2 teaspoons ground nutmeg

½ teaspoon ground ginger

½ teaspoon ground cloves

2 eggs

¼ cup vegetable oil

¾ cup skim milk

1 cup cold mashed pumpkin

Preheat oven to 200°C. Grease muffin tins.

In a large bowl, sift together dry ingredients.

In a separate bowl, beat together eggs, oil, milk and pumpkin.

Add to dry ingredients and stir until just combined.

Spoon into prepared muffin tins.

Bake for 20–25 minutes.

MAKES 16

Spicy slice

250 g softened butter

1 cup soft brown sugar

1 teaspoon vanilla extract

1 egg, separated

2 cups plain flour

1 teaspoon ground cinnamon

¼ teaspoon ground ginger

¼ teaspoon ground nutmeg

1 cup ground walnuts

Preheat oven to 180°C. Grease a 19-cm × 29-cm slice tin and dust with flour.

Cream butter, sugar and vanilla until light and fluffy. Add egg yolk and beat well.

Sift together the flour and spices, and stir into the creamed mixture. Mix in half the ground walnuts.

Spread mixture into the prepared tin.

Beat egg white until frothy but not stiff, and spread over the mixture. Sprinkle with the remaining nuts.

Bake for 25 minutes. Cool slightly, then cut into squares.

MAKES 24

Spinach & caramelised onion muffins

2 onions, diced

1 teaspoon olive oil

1 bunch spinach, washed
and spun dry

2½ cups plain flour

1 teaspoon baking powder

2 teaspoons salt

¼ cup castor sugar

2 eggs

¾ cup milk

⅔ cup vegetable oil

½ cup grated parmesan
cheese, for sprinkling

Preheat oven to 215°C. Grease muffin tins.

Cook the diced onions in olive oil over medium-high heat, until they become richly caramelised. Remove from the pan and set aside to cool.

Add the spinach to the pan and cook over high heat until the leaves become completely wilted. Remove from the pan and set aside to cool. When cool, chop finely.

Sift the flour, baking powder and salt into a large bowl. Stir in sugar.

Add eggs, milk and oil to dry ingredients along with cooled onions and spinach. Mix together until just combined.

Spoon batter into prepared muffin tins, filling two-thirds full. Sprinkle tops with parmesan cheese.

Bake for about 15 minutes.

MAKES 20

Spinach & feta muffins

2 cups self-raising flour

1 egg

¾ cup water

½ teaspoon salt

1 clove garlic, crushed

100 g feta cheese, crumbled

1 cup finely shredded
spinach

⅔ cup grated cheddar
cheese

¼ cup grated parmesan
cheese, for sprinkling

Preheat oven to 180°C. Grease muffin tins.

Sift flour into a large bowl. Mix in remaining ingredients (except parmesan cheese), until just combined.

Spoon into prepared muffin tins and sprinkle with parmesan.

Bake for 15–20 minutes.

MAKES 16

Spring onion muffins

2 cups plain flour

1 tablespoon white sugar

2 teaspoons baking powder

1 teaspoon garlic powder

1 teaspoon mustard powder

½ teaspoon salt

2 egg whites, lightly beaten

1 cup skim milk

½ cup grated carrot

¼ cup chopped spring
onion

2 tablespoons olive oil

2 tablespoons non-fat plain
yoghurt

Preheat oven to 190°C. Grease muffin tins.

In a large bowl, sift together flour, sugar, baking
powder, garlic powder, mustard powder and salt.

In a small mixing bowl, combine egg whites and
remaining ingredients.

Blend egg mixture gently into flour mixture.

Spoon batter into prepared muffin tins.

Bake for 18–20 minutes.

MAKES 16

Squashed fly slice

2 sheets frozen shortcrust
   pastry, thawed

½ cup currants

½ cup raisins, chopped

1½ cups sultanas, chopped

1 tablespoon sherry

1 egg, lightly beaten

white sugar, for sprinkling

Preheat oven to 180°C. Grease and line a baking tray.

Lay a sheet of pastry on the tray and spread the combined fruit evenly across it. Sprinkle with the sherry.

Place remaining sheet of pastry over the top, and press down to remove any trapped air. Press edges of pastry together with a fork to seal.

Prick pastry all over with a fork, then brush with egg and sprinkle with sugar.

Bake for about 10 minutes, then reduce the temperature to 160°C and cook for a further 20 minutes, or until golden brown.

When cool, cut into squares.

MAKES 16

Strawberry muffins

3 cups plain flour

½ cup castor sugar

½ cup soft brown sugar

1 tablespoon baking powder

125 g butter, melted and
   cooled slightly

3 eggs

1 cup milk

1½ cups chopped
   strawberries

icing sugar, for dusting

Preheat oven to 200°C. Brush oil onto bottoms of muffin tins only.

In a large bowl sift together flour, sugars and baking powder.

In a separate bowl mix together butter, eggs and milk.

Add egg mixture to dry ingredients, then fold in berries.

Spoon batter into prepared tins and bake for 20 minutes.

Serve hot, dusted with icing sugar.

VARIATION
Allow muffins to cool and serve with whipped cream and fresh strawberries.

MAKES 30

Strawberry rhubarb muffins

1 cup rolled oats

1 cup strawberry yoghurt

125 g butter, melted

½ cup soft brown sugar

1 egg

1 cup plain flour

½ teaspoon salt

1 teaspoon baking powder

½ teaspoon bicarbonate
of soda

1 teaspoon ground
cinnamon

¾ cup bran

¾ cup finely chopped
rhubarb

½ cup strawberry jam

Preheat oven to 190°C. Grease muffin tins.

Soak rolled oats in strawberry yoghurt for 5 minutes.

Stir melted butter and brown sugar into yoghurt.

Lightly beat egg and add to yoghurt mixture.

Sift together flour, salt, baking powder, bicarbonate
of soda and cinnamon and add with bran to yoghurt
mixture. Stir until dry ingredients are just moistened.

Fold in chopped rhubarb and strawberry jam.

Three-quarters fill prepared muffin tins and bake
for 15–20 minutes.

MAKES 12–16

Strawberry shortcake

1½ cups self-raising flour

½ teaspoon baking powder

good pinch of salt

75 g softened butter

½ cup castor sugar

1 egg, beaten

¼ cup buttermilk

250 g strawberries, hulled, halved and mixed with 1 dessertspoon castor sugar

200 ml cream

icing sugar, for dusting

Preheat oven to 190°C. Lightly grease two 20-cm round cake tins and line the bases with non-stick baking paper.

For pastry, combine the sifted flour, baking powder and salt in a large mixing bowl. Add the butter and rub in until the mixture resembles coarse breadcrumbs. Mix in the sugar and the egg.

Stir in enough buttermilk to form a soft dough.

Divide dough into two pieces and, with floured hands, press lightly into the tins.

Bake for 20–25 minutes or until firm and lightly browned. Turn out onto a wire rack to cool.

Fill pastry with strawberries and whipped cream, and dust with icing sugar.

Strawberry yoghurt muffins

1¾ cups wholemeal
   self-raising flour

½ cup castor sugar

2 eggs, beaten

60 g butter, melted and
   cooled slightly

⅔ cup milk

⅓ cup strawberry yoghurt

desiccated coconut,
   for sprinkling

Preheat oven to 190°C. Grease muffin tin.

In a large bowl sift together flour and sugar.

In a separate bowl mix together eggs, butter and milk.

Add milk mixture to dry ingredients and stir until just combined.

Spoon batter into prepared muffin tin and bake for 15–20 minutes.

Allow to cool, then slice off tops and cut each top in half. Drop a teaspoonful of yoghurt onto cut surface of muffin and push straight edges of tops into yoghurt. Sprinkle with coconut.

MAKES 12

Streusel pumpkin cake

60 g softened butter

⅓ cup castor sugar

⅓ cup mashed pumpkin

¼ cup sour cream

1 egg, lightly beaten

1¼ cups plain flour

¼ teaspoon ground nutmeg

1 tablespoon baking powder

½ teaspoon bicarbonate
   of soda

⅓ cup orange juice

2 teaspoons finely grated
   orange zest

TOPPING

¼ cup soft brown sugar

45 g cold butter, cut into
   small pieces

2 tablespoons plain flour

½ teaspoon ground
   cinnamon

⅓ cup pecans, roughly
   chopped

Preheat oven to 180°C. Lightly grease a 22-cm round springform cake tin and line the base with non-stick baking paper.

Beat the butter, sugar, pumpkin, sour cream and egg until well combined.

Sift the flour, nutmeg, baking powder and bicarbonate of soda into another bowl. Make a well in the centre and stir in the pumpkin mixture and orange juice, alternating between the two, until well combined. Stir in the grated orange zest.

Pour the batter into the prepared tin.

Combine the streusel topping ingredients in a bowl until the mixture resembles coarse breadcrumbs. Sprinkle the mixture over the cake batter.

Bake for 45 minutes or until firm and cooked through. Cool in the tin and then turn out onto a wire rack.

Serve warm or cold with cream or yoghurt.

Sugared Brazil bars

BASE

60 g cold butter, cut into
    small pieces

1 cup plain flour

FILLING

¼ cup soft brown sugar

2 eggs, beaten

1 cup Brazil nuts, finely
    chopped

½ cup desiccated coconut

1 teaspoon vanilla extract

TOPPING

185 g dark cooking
    chocolate, chopped

⅓ cup golden syrup

1 tablespoon water

½ cup Brazil nuts, finely
    chopped

Preheat oven to 180°C. Lightly grease a 23-cm square cake tin.

For the base, rub butter into sifted flour with your fingertips until crumbly. Press into tin and bake for 15 minutes. Remove. (Leave oven on.)

For the filling, beat sugar and eggs until frothy, then mix in nuts, coconut and vanilla. Spread filling over base and bake for a further 15 minutes. Set aside to cool in the tin.

For the topping, melt chocolate in a double boiler over simmering water, or on MEDIUM in the microwave. Add golden syrup and water and blend well.

Spread over the slice and sprinkle with remaining nuts. Let stand until firm, then cut into bars.

MAKES 24

Sultana Bran muffins

1⅓ cups plain flour

1½ tablespoons baking powder

¼ teaspoon salt

½ teaspoon ground cinnamon

1⅓ cups milk

3 cups Sultana Bran

2 eggs, well beaten

60 g butter, melted

½ cup honey

Preheat oven to 200°C. Grease muffin tins.

Sift together flour, baking powder, salt and cinnamon.

Pour milk over Sultana Bran, stir, and let stand 5 minutes.

Stir eggs, melted butter and honey into Sultana Bran mixture.

Add dry ingredients and stir just until moistened.

Spoon batter into prepared muffin tins.

Bake for 20 minutes.

MAKES 12

Sultana choc-chip biscuits

125 g softened butter

1½ cups soft brown sugar

½ teaspoon vanilla extract

1 egg, beaten

1¾ cups self-raising flour

½ cup sultanas

½ cup chocolate chips

Preheat oven to 180°C. Lightly grease baking trays.

Cream butter, sugar and vanilla until light and fluffy. Beat in egg, then stir in sifted flour, sultanas and chocolate chips to form a stiff dough.

Roll dough into small balls and place on baking trays. Flatten slightly with a fork.

Bake for 15–20 minutes, until lightly browned.

MAKES 36

Sultana lunch cake

350 g sultanas

225 g softened butter

1 cup castor sugar

3 eggs

3⅓ cups plain flour

3 teaspoons baking powder

½ teaspoon salt

½ cup milk

Preheat oven to 180°C. Lightly grease a 20-cm cake tin and line the bottom with non-stick baking paper.

Cover sultanas with water and boil for 10 minutes. Strain and cool.

Cream butter and sugar until light and fluffy, then add eggs one at a time, beating well.

Add sultanas, sifted flour, baking powder and salt. Stir in milk.

Pour into prepared tin and bake for 90 minutes, or until a skewer inserted into the centre of the cake comes out clean.

Sultana & pineapple muffins

1 × 450-g tin crushed
   pineapple

1 cup sultanas

1 cup castor sugar

125 g butter

1 teaspoon mixed spice

¼ teaspoon salt

2 eggs

2 cups plain flour

1½ teaspoons baking powder

icing sugar, for dusting

Preheat oven to 180°C. Grease muffin tins.

Tip crushed pineapple into a saucepan and add sultanas, sugar, butter, mixed spice and salt. Bring to the boil, stirring, until butter melts. Simmer for 5 minutes, then allow to cool slightly.

Beat in eggs.

Sift together flour and baking powder and add to pineapple mixture. Stir to combine.

Spoon batter into prepared muffin tins and bake for 15–20 minutes.

Serve dusted with icing sugar.

VARIATION
If desired, fill with whipped cream mixed with drained crushed pineapple.

MAKES 16

Sultana sesame muffins

2 cups plain flour

¼ cup castor sugar

1 tablespoon baking powder

1 teaspoon salt (optional)

½ teaspoon ground ginger

¼ teaspoon ground
  cinnamon

¾ cup chopped sultanas

1 egg

1 cup milk

80 g butter, melted

TOPPING

1 tablespoon sesame seeds

1 tablespoon soft brown
  sugar

pinch of ground ginger

Preheat oven to 220°C. Grease muffin tins.

Sift together flour, sugar, baking powder, salt, ginger and cinnamon. Add sultanas and mix well.

In a small bowl, beat egg and add milk and melted butter. Stir into flour mixture until just combined.

Three-quarters fill prepared muffin tins.

For topping, combine sesame seeds, brown sugar and ginger and sprinkle over muffins.

Bake for 20–25 minutes.

MAKES 16

Sultana slice

125 g butter

1 cup soft brown sugar

1 egg, beaten

2 cups sultanas

1½ cups self-raising flour

Preheat oven to 190°C. Lightly grease and line a 20-cm × 30-cm lamington tin.

Melt the butter in a saucepan, then add sugar and stir until dissolved. Remove from heat and cool for a few minutes so egg doesn't scramble when added.

Mix in egg, sultanas and sifted flour. Mix thoroughly.

Press into prepared tin and bake for 20 minutes, or until a golden crust has formed.

Cool before cutting into squares or bars.

MAKES 24

Sun-dried tomato & herb muffins

1 cup plain flour

¼ teaspoon salt

1 tablespoon baking powder

1 egg, beaten

2 tablespoons chopped
    fresh herbs

1½ cups grated tasty cheese

½ cup sun-dried tomatoes,
    chopped

Preheat oven to 200°C. Grease muffin tins.

Sift together flour, salt and baking powder.

Make egg up to 1 cup with water and mix with flour
and remaining ingredients until just combined.

Three-quarters fill prepared muffin tins and bake for
12–15 minutes.

MAKES 12

Sweet potato & walnut muffins

¾ cup milk

2 eggs

¼ cup honey

2 tablespoons vegetable oil

1 cup mashed sweet potato

2 cups wholemeal plain flour

2 teaspoons baking powder

½ teaspoon salt

1 teaspoon ground cinnamon

½ cup chopped walnuts

Preheat oven to 200°C. Grease muffin tins.

Beat milk, eggs, honey and oil in large bowl. Stir in sweet potato.

Sift together flour, baking powder, salt and cinnamon and stir into sweet potato mixture. Add walnuts.

Spoon mixture into prepared muffin tins.

Bake for 20 minutes or until a skewer inserted comes out clean.

MAKES 16

Sweet sesame biscuits

¾ cup self-raising flour

1¼ cups plain flour

¼ teaspoon salt

185 g cold butter, cut into
    small pieces

¾ cup castor sugar

1 egg yolk

1 teaspoon vanilla extract

1 tablespoon milk

125 g toasted sesame seeds,
    for coating

Preheat oven to 180°C. Lightly grease baking trays.

Sift together flours and salt, then rub in butter with
your fingertips until crumbly.

Add sugar, egg yolk, vanilla and milk and mix to form
a soft dough.

Roll teaspoonfuls of mixture into balls about 2 cm
in diameter. Roll balls in sesame seeds to coat, place
on baking trays and press down gently with the back
of a spoon.

Bake for 12–15 minutes or until golden.

MAKES 48

Swiss lemon slice

1 cup self-raising flour

1 cup desiccated coconut

115 g butter, melted

⅓ cup soft brown sugar

lemon glacé icing
   (page 679)

Preheat oven to 180°C. Lightly grease and line a 19-cm × 29-cm slice tin.

Sift self-raising flour, then mix with coconut, butter and sugar.

Press into the tin. Bake for 15 minutes. When cold, ice with lemon icing.

MAKES 24

Sydney specials

125 g butter, melted

1 cup soft brown sugar

1 cup desiccated coconut

2 cups rolled oats

Preheat oven to 180°C. Lightly grease a 23-cm square slab tin.

Mix all ingredients together until well combined. Press into the tin.

Bake for 20 minutes or until golden brown. Cut into slices or squares while still warm.

MAKES 24

Syd's lamingtons

150 g softened butter

⅔ cup castor sugar

2 eggs

⅓ cup vanilla extract

⅓ cup milk

275 g self-raising flour

2½ cups desiccated coconut,
  for coating

ICING

3 tablespoons cocoa

3 tablespoons drinking
  chocolate powder

¼ cup water

3 tablespoons castor sugar

30 g butter

Preheat oven to 180°C. Lightly grease and line a 25-cm × 20-cm lamington tin.

Cream the butter and sugar until light and fluffy.

In another bowl, beat the eggs, vanilla extract and milk. Slowly beat this mixture into the butter mixture.

Fold in the sifted flour and add more milk if necessary to form a smooth batter.

Pour into the prepared tin and bake for 30 minutes or until golden. Cool for 5 minutes before turning out onto a wire rack to cool completely.

Meanwhile, stir all the icing ingredients in a saucepan over a gentle heat for 5–6 minutes, until the mixture is smooth and glossy. Remove and cool a little.

When the cake is completely cold, cut into twenty squares. Using tongs or piercing the cake with a metal skewer, dip each square into the icing to completely cover it, then roll in the coconut to coat.

MAKES 20

Tabitha's royal slice

BASE

1 cup plain flour

1 cup self-raising flour

125 g cold butter, cut into
  small pieces

½ cup white sugar

1 egg, beaten

½ teaspoon vanilla extract

FILLING

1 cup water

2 dessertspoons gelatine

1 cup white sugar

pinch of cream of tartar

few drops red food
  colouring

TOPPING

250 g white vegetable
  shortening

1 cup drinking chocolate
  powder

Preheat oven to 180°C. Lightly grease and line a 19-cm × 29-cm slice tin.

For the base, sift flours together, then rub in butter with your fingertips until crumbly. Add sugar, egg and vanilla and mix to a firm dough.

Press into tin and bake for about 20 minutes, or until golden. Allow to cool.

For the marshmallow filling, pour water into a saucepan and sprinkle over gelatine. Leave to soak for a few minutes. Add sugar and bring to boil. Reduce heat and simmer for 10 minutes.

Add cream of tartar and mix. Remove from heat. When liquid is cool, add a few drops of food colouring and beat with an electric mixer until thick and pink. Pour over base and leave to set.

For the topping, melt vegetable shortening in a double boiler over simmering water or on MEDIUM in the microwave, then mix in drinking chocolate.

Pour topping over marshmallow layer. Leave to cool. Cut into squares once completely set.

MAKES 36

Tamarillo nut cake

100 g softened butter

¾ cup castor sugar

2 eggs, beaten

¾ cup drained cooked
   tamarillos

1½ cups plain flour

½ teaspoon bicarbonate
   of soda

pinch of ground nutmeg

1 teaspoon ground
   cinnamon

¼ cup chopped walnuts,
   plus extra for decorating

½ cup sultanas

ICING

1 cup icing sugar

1 tablespoon lemon juice

1–2 tablespoons water

Preheat oven to 180°C. Lightly grease and flour an 18-cm ring tin.

In a large bowl cream butter and sugar until light and fluffy. Add eggs and combine well.

Finely chop cooked tamarillos and add to creamed mixture alternately with sifted dry ingredients.

Fold in chopped walnuts and sultanas.

Pour into prepared tin and bake for 75 minutes or until a skewer inserted into the centre of the cake comes out clean.

Allow to cool in tin.

Combine icing ingredients and drizzle over cake. Decorate top with walnuts.

NOTE
To cook tamarillos, peel, chop and stew gently until soft.

Tamarillo & spice muffins

2 cups plain flour

½ cup castor sugar

2½ teaspoons baking
powder

2 teaspoons mixed spice

1 egg, beaten

½ cup milk

100 g butter, melted and
cooled slightly

4 tamarillos, peeled
and chopped

Preheat oven to 200°C. Grease muffin tins.

In a large bowl sift together flour, sugar, baking powder
and mixed spice.

In a separate bowl mix together egg, milk and butter.

Add milk mixture and tamarillos to dry ingredients and
stir to just combine.

Spoon batter into prepared muffin tins and bake for
20 minutes.

If desired, serve filled with sweetened whipped cream
into which chopped tamarillo has been folded.

MAKES 16

Tapenade & olive muffins

1 cup plain flour

1 tablespoon baking powder

¼ teaspoon salt

1 egg, beaten

½ cup tapenade

½ cup grated tasty cheese

1 cup pitted green olives

Preheat oven to 200°C. Grease muffin tins.

Sift together flour, baking powder and salt.

Make egg up to 1 cup with water. Add tapenade, then stir in flour mixture and remaining ingredients until just combined.

Three-quarters fill prepared muffin tins and bake for 12–15 minutes.

MAKES 12

Tell my fortune cookies

3 egg whites

½ cup icing sugar

45 g unsalted butter, melted

½ cup plain flour

¼ teaspoon almond essence

strips of non-toxic paper
with fortunes written
on them

Preheat oven to 180°C. Cut a sheet of baking paper to fit your baking tray, then draw three 8-cm circles onto the paper. Place the sheet upside-down on the tray.

Beat egg whites until frothy. Add the sifted icing sugar and butter and stir until smooth. Stir in the sifted flour and then add the almond essence. Set mixture aside for 15 minutes.

Using a spatula, spread 1½ teaspoons of the mixture evenly into each circle. Bake for 5 minutes or until starting to colour around the edges.

Remove cookies from the tray one at a time, using a spatula. While still warm, place a fortune in the centre of each cookie. Bring sides up to meet in the middle and press to seal, then bend into a crescent shape.

Pack each cookie into a muffin tray hole or a small glass until set and cold (this will help them keep their shape). Repeat until all mixture is used up.

(You can't bake too many of these cookies at once, as they must be hot in order to be shaped. Prepare the next tray while the previous one is cooking.)

MAKES 20

Toasted pine nut muffins

2 cups plain flour

1 tablespoon baking powder

1 egg

¼ cup water

1 cup natural yoghurt

50 g butter, melted

2 tablespoons honey, plus
   extra for pouring

90 g ground almonds

⅓ cup castor sugar

¾ cup pine nuts, toasted

Preheat oven to 190°C. Grease muffin tins.

Sift flour and baking powder into a large bowl.
Add remaining ingredients and mix until just combined.

Spoon into prepared muffin tins and bake for
15–20 minutes.

To serve, pour a little warmed honey over each muffin
while still hot.

MAKES 16

Toffee crackle fruit slice

BASE

125 g softened butter

½ cup white sugar

1 teaspoon vanilla extract

1 egg yolk

1½ cups plain flour

FILLING

1 × 375-g packet mixed
 dried fruit

60 g glacé cherries

2 tablespoons plain flour

1 egg

2 tablespoons soft brown
 sugar

1 teaspoon vanilla extract

1 tablespoon brandy

TOPPING

1 cup white sugar

½ cup water

1 tablespoon butter

Preheat oven to 180°C. Lightly grease and line a
19-cm × 29-cm slice tin.

For the base, cream butter, sugar and vanilla until light
and fluffy. Add egg yolk and beat well. Add sifted flour
and beat until well combined.

Spread mixture into tin and bake for about 15 minutes,
or until golden. Set aside to cool a little. (Leave oven on.)

For the filling, combine the dried fruit, cherries and sifted
flour. In a separate bowl, beat together the egg, sugar,
vanilla and brandy. Add egg mixture to fruit mixture and
combine thoroughly.

Spread filling over base. Return to oven and bake for
20 minutes.

For the toffee topping, combine sugar and water in
saucepan. Stir over low heat until sugar has dissolved,
then bring to the boil. Continue boiling gently, without
stirring, until it turns a light toffee colour. Remove from
heat, add butter and swirl pan until butter has melted.

While slice is still hot, pour toffee evenly over the top.
Leave to set slightly, then score squares with a sharp
knife. Cool in the tin before cutting into squares.

MAKES 36

Toffee muffins

1¼ cups castor sugar

½ cup water

⅓ cup vegetable oil

1 egg

¾ cup milk

1¾ cups plain flour

1½ teaspoons baking powder

Preheat oven to 190°C. Grease a sheet of aluminium foil and place on a baking tray or chopping board. Grease muffin tins.

Gently boil ½ cup of the sugar with water until mixture turns golden brown.

Pour onto greased aluminium foil and leave to set.

Once set, break toffee into small pieces. Reserve some larger pieces for decorating cooked muffins.

Whisk together oil, remaining sugar, egg and milk.

Add toffee, sifted flour and baking powder and mix until just combined.

Spoon into prepared muffin tins and bake for about 20 minutes.

MAKES 12–14

Toffee walnut muffins

1¼ cups castor sugar

½ cup water

⅓ cup vegetable oil

1 egg

¾ cup milk

2¼ cups plain flour

1½ teaspoons baking powder

1 cup walnut pieces

12 walnut halves, for
  decorating

Preheat oven to 190°C. Grease a sheet of aluminium foil and place on a baking tray or chopping board. Grease muffin tins.

Gently boil ½ cup of the sugar with water until mixture turns golden brown.

Pour onto greased aluminium foil and leave to set.

Once set, break toffee into small pieces.

Whisk together oil, remaining sugar, egg and milk.

Add toffee, sifted flour, baking powder and walnut pieces, mixing until just combined.

Three-quarters fill prepared muffin tins and put a walnut half on top of each.

Bake for 20 minutes.

MAKES 16–18

Tomato, cheese & oregano muffins

1½ cups self-raising flour

1 egg

¾ cup water

1 cup grated cheddar cheese

¼ cup grated parmesan
   cheese

1 tablespoon chopped fresh
   oregano (or 1 teaspoon
   dried oregano)

3 tomatoes, seeded and
   chopped

Preheat oven to 190°C. Grease muffin tins.

Mix sifted flour with remaining ingredients until just
combined.

Spoon into prepared muffin tins and bake for 15 minutes.

MAKES 12

Tomato cheese squares

BASE

75 g butter, melted

150 g wholemeal
   breadcrumbs

FILLING

125 g baby spinach leaves

100 g feta, crumbled

100 g mozzarella, diced

12 sun-dried tomatoes,
   chopped

3 eggs, beaten

1 × 375-g tin evaporated
   milk

2 tablespoons chopped
   fresh basil

salt and freshly ground
   black pepper

Preheat oven to 200°C. Lightly grease and line a deep
19-cm × 29-cm slice tin.

For the base, mix melted butter and breadcrumbs and
press into the base of the tin. Bake for 15 minutes.
Set aside to cool.

For the filling, cover the cooled base with a layer
of spinach leaves, then sprinkle over half the cheese
and sun-dried tomatoes. Cover with remaining spinach,
then remaining cheese and tomato.

Beat the eggs with the evaporated milk and basil and
season well with salt and pepper. Pour over slice.

Bake for 20 minutes, then reduce heat to 180°C and
cook for a further 30 minutes or until set and golden.

MAKES 36

Traditional baked cheesecake

BASE

50 g rolled oats

100 g sweet biscuit crumbs

75 g butter, melted

FILLING

3 eggs, separated

⅔ cup castor sugar

300 g cream cheese

1 tablespoon plain flour

grated zest and juice
   of 1 lemon

50 g sultanas

100 ml sour cream

Preheat oven to 170°C. Lightly grease a 20-cm springform cake tin and line the base with non-stick baking paper.

Combine the base ingredients and press into the base of the prepared tin. Refrigerate while you make the filling.

Whisk the egg yolks together with the sugar until thick and creamy.

Beat in the cream cheese, sifted flour, zest and juice. Fold in the sultanas and the sour cream.

Whip the egg whites until stiff and then carefully fold them through the egg-yolk mixture.

Pour into the prepared tin and bake for 60 minutes or until firm to the touch.

Cool completely before serving with orange segments and chopped strawberries.

Treacle, prune & walnut loaf

175 g self-raising flour

175 g wholemeal plain flour

½ teaspoon salt

½ teaspoon bicarbonate
of soda

50 g walnuts, roughly
chopped

75 g pitted prunes,
roughly chopped

275 ml buttermilk

2 tablespoons treacle

Preheat oven to 200°C. Lightly grease and line a 25-cm × 15-cm loaf tin.

Sift the flours into a mixing bowl with the salt and bicarbonate of soda. Mix in the chopped walnuts and prunes.

Warm the buttermilk in a saucepan and stir in the treacle until it has dissolved. Make a well in the centre of the flour mixture and stir in the buttermilk mixture. Fold quickly to make a soft dough.

Pour into the prepared tin and bake for 30–35 minutes or until firm and cooked through. Cool in the tin and then turn out onto a wire rack.

This loaf is delicious served with cheddar cheese or a salty blue cheese.

Treacle snaps

185 g softened butter

1 cup white sugar, plus extra
    for coating

¼ cup treacle

1 egg

2 cups plain flour

pinch of salt

1 teaspoon bicarbonate
    of soda

1 teaspoon ground
    cinnamon

1 teaspoon ground cloves

1 teaspoon ground ginger

Cream butter, sugar and treacle until light and fluffy. Beat in the egg.

In a separate bowl, sift together flour, salt, bicarbonate of soda and spices. Add to creamed mixture and beat until combined. Chill for 1 hour.

Preheat oven to 190°C. Lightly grease baking trays.

Roll spoonfuls of mixture into balls 2.5 cm in diameter, then roll in sugar to coat.

Place on trays and bake for about 10 minutes, or until lightly browned.

Cool on trays for 5 minutes, then transfer to a wire rack.

MAKES 40

Tuna lunchbox slice

½ cup olive oil

675 g potatoes, diced

2 bay leaves

1 onion, chopped

2 cloves garlic, crushed

1 cup frozen peas

1 red capsicum, diced

salt and black pepper

2 teaspoons ground paprika

1 × 425-g tin tuna, drained

½ × 400-g tin whole peeled
tomatoes

1 cup white wine

handful fresh parsley,
chopped

500 g frozen shortcrust
pastry sheets

milk, for brushing

Heat oil in a large frying pan and stir-fry potatoes and bay leaves for 5 minutes. Add onion and garlic and cook for 5 minutes. Add peas and capsicum and cook for 5 minutes. Season with salt, pepper and paprika.

Add tuna, tomatoes, wine and parsley, and simmer until most of the liquid has evaporated. Remove bay leaves and set aside to cool.

Preheat oven to 200°C. Lightly grease a large shallow baking tin.

Cut pastry sheets to cover base and sides of tin. Pour in tuna mix. Moisten pastry edges and cover filling with more pastry, pressing the top and bottom edges together with a fork to seal. Brush the top with milk and bake until golden brown.

Cut into squares and eat hot or cold.

MAKES 16

Turkish fig & chocolate cake

¾ cup chopped dried figs

½ cup brandy

120 g softened butter

⅔ cup castor sugar

3 eggs

125 g dark cooking
  chocolate, chopped

1½ cups roasted hazelnuts,
  finely chopped

¼ cup dried breadcrumbs

TOPPING

⅓ cup castor sugar

100 g milk chocolate,
  chopped

½ cup cream

Preheat oven to 160°C. Lightly grease a 23-cm springform tin and line the base with non-stick baking paper.

Combine figs and brandy in a saucepan and boil until brandy has evaporated. Allow to cool.

Cream butter and sugar until light and fluffy, add eggs and beat well. Add figs and brandy. (Don't worry if this mixture looks curdled.)

Melt chocolate in a double boiler over simmering water or on MEDIUM in the microwave. Stir nuts, melted chocolate and breadcrumbs into fig mixture.

Pour into prepared tin and bake for 60–75 minutes. Allow to cool on a wire rack.

To make topping, heat sugar in saucepan until brown. Add chocolate and heat gently until melted – don't boil. Remove from heat, add cream and mix well. Allow mixture to cool to room temperature before icing – it will thicken as it cools.

Upside-down caramel banana pudding

310 g butter

1¾ cups soft brown sugar

3 large ripe bananas, thinly
sliced

40 g walnut halves

1⅓ cups self-raising flour

2 teaspoons baking powder

50 g chopped walnuts

¼ cup milk

Preheat oven to 180°C. Lightly grease a 2-litre shallow ovenproof dish or cake tin.

Melt 60 g of the butter and ¼ cup of the sugar in a saucepan over a low heat. Spread over the base and sides of the prepared dish and lay the banana slices over the top. Place the walnut halves into any gaps.

Blend the remaining ingredients together in a food processor or using an electric mixer.

Spread the mixture over the bananas and bake for 50 minutes or until the pudding is cooked through and golden brown on top. Run a knife around the edges and turn out onto a hot dish.

Serve warm or cold.

SERVES 6

Upside-down rhubarb muffins

60 g butter, melted

1 cup finely chopped
   rhubarb

½ cup soft brown sugar

80 g softened butter

⅓ cup castor sugar

1 egg

1½ cups plain flour

2 teaspoons baking powder

½ teaspoon salt

½ teaspoon ground nutmeg

½ cup milk

Preheat oven to 190°C. Grease muffin tins.

Combine melted butter, rhubarb and brown sugar in a small bowl and mix well.

Spread evenly into prepared muffin tins.

Beat together softened butter, castor sugar and egg until fluffy.

Sift together flour, baking powder, salt and nutmeg and add to creamed mixture alternately with milk.

Stir to just moisten, then spoon on top of rhubarb mixture.

Bake for 20–25 minutes.

Invert onto a serving plate and leave tin over muffins for a few minutes so all the rhubarb sauce runs out. Serve warm.

MAKES 12

Vanilla butter drops

185 g softened butter

1¼ cups white sugar

1 teaspoon vanilla extract

2 eggs, beaten

3 cups plain flour

3 teaspoons baking powder

¾ teaspoon salt

⅔ cup milk

Preheat oven to 180°C. Lightly grease baking trays.

Cream butter and sugar until light and fluffy. Add vanilla, then gradually beat in eggs.

In a separate bowl, sift together flour, baking powder and salt. Gradually fold into the creamed mixture, alternately with the milk.

Drop teaspoonfuls of mixture onto prepared trays. Bake for about 15 minutes or until pale golden.

VARIATIONS
For chocolate drops, add 60 g melted chocolate when you add the vanilla. For cherry drops, add ⅓ cup chopped glacé cherries with the flour and milk. For nut drops, add ½ cup chopped nuts (almonds, walnuts or pecans) with the flour and milk. For orange drops, add 2 teaspoons finely grated orange zest with the flour, and replace milk with orange juice.

MAKES 60

Vanilla & coconut muffins

1 cup plain flour

1¾ teaspoons baking
   powder

3 tablespoons soft brown
   sugar

1 cup desiccated coconut,
   plus extra for sprinkling

40 g butter, melted and
   cooled slightly

½ cup milk

1 egg

½ teaspoon vanilla extract

ICING

2 cups icing sugar

1 teaspoon vanilla extract

1 tablespoon butter

milk, to mix

Preheat oven to 190°C. Grease muffin tins.

In a large bowl sift together flour, baking powder
and brown sugar. Stir in coconut.

In a separate bowl mix together butter, milk, egg
and vanilla.

Make a well in the centre of the dry ingredients
and add milk mixture. Stir to just combine.

Spoon batter into prepared muffin tins and bake for
10–15 minutes.

To make vanilla icing, mix sifted icing sugar with
remaining ingredients, adding enough milk to create
desired consistency.

Top muffins with vanilla icing and sprinkle with coconut.

MAKES 12

Vanilla poppy seed muffins

150 g softened butter

¾ cup castor sugar

1½ cups plain flour

1 teaspoon baking powder

1 teaspoon bicarbonate
of soda

1 egg, beaten

150 g vanilla yoghurt

1 teaspoon vanilla extract

3 tablespoons poppy seeds

Preheat oven to 160°C. Grease muffin tins.

Cream butter and sugar until light and fluffy.

In a separate bowl, sift together flour, baking powder and bicarbonate of soda. Add to creamed mixture with remaining ingredients and stir until just combined.

Spoon into prepared tins and bake for 15–20 minutes.

MAKES 12

Vintage Victoria sponge cake with cream & jam

225 g softened butter

1 cup castor sugar

4 eggs

1½ cups self-raising flour

2 teaspoons baking powder

¼ cup strawberry or
  raspberry jam

150 ml cream

icing sugar, for dusting

Preheat oven to 180°C. Lightly grease two 20-cm sandwich cake tins and line the bases with non-stick baking paper.

Combine the butter, sugar, eggs, sifted flour and baking powder and beat until well blended and thoroughly mixed to a creamy batter. Divide the mixture between the two cake tins.

Bake for 25–30 minutes or until lightly browned and cooked through.

Cool in the tins for 10 minutes. Turn out onto a wire rack to cool completely.

Once cold, fill with jam and whipped cream and dust with icing sugar.

Walnut fudge cake

¾ cup soft brown sugar

150 g butter

100 g dark cooking
  chocolate, chopped

½ cup condensed milk

2 cups chopped walnuts

¾ cup self-raising flour

¼ cup milk

1 egg, lightly beaten

icing sugar, for dusting

Preheat oven to 180°C. Lightly grease a 20-cm round cake tin and line the base with non-stick baking paper.

Heat the sugar, butter, chocolate, condensed milk and walnuts in a saucepan over low heat. Stir until the mixture has thickened and the sugar has dissolved.

Remove from the heat and cool a little. Pour into a mixing bowl. Stir in the sifted flour, milk and egg until well combined. Spoon into the prepared tin and smooth the top.

Bake for 30–40 minutes or until cooked through but still moist in the middle. Cool in the tin before cutting and dusting with icing sugar.

Serve with ice-cream.

Walnut Victoria sandwich

175 g softened butter

¾ cup castor sugar

3 eggs, beaten

175 g self-raising flour

pinch of salt

2 tablespoons warm water

jam, for filling

glacé icing (page 679)

walnuts, for decorating

Preheat oven to 190°C. Lightly grease and line two 18-cm sandwich tins.

Cream butter and sugar until light and fluffy. Beat in eggs, one at a time.

Sift flour and salt. Stir 1 tablespoon of flour into butter mixture until well mixed. Gradually beat in remaining flour. Add enough water to give a soft dropping consistency.

Pour into prepared tins and bake for 20 minutes, or until well risen and golden. Turn out onto a wire rack to cool.

Fill with jam. Ice with glacé icing and decorate with walnuts.

Walnut whiteys

225 g white cooking
  chocolate

75 g butter

200 ml condensed milk

3 eggs, separated

1⅓ cups self-raising flour

100 g chocolate-chip
  biscuits, crushed

100 g walnuts, roughly
  chopped

225 g white chocolate
  buttons

Preheat oven to 180°C. Lightly grease and line a
25-cm × 31-cm slice tin.

Melt the white chocolate with the butter in a double
boiler over simmering water, or on MEDIUM in the
microwave. Set aside to cool.

In a large bowl, combine the condensed milk, egg yolks,
sifted flour, biscuit crumbs, nuts and chocolate buttons.
Add the melted chocolate and mix well.

Whisk the egg whites until soft peaks form, then gently
fold into the mixture.

Pour into prepared tin and bake for 30 minutes or until
risen and golden. Cool on a wire rack before cutting into
squares.

MAKES 20

Warm upside-down ricotta cakes with Melba sauce

BASE

1 cup sweet biscuit crumbs

3 tablespoons softened
  butter

CAKE

¼ cup cream cheese

1 cup ricotta

½ teaspoon vanilla extract

½ teaspoon almond essence

2 eggs, lightly beaten

3 tablespoons castor sugar

SAUCE

300 g tinned or frozen
  raspberries

2 tablespoons redcurrant
  jelly

½ tablespoon icing sugar

1 tablespoon arrowroot,
  mixed with 1 tablespoon
  cold water

Preheat oven to 180°C. Lightly grease a six-cup jumbo
muffin tin.

For the bases, combine the biscuit crumbs and butter
and press into the bases of the muffin cups.

Beat all the cake ingredients until smooth. Spoon evenly
into the muffin cups. Bake for 15–20 minutes or until set.
Cool for 10 minutes before turning out.

To make Melba sauce, rub the raspberries through a
sieve to remove all the seeds. Place in a saucepan and
add the redcurrant jelly and icing sugar. Slowly bring
to the boil and then turn the heat down and stir in the
arrowroot. Continue stirring until the sauce has thickened
(2–3 minutes).

Serve cakes upside down, drizzled with Melba sauce.

MAKES 6

Whisked sponge cake with coffee icing

3 eggs

125 g castor sugar

85 g self-raising flour

½ cup chocolate-coated coffee beans, for decorating

ICING

2 cups icing sugar

200 g softened butter

2 teaspoons instant coffee granules dissolved in 2 tablespoons boiling water

Preheat oven to 190°C. Lightly grease a 20-cm round cake tin and line the base with non-stick baking paper.

Whisk the eggs and sugar until pale and thick. Sift the flour into the mixture and carefully fold through.

Pour into the cake tin and bake for 30–35 minutes or until firm and cooked through.

Turn out onto a wire rack to cool. When cold, cut in half horizontally using a long bread knife.

To make icing, place icing sugar in a food processor and pulse to remove any lumps. Add butter and coffee and process until smooth.

Using a palette knife, carefully spread about one-third of the icing as a filling for the cake. Spread the rest of the icing to cover the whole cake.

Decorate the top and sides with chocolate-coated coffee beans.

Whisky raisin muffins

1 cup raisins

¼ cup whisky

2 cups plain flour

2 tablespoons honey

1 cup natural yoghurt

¼ cup milk

50 g butter, melted

1 egg

2 teaspoons baking powder

⅓ cup castor sugar

Gently heat raisins and whisky, then leave to soak for at least an hour.

Preheat oven to 180°C. Grease muffin tins.

Add sifted flour and remaining ingredients to raisins and mix until just combined.

Spoon into prepared muffin tins and bake for 15–20 minutes.

MAKES 16

White chocolate button biscuits

100 g softened butter

½ cup castor sugar

1 cup soft brown sugar

1 egg

1 teaspoon vanilla extract

1½ cups plain flour

½ teaspoon baking powder

pinch of salt

175 g white chocolate buttons

Preheat oven to 190°C. Line baking trays with baking paper.

Cream butter and sugars until light and fluffy. Whisk together the egg and vanilla and beat into the creamed mixture.

In a separate bowl, sift together the flour, baking powder and salt. Add to the creamed mixture and combine well.

Place chocolate buttons in a plastic bag and break into small pieces using a rolling pin or mallet. Stir chocolate into the dough.

Roll dough into walnut-sized balls. Place onto trays, leaving plenty of space for spreading.

Bake for 10–12 minutes.

MAKES 36

White Christmas

1 cup powdered milk

1 cup icing sugar

1 cup Rice Bubbles

1 cup mixed dried fruit

250 g white vegetable
   shortening, melted

2 teaspoons vanilla extract

Lightly grease a 23-cm square slab tin.

Sift together powdered milk and icing sugar. Mix in Rice Bubbles and dried fruit. Add vegetable shortening and mix well, then stir in vanilla.

Pour into tin. Chill in refrigerator until firm, then cut into small squares.

MAKES 36 | NO BAKE

Wholemeal banana bars

1½ cups wholemeal
   self-raising flour

pinch of salt

1 cup wheatgerm

½ cup soft brown sugar

250 g pitted dates, chopped

1¼ cups milk

125 g butter

2 eggs, beaten

3 bananas, mashed

lemon glacé icing
   (page 679)

Preheat oven to 190°C. Lightly grease two 19-cm square cake tins.

Combine sifted flour and salt with wheatgerm, sugar and dates in a bowl.

Bring ¼ cup of the milk to the boil in a small saucepan. Add butter and stir until it melts. Add beaten eggs and remaining milk.

Pour liquid into dry ingredients and beat well. Add mashed banana and stir until well combined.

Spoon into prepared tins and cook for 40–45 minutes or until risen and browned.

Once cool, top with lemon icing. Cut into bars.

MAKES 24

Wholemeal banana muffins

2 ripe bananas

1 egg

75 g butter, melted

½ teaspoon bicarbonate
of soda

½ cup hot milk

1½ cups wholemeal plain
flour

2 teaspoons baking powder

¼ teaspoon ground
cinnamon

¼ teaspoon ground nutmeg

½ cup soft brown sugar

½ cup sultanas

Preheat oven to 200°C. Grease muffin tins.

Mash bananas and add egg, butter and bicarbonate
of soda dissolved in milk.

Add sifted flour and remaining ingredients and mix
until just combined.

Three-quarters fill prepared muffin tins and bake
for 15–20 minutes.

MAKES 12–14

Wholemeal crackers

4 cups wholemeal plain
   flour

1 teaspoon salt

1½–1¾ cups sour cream

Preheat oven to 180°C. Lightly grease baking trays.

Sift together flour and salt, then add just enough sour cream to make a soft and pliable dough.

On a lightly floured surface, roll out the dough thinly. Cut into squares with a knife, or cut into rounds using a biscuit cutter.

Bake for 10–12 minutes or until pale golden.

MAKES 48

Wholemeal spicy pumpkin muffins

½ cup soft brown sugar,
  firmly packed

¼ cup vegetable oil

1 egg

½ cup mashed pumpkin

½ cup sultanas

1½ cups wholemeal
  self-raising flour

½ teaspoon salt

¼ teaspoon ground nutmeg

¼ teaspoon mixed spice

½ cup milk

Preheat oven to 200°C. Grease muffin tins.

Beat together sugar, oil, egg and mashed pumpkin until well blended. Stir in sultanas.

Sift together flour, salt and spices.

Stir flour into pumpkin mixture alternately with milk until just combined (add a little extra milk if needed).

Three-quarters fill prepared muffin tins and bake for 15–20 minutes.

MAKES 12

Wicked marbled chocolate pudding

50 g dark cooking chocolate, chopped

50 g white chocolate, chopped

110 g softened butter

⅔ cup soft brown sugar

2 eggs, beaten

¾ cup self-raising flour

SAUCE

100 g dark cooking chocolate, chopped

150 ml cream

Preheat oven to 190°C, or fill a steaming pan with water. Lightly grease a 900-ml pudding basin.

Melt the chocolates separately in bowls over hot water or on MEDIUM in the microwave.

Cream the butter and sugar until light and fluffy. Add the eggs, a little at a time and then fold in the sifted flour.

Spoon half of the mixture into another bowl and stir in the melted dark chocolate. Stir the white chocolate into the other half of the mixture.

Spoon the white and dark chocolate mixtures into the prepared pudding basin alternately. Using a wooden skewer, swirl through the mixture to create a marbled effect.

Cover basin with greased, pleated foil. Bake for 90 minutes in the oven, or steam for 90 minutes on top of the stove, topping up with water as necessary.

To make hot chocolate sauce, place ingredients in a saucepan over a gentle heat and stir until the sauce is smooth and glossy.

SERVES 6

Yoghurt bars

BASE

1 cup wholemeal plain flour

40 g cold butter, cut into
small pieces

2 tablespoons water

1 tablespoon lemon juice

FILLING

500 g natural yoghurt

200 g cottage cheese

3 tablespoons honey

¼ cup wholemeal plain
flour

1 tablespoon finely grated
lemon zest

1 tablespoon lemon juice

2 eggs, lightly beaten

TOPPING

60 g cold butter, cut into
small pieces

1 cup wholemeal self-raising
flour

¼ cup soft brown sugar

2 tablespoons chopped or
flaked almonds

Preheat oven to 220°C. Lightly grease a 23-cm square cake tin.

For the base, sift flour into a large mixing bowl. Add butter and rub in with your fingertips until crumbly. Add the water and lemon juice and mix to form a stiff dough.

Knead dough lightly on a floured surface. Roll out and use to line the base of the cake tin. Chill in the refrigerator while preparing the filling.

For the filling, mix together the yogurt, cottage cheese and honey until smooth. Fold in the sifted flour and lemon zest. Add lemon juice and eggs and mix well. Spread over the chilled base.

For the topping, rub butter into sifted flour and sugar until crumbly. Spread over the filling and sprinkle with the nuts.

Place in the preheated oven, then reduce temperature immediately to 200°C and bake for 45 minutes. Cool a little, then refrigerate until cold. Cut into bars to serve.

MAKES 24

Yoghurt & sultana muffins

1 cup plain flour

½ teaspoon baking powder

½ teaspoon salt

¼ teaspoon bicarbonate
of soda

¾ cup wheatgerm

⅓ cup soft brown sugar,
firmly packed

1 egg, beaten

1 cup natural yoghurt

75 g butter, melted and
cooled slightly

½ cup sultanas

1 tablespoon milk (optional)

Preheat oven to 190°C. Grease muffin tins.

Sift together flour, baking powder, salt and bicarbonate of soda. Stir in wheatgerm and brown sugar.

In a separate bowl, combine beaten egg, yoghurt (adding a little milk if very thick) and cooled melted butter. Add to dry ingredients.

Add sultanas and stir until dry ingredients are just moistened. Do not over mix.

Three-quarters fill prepared muffin tins and bake for 20–25 minutes.

MAKES 12

Yoyos

190 g softened butter

⅓ cup icing sugar

1 cup plain flour

1 cup custard powder

pinch of salt

½ teaspoon vanilla extract

butter icing (page 677)
   or jam, for filling

Preheat oven to 180°C. Lightly grease baking trays.

Cream butter and sifted icing sugar until light and fluffy.

In a separate bowl sift together flour, custard powder and salt. Add to creamed mixture with vanilla to form a soft dough.

Roll dough into balls, place onto baking trays and flatten slightly with a fork.

Bake for 15–20 minutes, until a pale beige colour.

Once cold, sandwich biscuits together with jam or butter icing that has been flavoured with a little vanilla extract or lemon essence.

MAKES 36

Zucchini cake

500 g grated zucchini

1 cup vegetable oil

1½ cups soft brown sugar

2½ cups plain flour

1½ teaspoons baking powder

1½ teaspoons ground
   cinnamon

1 teaspoon freshly grated
   nutmeg

½ teaspoon salt

3 eggs, beaten

1 cup chopped walnuts

½ cup sultanas

icing sugar, for dusting

Preheat oven to 160°C. Lightly grease and flour a 23-cm round tin.

Combine zucchini, oil and sugar. Allow to stand for 5 minutes. Add sifted dry ingredients, eggs, walnuts and sultanas.

Pour into prepared tin and bake for 90 minutes, or until a skewer inserted into the centre of the cake comes out clean.

Dust with icing sugar or ice as required.

Zucchini muffins

1 egg

¼ cup castor sugar

2 tablespoons vegetable oil

½ cup buttermilk

1¼ cups wholemeal plain flour

1 teaspoon baking powder

½ teaspoon bicarbonate of soda

2–3 teaspoons ground cinnamon

2 cups grated zucchini

Preheat oven to 180°C. Grease muffin tins.

Beat together egg, sugar, oil and buttermilk.

Sift dry ingredients into a large bowl.

Add zucchini and wet ingredients to dry ingredients.

Mix until all ingredients are just combined.

Spoon into prepared muffin tins and bake for 20–30 minutes.

MAKES 12

Zucchini nut muffins

3 cups plain flour

1 teaspoon baking powder

1 teaspoon bicarbonate
    of soda

½ teaspoon salt

1 teaspoon ground
    cinnamon

2 cups castor sugar

4 eggs

1 cup canola oil

2 cups grated zucchini

½ teaspoon vanilla extract

1 cup chopped walnuts

½ cup raisins

Preheat oven to 180°C. Grease muffin tins.

Sift together all dry ingredients (except sugar).

In a separate bowl, combine sugar and eggs.
Beat for 2 minutes. Add oil and beat for 3 minutes.

Add zucchini, vanilla, nuts and raisins to egg mixture.

Fold in dry ingredients until just combined.

Fill muffin tins two-thirds full and bake for 25 minutes.

Serve with berry jam if desired.

MAKES 24

Zucchini ricotta muffins

1½ cups plain flour

3 teaspoons baking powder

½ teaspoon salt

2 tablespoons castor sugar

¾ teaspoon dried dill

¼ cup milk

120 g butter, melted

2 eggs

⅔ cup ricotta

½ cup grated zucchini

Preheat oven to 200°C. Grease muffin tins.

In a large bowl, sift together flour, baking powder and salt. Stir in sugar and dill. Mix well.

In a medium bowl combine milk, butter and eggs.

Stir in ricotta and zucchini and beat well.

Add milk mixture to dry ingredients, stirring until just moistened (batter will be stiff).

Fill prepared muffin tins two-thirds full. Bake for 20–25 minutes or until golden brown.

MAKES 12

Icings & sauces

Butter icing

125 g softened butter

2 cups icing sugar

1–2 tablespoons warm milk

food colouring and
    flavouring (optional)

Cream the butter in a bowl. Gradually add sifted icing sugar, alternately with the milk, until soft and creamy. Beat in flavouring and colouring, if using.

NOTE
Butter icing is soft with a matt finish, and it's much richer in flavour than glacé icing. It stays relatively moist and can be used for sandwiching biscuits together.

MAKES ¾ CUP

Lemon butter icing

125 g softened butter

2 cups icing sugar

1–2 tablespoons warm
    lemon juice

Cream the butter in a bowl. Gradually add sifted icing sugar, alternately with the lemon juice, until soft and creamy.

MAKES ¾ CUP

Orange butter icing

125 g softened butter

2 cups icing sugar

1–2 tablespoons warm
orange juice

Cream the butter in a bowl. Gradually add sifted icing sugar, alternately with the orange juice, until soft and creamy.

MAKES ¾ CUP

Chocolate butter icing

60 g dark cooking chocolate,
chopped

125 g softened butter

2 cups icing sugar

1–2 tablespoons warm milk

Melt chocolate in a double boiler over simmering water or on MEDIUM in the microwave. Cool.

Cream the butter in a bowl. Gradually add sifted icing sugar, alternately with the milk, until soft and creamy. Beat in melted chocolate.

VARIATION
Substitute the chocolate with 1 tablespoon cocoa if desired – add it with the icing sugar.

MAKES ¾ CUP

Glacé icing

2 cups icing sugar

2 tablespoons warm water

food colouring and
  flavouring (optional)

Sift the icing sugar into a bowl. Gradually add the water, beating until the icing is smooth and thick enough to coat the back of a spoon. Flavour and colour as required and use immediately.

NOTE
Glacé icing is a smooth, glossy icing that should have a fairly runny consistency. It works best when poured over warm slices, muffins, cakes or biscuits, as the surface becomes dull if you spread it.

MAKES ¾ CUP

Lemon glacé icing

2 cups icing sugar

2 tablespoons warm
  lemon juice

Sift the icing sugar into a bowl. Gradually add the lemon juice, beating until the icing is smooth and thick enough to coat the back of a spoon. Use immediately.

MAKES ¾ CUP

Orange glacé icing

2 cups icing sugar

2 tablespoons warm
  orange juice

Sift the icing sugar into a bowl. Gradually add the orange juice, beating until the icing is smooth and thick enough to coat the back of a spoon. Use immediately.

MAKES ¾ CUP

Chocolate glacé icing

60 g dark cooking chocolate

2 cups icing sugar

2 tablespoons warm water

1 teaspoon butter, melted

1 teaspoon vanilla extract

Melt chocolate in a double boiler over simmering water or on MEDIUM in the microwave. Cool.

Sift the icing sugar into a bowl. Gradually add the water, beating until the icing is smooth and thick enough to coat the back of a spoon. Mix in melted chocolate, butter and vanilla. Use immediately.

MAKES ¾ CUP

Coffee glacé icing

2 cups icing sugar

2 tablespoons warm strong
   black coffee

Sift the icing sugar into a bowl. Gradually add the coffee, beating until the icing is smooth and thick enough to coat the back of a spoon. Use immediately.

VARIATION
Substitute the strong black coffee with 1 dessertspoon coffee essence plus 1 tablespoon warm water.

MAKES ¾ CUP

Cream cheese icing

250 g softened cream cheese

50 g softened butter

1 teaspoon vanilla extract

3 cups icing sugar

Using a food processor or electric mixer, blend the cream cheese and butter.

Add the vanilla extract, then mix in the sifted icing sugar until smooth.

Refrigerate until ready to use.

MAKES 1½ CUPS

Butterscotch sauce

¾ cup castor sugar

¼ cup boiling water

¾ cup soft brown sugar

50 g butter

few drops vanilla extract

100 ml cream

Dissolve the castor sugar in a saucepan over a gentle heat and bring to the boil. Cook until the syrup turns a golden brown.

Take pan off the heat, then pour in the boiling water and stir. Stir in the brown sugar and butter and return to the heat until the mixture is smooth and the sugar is dissolved.

Stir in the vanilla and cream and cool until ready to serve.

MAKES 1 CUP

Pouring custard

2 eggs

1 tablespoon castor sugar

1 cup milk

few drops vanilla extract

Using a whisk, mix the eggs and sugar lightly.

Heat the milk and vanilla extract in a saucepan until just warmed through. Remove from heat and pour over the eggs.

Tip the mixture back into the saucepan and, stirring all the time, slowly bring to the boil. Turn down immediately to a simmer and cook, still stirring constantly, until the custard is thick enough to coat the back of a spoon.

Serve hot or cold.

To serve cold, whisk hot custard in a stainless steel bowl over a bowl of ice until cool, to avoid splitting.

MAKES 1½ CUPS

Conversions

Centimetres	Inches
1 cm	⅖ in
1.5 cm	⅗ in
2 cm	⅘ in
2.5 cm	1 in
3 cm	1⅕ in
4 cm	1⅗ in
5 cm	2 in
6 cm	2⅖ in
7 cm	2⅘ in
8 cm	3 in
9 cm	3½ in
10 cm	4 in
18 cm	7 in
19 cm	7½ in
20 cm	8 in
23 cm	9 in
25 cm	10 in
28 cm	11 in
30 cm	12 in

LIQUIDS

Millilitres	Fluid ounces
20 ml	½ fl oz
60 ml	2 fl oz
100 ml	3 fl oz
250 ml	8½ fl oz
300 ml	10 fl oz
375 ml	13 fl oz
500 ml (½ litre)	17 fl oz
750 ml	27 fl oz
1 litre	35 fl oz

Spoon/cup	Millilitres
1 teaspoon	5 ml
1 tablespoon	20 ml
¼ cup	60 ml
⅓ cup	80 ml
½ cup	125 ml
⅔ cup	160 ml
¾ cup	180 ml
1 cup	250 ml

WEIGHTS

Grams	Ounces
15 g	½ oz
25 g	1 oz
50 g	2 oz
80 g	3 oz
100 g	3½ oz
150 g	5 oz
175 g	6 oz
200 g	7 oz
250 g	9 oz
375 g	13 oz
500 g	16 oz (1 lb)
750 g	1⅔ lb
1 kg	2 lb

OVEN TEMPERATURES

Celsius	Fahrenheit
150°C	300°F
160°C	320°F
170°C	340°F
180°C	360°F
190°C	375°F
200°C	390°F
220°C	430°F

Index

PENGUIN BOOKS

Published by the Penguin Group
Penguin Group (Australia)
250 Camberwell Road, Camberwell, Victoria 3124, Australia
(a division of Pearson Australia Group Pty Ltd)
Penguin Group (USA) Inc.
375 Hudson Street, New York, New York 10014, USA
Penguin Group (Canada)
90 Eglinton Avenue East, Suite 700, Toronto ON M4P 2Y3, Canada
(a division of Pearson Penguin Canada Inc.)
Penguin Books Ltd
80 Strand, London WC2R 0RL, England
Penguin Ireland
25 St Stephen's Green, Dublin 2, Ireland
(a division of Penguin Books Ltd)
Penguin Books India Pvt Ltd
11 Community Centre, Panchsheel Park, New Delhi – 110 017, India
Penguin Group (NZ)
67 Apollo Drive, Rosedale, North Shore 0632, New Zealand
(a division of Pearson New Zealand Ltd)
Penguin Books (South Africa) (Pty) Ltd
24 Sturdee Avenue, Rosebank, Johannesburg 2196, South Africa

Penguin Books Ltd, Registered Offices: 80 Strand, London, WC2R 0RL, England

Muffin Bible first published by Penguin Group (NZ) Ltd, 2001. Illustrated edition published by Penguin Group (Australia), 2006.
Cake Bible first published by Penguin Group (Australia), 2006.
Biscuit & Slice Bible first published by Penguin Group (Australia), 2007.
This omnibus edition published by Penguin Group (Australia), a division of Pearson Australia Group Pty Ltd, 2008.

10 9 8 7 6 5 4 3 2 1

Cover and text design by Claire Tice © Penguin Group (Australia)
Photographs by Julie Renouf
Food prepared by Julie Lanham, Kerryn Vilinskis and Linda Brushfield
Typeset by Post Pre-press, Brisbane, Queensland
Scanning and separations by Splitting Image P/L, Clayton, Victoria
Printed in China by Everbest Printing Co. Ltd

National Library of Australia
Cataloguing-in-Publication data:

   Baking bible.
   Omnibus ed.
   Includes index.
   ISBN 978 0 14 300825 5 (pbk.).
   1. Baked products. 2. Muffins. 3. Cake. 4. Biscuits.

   641.815

penguin.com.au